UNIVERSAL
KITCHEN
&
BATHROOM
PLANNING

The National Kitchen & Bath Association

presents

UNIVERSAL

KITCHEN

&

BATHROOM

PLANNING

Design That Adapts To People

by

Mary Jo Peterson, CKD, CBD, CHE

McGraw-Hill

New York San Francisco Washington, D.C. Auckland Bogotá
Caracas Lisbon London Madrid Mexico City Milan
Montreal New Delhi San Juan Singapore
Sydney Tokyo Toronto

Library of Congress Catalog-in-Publication Data

Peterson, Mary Jo.
    The National Kitchen & Bath Association presents universal kitchen
    & bathroom planning: design that adapts to people/by Mary Jo Peterson.
          p.   cm
    Includes index.
    ISBN 0-07-049980-2
    1. Kitchens—Design and construction. 2. Bathrooms—Design and
    construction. 3. Architecture—Human factors. I. National Kitchen
    and Bath Association (U.S.) II. Title.
    TH4816.3.K58P48 1998
    747.7′97—dc21   98-20250
                                                         CIP

McGraw-Hill

A Division of The McGraw·Hill Companies

1 2 3 4 5 6 7 8 9 0   KGP/KGP   9 0 3 2 1 0 9 8

ISBN 0-07-049980-2

The sponsoring editor for this book was Wendy Lochner and the production supervisor was Pamela A. Pelton.

Printed and bound by Quebecor/Kingsport.

McGraw-Hill books are available at special quantity discounts to use as premiums and sales promotions, or for use in corporate training programs. For more information, please write to the Director of Special Sales, McGraw-Hill, 11 West 19th Street, New York, N.Y. 10011. Or contact your local bookstore.

About NKBA® Membership

NKBA® is the leading organization for the kitchen and bathroom industry, known for its quality education programs and materials and its exceptional promotion of the kitchen and bathroom profession to consumers. We applaud your entrance into the kitchen and bathroom design field and congratulate you for beginning or expanding your education with the widely recognized and respected information included herein.

NKBA® membership is the first step toward building close, powerful working relationships with other NKBA® members as well as with clients. You'll benefit from:

- **Networking with the best and brightest.** Exchange ideas, insights and strategies you can use immediately to build business.

- **Consumer advertising and publicity programs.** NKBA® consumer marketing programs are designed to link you with qualified prospects pursuing kitchen and bathroom projects. Advertising, publicity, our own quarterly magazine and our exclusive consumer referral program, Direct to Your Door™ make NKBA® a powerful enhancement to your existing marketing program.

- **Business management tools.** Supplies that streamline your day-to-day operation, reduce costs and enhance your professionalism.

- **Certification.** Certified Kitchen Designer (CKD) and Certified Bathroom Designer (CBD) designations bring you added professional recognition, prestige and credibility.

- **Nationally acclaimed trade shows.** Where you can be among the first to see the latest in design and technology.

- **Prestigious design competitions.** Creating valuable publicity for NKBA® members only.

Consumer research confirms that NKBA® membership creates credibility and confidence among homeowners who plan to remodel their kitchens or bathrooms. It evokes a powerful image of stability and security. A feeling of confidence that delivers business!

Take advantage of the opportunities NKBA® affiliation can create!

Call **1-800-THE-NKBA** for a free brochure and membership application; or visit us on-line at: www.nkba.org

NKBA®
687 Willow Grove Street
Hackettstown, New Jersey 07840
e-mail: educate@nkba.org

Preface

Designing rooms that suit the needs of all users throughout their lifecycle is the purpose of universal design. The ability to create rooms that can be used by more types of people, including people with children, people with disabilities and people who are aging, is essential for success in today's marketplace. As the baby boomer generation - the largest segment of the population, - grows older, these design concepts will become even more important.

The National Kitchen & Bath Association (NKBA) recognizes that universal design is a fact of life and that all members of the kitchen and bathroom industry need comprehensive, up-to-date information on this subject. Providing that information is the purpose of <u>"Universal Kitchen & Bathroom Planning, Design That Adapts To People."</u>

To create this book, NKBA teamed up with experts in the field of universal design. The collective knowledge, expertise and ideas of all the industry and design professionals involved ensure that the information found within this book is accurate, thorough and practical.

Every aspect of universal design as it applies to kitchen and bathroom planning is covered in the following pages including: history, demographics, the definition of universal design; assisting the universal design client; design guidelines; cabinets, countertops, fixtures and equipment; safety; laws and standards; and marketing universal design services.

<u>"Universal Kitchen & Bathroom Planning, Design That Adapts To People"</u> is intended to help you understand universal design concepts. It will also help build your business by increasing your expertise, allowing you to provide greater value and superior service to all of your clients. With this book, you will learn how to create functional, universally designed kitchens and bathrooms without sacrificing aesthetics.

Nick Geragi, CKD, CBD, NCIDQ
Publisher, NKBA Books
Director of Education and Product Development

A Special Thanks ...

The author would like to thank Ron Mace, FAIA, and the Center for Universal Design, Ed Steinfeld and Abir Mullick, Center for Inclusive Design and Environmental Access, School of Architecture and Planning at SUNY Buffalo, for their continued reference and personal support.

NKBA would like to thank many other individuals and organizations that have contributed to the content and preparation of this book.

NKBA's Universal Design Committee; Margaret Wylde, Institute for Technology Development; Joan Eisenberg, CKD, CBD, CHE, JME Consulting Inc; James Krengel, CKD, CBD, Kitchens by Krengel; Abir Mullick, Dept. of Architecture, State University of NY at Buffalo; Ken Smith, CKD, CBD; Doris LaCroix, CKD, CBD, Canac Kitchens; Ron Mace, FAIA, Center for Universal Design, North Carolina State University and Nick Geragi, CKD, CBD, NCIDQ, National Kitchen & Bath Association and Mary Jo Peterson, CKD, CBD, CHE, Mary Jo Peterson Design Consultants.

Other Contributors ...

- Illustrations: Kate Erwin, CKD, Sharon Coughlin, CKD

- Electronic Publishing/Design: Beth A. Treen

- Abir Mullick, Mark Eberle, Glenn Goatha, Sherry Altman
                IDEA SUNY Buffalo, Bath Seat and Lift Ideas

- American Standard Inc. - Heather Bathroom Project Photography

- Annette DePaepe, CKD, CBD, ASID, - Kline Bathroom Project

- Dee Reis-Braaten, MS Occupational Therapy

- Gordon Beall - Dobkin Bathroom Project Photography

- Linda Eggers - The Maytag Company

- Joy Myers-Piske, CKD

- Marsha A. Raisch - Kitchen & Bath Editor - Better Homes & Gardens Magazine

- Mary Seymour

- Brian Sherry - General Electric Appliances

- Carolyn Verwyst - Whirlpool Corporation

- Wilsonart International - Kline Bathroom Project Photography

Foreword

by
Ron Mace, FAIA
Ed Steinfeld, AIA

The concept of universal design is not new. It was first promoted in the mid 1970's as a common sense idea to help eliminate some of the extra costs and stigma associated with *"special"* spaces and facilities for *"handicapped"* people. Many of these special features were known to be helpful to people other than those with a disability.

Almost everyone experiences some form of disability during their lifetime. Therefore, it seems reasonable to make such helpful features attractive, marketable to everyone and part of common practice for all designers.

Universal Design is receiving attention all over the world. The concept has been gaining acceptance in recent years with the recognition of our burgeoning older population, proving to us that specialty design is not limited to people with a disability. It has sparked interest among advocates of disability rights and the aged. Corporations view it as a means to extend their market for products and services. Computer software and hardware designers are using it to insure that everyone will get ready access to the information highway.

Design professionals have long needed the support of their professional associations on this approach to design. The best information on methods for integrating universal design into common practice has been difficult to find. The National Kitchen & Bath Association is leading the way by adopting universal design as an integral part of its training and certification for kitchen and bathroom designers, and by authoring this useful book.

NKBA® has compiled the best available information on the topic and created the most comprehensive single source of technical data on universal design for the kitchen and bathroom. This book covers background issues, data on disability type and advice on working with clients who have disabilities, design specifications, marketing advice, related legislation and information on unique products useful for creating adjustable or adaptable features. It is a comprehensive presentation of the universal design idea in a form that designers will find very useful. Not only does it communicate the concept of detail that a designer needs to do it right. It is filled with good ideas and information to design kitchens and bathrooms that will fulfill the needs of the entire population for years to come.

Kitchen and bathroom designers will benefit from the practice of universal design. All clients will appreciate the added functionality and the attention to details that results. But, most importantly, universally designed kitchens and bathrooms will have lasting value because they meet the needs of individuals over their entire life span.

Ronald L. Mace, FAIA
Director, The Center for Universal Design
N.C. State University, School of Design

Ed Steinfeld, AIA
Center for Inclusive Design & Environmental Access
School of Architecture, SUNY Buffalo

Table Of Contents

UNIVERSAL KITCHEN & BATHROOM PLANNING

chapter 1

The Move Toward Universal Design

The world is changing and it's time for designers to respond. Our growing awareness of changing life styles and diversity must change the way we design kitchens and bathrooms.

Traditionally, the built environment has been designed for an idealized, able-bodied, non-elderly adult. Since that description fits less than 15% of our population, the result is environments, including bathrooms, which create handicaps or barriers for the rest of us.

Demographics, legislation, public awareness and personal experience are pressing us to examine the basic assumptions we have used in design. Through this examination and a growing appreciation for diversity, a trend has emerged that calls for more flexibility and adaptability in design, allowing for use by more kinds of people more often. This trend is towards universal design which, once incorporated, will be simply good design.

HISTORY

The history of universal design from the end of World War II to the present can be seen in legal changes and our ever-changing life-styles. The design implications of this history and the terminology relating to it are important to learn. Once understood, universal design will be at its best when not labeled or defined, but truly incorporated as an essential part of all good design.

Need For Universal Design

Awareness of the need for universal and accessible design has been growing since the end of World War II. Disabled veterans, polio epidemics and the booming population meant more people required specialized accessible design. In response to this, in 1961, the **American National Standards Institute (ANSI)** published the first design standard on accessibility, the *"Specifications for Making Buildings and Facilities Accessible to and Usable by the Physically Handicapped,"* **(ANSI 117.1-1961)**. Since then, the awareness of the need for accessibility has grown. Recognition of the rights of minorities, including children, the disabled and the elderly has grown as well. Following the **ANSI Standard of 1961,** other laws and standards were developed on the state, local and federal levels, creating problems with inconsistency and interpretation.

From the fifties to the eighties, awareness of the need for accessibility in all aspects of life grew. Recognition of minority rights also continued to grow. In 1980, ANSI published a revised standard to create some consistency. In the mid-80's, the **Uniform Federal Accessibility Standards (UFAS)**, used for all federally funded construction subject to the **Architectural Barriers Act**, incorporated the revised ANSI standard, creating a standard that, for the most part, was indeed uniform. In 1988, the **Fair Housing Amendment** to the **Civil Rights Act** of 1968 was passed into law, with guidelines published in 1991 that reference the ANSI standard to some extent. This law impacted multiple housing units with four or more units under one roof.

In 1990, the **Americans with Disabilities Act (ADA)** was passed, with guidelines passed in 1991, again referencing the ANSI standard to a great extent. This law stipulated mandatory conditions for public places and truly changed the way we view the built environment. The intent of all these regulations is not *"separate but equal."* It is to recognize and defend the diversity of our culture and to incorporate this diversity in all aspects of life, including design. In 1992, ANSI again revised the standard. Design standards are constantly under review and revision, moving toward uniformity and the goal of making universal design concepts an integral part of every space and product we develop.

Changing Lifestyles

In terms of lifestyle, from post-World War II to the present, we have become a country where everyone shares in the responsibilities and activities of home life. In the 1950's, the bathroom was typically not flexible or luxurious, but simply a place where one performed certain basic functions. The standard American bathroom was 5' x 7' (152cm x 213cm) with a 30" (72cm) high vanity and lavatory, a water closet at 15" (38cm) high, and a combination bathtub/shower that was 30" x 60" (72cm x 152cm), with a curtain or sliding door. If a person was other than ideal height and physical ability, he would need assistance to adapt to this environment.

Today, the bathroom needs to be as varied as the characteristics of the people using it. Household members may include the children of the 50's, now middle-aged, as well as their parents and children, all with varying physical abilities, all needing to use the space safely and independently.

Todays bathroom may be a place to dress, to workout, to hear the morning news, or to relax, possibly by more than one person at a time and probably by people with varying physical characteristics.

The kitchen was a place where the lady of the house stayed home, was the sole cook and prepared meals to be served to the family, all of whom were seated together for each meal. She was 5'4" (163cm) tall and, as a sign of prosperity, had a kitchen very much like each of her peers. More than likely, her kitchen was designed by a man, taller than average height and not a cook.

Today, cooks come in all sizes, shapes and genders, and with varying physical abilities. Those who were children in the fifties are now middle-aged. Men, women and especially children are sharing in the activities in the kitchen, not only cooking, but homework, planning, bill-paying and family time. And now, the family doesn't necessarily eat together, nor do they even eat the same food.

Further changes in the needs of our clients center around independence for people with disabilities. The largest segment of people with disabilities is the group with impaired mobility or dexterity (whether injury- or illness-related). *"This group includes 37 million Americans with arthritis, 21 million of whom are under the age of 65. An estimated 21 million Americans have hearing impairments, and 16 million Americans have visual impairments."*

The number of people with disabilities is growing. People born with a disability or having injury - or illness - related disabilities are surviving at a greater rate. Life expectancies are longer, especially for women.

A major force in changing the needs of our clients is the aging process. By the year 2020, over 20% of our population will be over 65. According to an **American Association of Retired Persons (AARP)** survey, 84% of these people wish to stay in their homes and *"age in place."* Exploration of residential design options relating to independent living is part of the national health care reform movement.

These statistics become more real as we reflect on our own lifestyles and circumstances.

We can think of parents or grandparents who have moved out of their homes, perhaps into ours or into a group setting. We want to see them leading independent and dignified lives. We can recognize the roles of those elders and children in our daily household responsibilities. We can acknowledge the difficult or impossible barriers in our homes that become apparent only when we experience physical disabilities. Best of all, we can create bathrooms that are beautiful and flexible and allow for these differences in the lives of our home community.

DESIGN TERMS DEFINED

The following definitions of terms relating to universal design, adapted from the **Center for Universal Design**, should increase understanding and awareness. As universal design becomes incorporated into all good design, the need for labels will be eliminated.

Universal Design

Items that most people can use, regardless of their level of ability or disability, are considered universally usable. Many accessible and adaptable features are universally usable. *For example*, round door knobs are not usable by people with limited use of their hands, but lever handles, available in all price ranges, styles and colors, are usable by almost everyone, even people who have no hands.

Some items are made more universally usable by their placement. Light switches at lower heights and electrical receptacles raised to 15" - 48" (38cm - 122cm) above the floor are within reach of most people without requiring bending or stretching. Bathtub controls located off center, toward the outside of the tub, provide the same benefit.

Universal design addresses the scope of accessibility and suggests making all elements and spaces accessible to and usable by all people as much as possible. This is accom-plished through thoughtful planning and design at all stages of any design project. It need not increase costs or result in special, clinical or *"different"* looking facilities.

Universal design requires an understanding and consideration of the broad range of human abilities throughout life. Creative application of that knowledge results in products, buildings and facilities that are usable by more people, regardless of their level of ability or disability. By considering the needs of people with physical limitations in the design of products and spaces, we can make them not only easier and safer to use, but also more marketable and profitable. This universal design approach goes beyond the minimum requirements of accessibility law.

Accessible Design

Accessible generally means that the dwelling meets prescribed requirements for accessible housing. Accessible features in homes include wide doors, sufficient clear floor space for wheelchairs, lower countertop segments, lever- and loop- type hardware, seats at bathing fixtures, grab bars in bathrooms, knee spaces under sinks and counters, audible and visual signals, switches and controls in easily reached locations, entrances free of steps and stairs, and an accessible route throughout the house. Most *"accessible"* features are permanently fixed in place.

Adaptable Design

Adaptable features are either adjustable or capable of being easily and immediately added or removed to *"adapt"* the unit to individual needs or preferences. In an adaptable home, wide doors, no steps, knee spaces, control and switch locations, grab bar reinforcing and other access features must be built in.

- Grab bars, however, can be omitted and installed when needed. Because the necessary backing is already provided, the bars can simply be screwed in place without opening the existing walls to install reinforcing.

- Knee spaces can be concealed by installing a removable base cabinet that can simply be unscrewed from adjacent cabinets and slipped out when needed or by installing self-storing cabinet doors that fold and slide back.

- Countertops and closet rods can be placed on adjustable supports rather than fixed at lower heights as required for some wheelchair users.

Adaptable design means readily adjusted. It is best to remember adaptable features as those that can be adjusted in a short time by unskilled labor without involving structural or finish-material changes. In addition, the following terms are frequently used.

Barrier-Free Design.

Design that eliminates the obstacles in a space or product, making it fully usable by people of varying size and abilities.

Intergenerational or Lifespan Design

Design that allows people full function, regardless of changes due to age or current physical abilities.

Changes in our lifestyles and life-span have created a growing need for changes in the way we design kitchens and bathrooms. Recognition of the facts that we are aging and people with or without disabling conditions are living longer has precipitated this need for change.

Increased awareness and improved standards have provided for the expansion of universal design principles as presented in the NKBA Kitchen and Bathroom Guidelines included in Chapters 3 and 7 of this publication.

c h a p t e r 2

Space Planning A Closer Look

In some cases, universal design guidelines will be impacted by specific client needs. While the goal of universal design is to meet the needs of the greatest number of people, particular clients may have impairments that require *specific* design considerations. Your purpose may be to design a functional kitchen or bathroom for a client with a particular disability, or it may be simply to understand the minimum requirements of a person with a specific disability so as to better meet the goal of universal design. Either way, the following design criteria will help.

THE UNIVERSAL DESIGN APPROACH

A common misconception regarding universal design is that it is nothing more than design for people using wheelchairs. The opposite is true. To be considered universal, a design will be accessible not only to people in wheelchairs, but also to people of most sizes, shapes and abilities.

Reference is frequently made to clearances required for wheelchairs because these clearances are generally fine for most other users as well. *For example,*

- the clear floor space required at a kitchen sink for a person in a wheelchair is a minimum of 30" x 48" (76cm x 122cm), more than meeting the needs of most people, similarly,

- the clear floor space required at a bathroom lavatory for a person in a wheelchair is a minimum 30" x 48" (76cm x 122cm), enough for almost anyone.

In either case however, 30" (76cm) high countertops or work surfaces for the person in a wheelchair may also work well for a seated person, a shorter person or a child, but they will not work for a tall person or someone who cannot bend.

In this case, to be universal, the space must go beyond requirements for the person in a wheelchair, possibly by using adjustable-height counter surfaces or providing a variety of counter surface heights.

This chapter will address the following broad categories of persons with disabilities; mobility impaired, visually impaired, hearing impaired, dementia in terms of memory loss and confusion as well as grip and dexterity impairments.

In addition to functionality issues, we will address space planning and design issues as they relate to; clear floor space, knee and turning space, height and reach ranges, space planning for signals and controls, space planning for way-finding and space planning for visible and accessible storage.

Fixtures and Clear Floor Space

Although there are general universal standards for planning spaces, the exact appliance, equipment and fixture selected and the intended approach and use of the fixture will impact these standards. *For example*, the required clear floor space for a person using a wheelchair is 30" x 48" (76cm x 122cm), but when that person is approaching a bathtub, that dimension needs to be increased to allow for access to controls and safe transfer into the bathtub.

Space Planning

When planning space for a wheelchair user, you must measure the wheelchair(s) to be used. There is no standard wheelchair, but the following dimensions can be a guide when you have no wheelchair available, and want to plan for one.

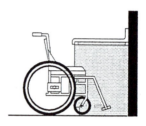

SPORT MODEL WHEELCHAIR

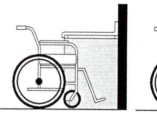

STANDARD ARM WHEELCHAIR   DESK ARM WHEELCHAIR

Figure 2 -   Common wheelchair styles.

Clear Floor Space

The following clearances are minimums for people who use walkers, crutches or wheelchairs, or stationary seats while working. People who use scooters or bathrooms where one of the users may use a mobility aid will benefit from more space. On the other hand people with vision impairments or low energy or balance will benefit from the minimum amount of space. Layouts that require more turning will require more space.

As noted before, the minimum clear floor space required for a wheelchair user is 30" x 48" (76cm x 122cm). This can be planned for parallel approach or perpendicular (forward) approach. Whenever possible the space for both should be allocated, but this is not always possible or practical in a bathroom.

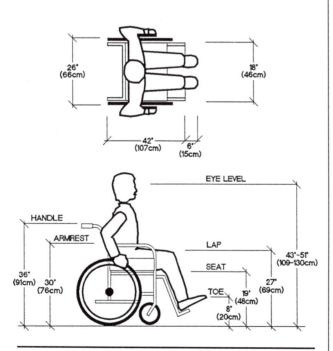

Figure 1 -   Dimensions of Adult- Sized Wheelchairs.

Attention must be given to the client's preference in bathing fixture and in approach or transfer. This should include consideration of a person's handedness, which is the hand or side that is stronger and most able.

PARALLEL APPROACH

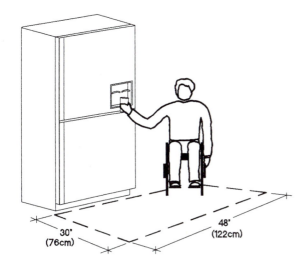

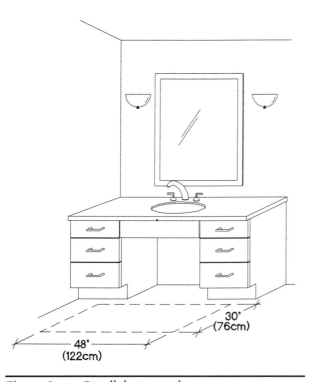

Figure 3 - Parallel approach.

PERPENDICULAR OR FORWARD APPROACH

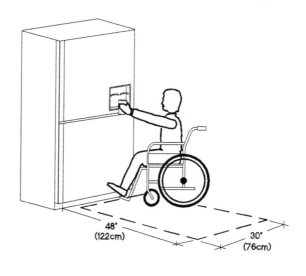

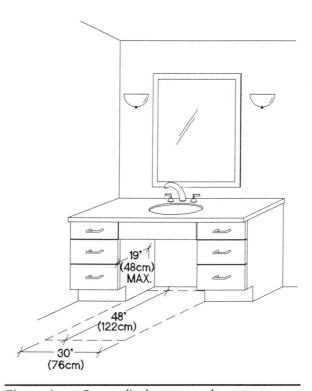

Figure 4 - Perpendicular approach.

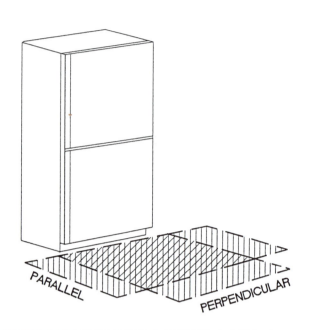

Figure 5 - Both parallel or perpendicular (or forward) approach.

Up to 19" (48cm) of this clear floor space may extend under a counter or into a knee space, as at a lavatory, sink or adjacent to a range.

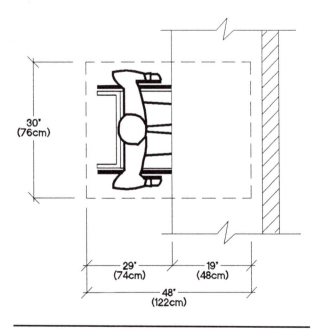

Figure 6 - Clear floor space under work surface.

Up to 6" (15cm) of the required 48" (122cm) of clear floor space can be cabinet toekick space, provided the toekick is a minimum 9" - 12" (23cm - 30cm) high.

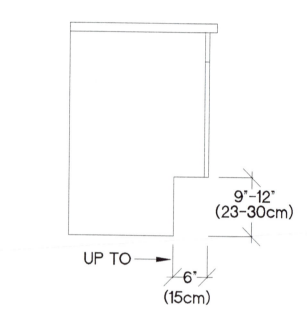

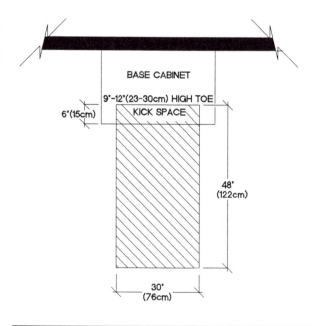

Figure 7 - Toekick recommendations

KNEE SPACE

Knee spaces are for people who need or wish to sit while using the lavatory or work space. They are desirable at or adjacent to all major workcenters/appliances in the kitchen, including the sink, cooktop, range, oven, dishwasher and refrigerator. The minimum dimensions for this knee space are 30" wide by 27" high by 48" deep (76cm x 69cm x 122cm) (maximum 19" (48cm) under the counter).

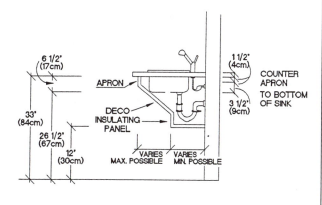

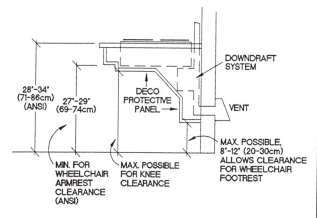

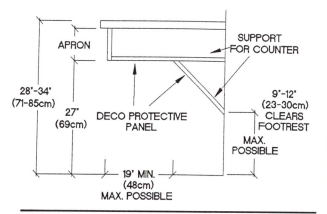

Figure 8 - Kneespace considerations.

Measuring the Dimensions

When measuring the dimension of the knee space, there are several points to measure.

• At the front edge or apron, the height must be the greatest (27" (69cm) minimum) to allow wheelchair arm clearance. If there is a fixture (sink or countertop) that obstructs this kneespace, it may be beneficial to set the fixture back in the counter to allow maximum wheelchair armrest clearance (provided you do not move it out of functional reach).

• The second height, under the obstruction, must clear knees and should be the maximum possible.

• The third dimension is the depth, which should be clear all the way to the wall, but when there is an obstruction, a minimum of 19" (48cm) allows clearance for wheelchair footrests. If possible a 9" - 12" (23cm - 30 cm) height space off the floor at the back wall will allow greater clearance of the wheelchair footrests.

Depth: Generally a vanity counter is 21" - 24" (53cm - 61cm) deep. A kitchen counter is generally 24" (61cm) plus in depth. However, only 19" (48cm) of either of these can be counted in the total of 48" (122cm) clear floor space at the knee space.

Width: Although 30" (76cm) is given as a minimum, 36" (91cm) works much better as it allows for the possibility of a 3-point turn for a wheelchair user.

Height: A minimum knee space height of 27" - 29" (69cm - 74cm) is recommended, and the exact minimum for a specific client will be determined by the height of the arm of his/her wheelchair. While each wheelchair is custom, several styles with variations in the armrests allow flexibility in the required knee space height.

Consequently, the knee space under a lavatory or sink has special considerations. The dimensions of the clear knee space are affected by the height of the counter and the depth of the sink as well as the drain and plumbing location. ANSI recommends sinks be no deeper than 6 1/2" (17cm).

Any exposed electrical or plumbing systems (drain pipes, shut off valves, wires) should be insulated or padded and concealed to improve the look and protect users from contact with hot or sharp surfaces.

In the case where a disposer is part of one sink bay, that section may be enclosed in cabinetry, and the second bay of the sink plus adjacent space on the side of the sink away from the disposer can make up the minimum 30" - 36" (76cm - 91cm) width.

Turning Space

A space that requires as few turns as necessary provides easier maneuvering for a person in a wheelchair in the kitchen or bathroom. It is desirable that space be provided for a person using a wheelchair to turn 180°. Two types of clear floor spaces for two types of turns make this possible.

The first is the easily recognized 60" (152cm) diameter circle and the second is a

36" x 36" x 60" (91cm x 91cm x 152cm) T-turn. The full 60" (152cm) circle is usually the preferred, but if space or energy levels make this difficult or if visual impairments exist, a T-turn that takes less space and allows for easier *way-finding* may be the choice.

The actual space required for a 360° pivoting turn is 60" (152cm) at the floor and less as you rise above the floor. At approximately 12" (30cm) off the floor, the required space gets smaller because it is above the wheelchair footrests. At 30" (72cm) off the floor the required space again becomes smaller because it has cleared the wheelchair armrest.

This information can be useful when working with limited space. Up to 6" (15cm) of the required 60" (152cm) can be provided by a toekick that is a minimum 6" (15cm) deep and 9" - 12" (23cm - 30cm) high. Up to 19" (48cm) of the required 60" (152cm) can be provided by the clear floor of a knee space if the knee space is a minimum of 48" - 54" (122cm - 137cm) wide. Considering that smaller spaces will sometimes work better for a person with visual impairments or reduced stamina, this can provide a better option.

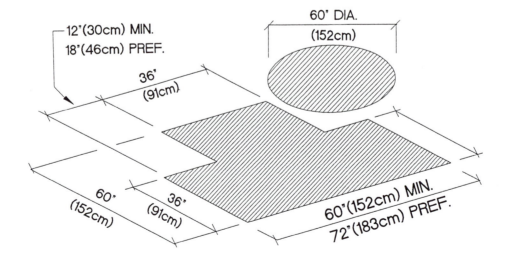

Figure 9 -   Clear floor space for turning wheelchairs.

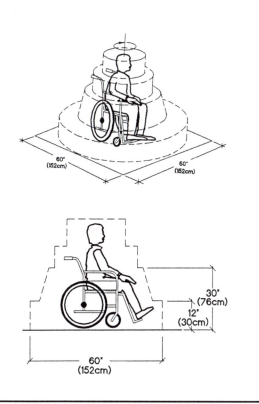

Figure 10 -   Clear floor space for a circular turn.

The other type of turn, the T-turn, requires minimum clear floor space of 36" x 36" x 60" - 72" (91cm x 91cm x 183cm). The turn is made by pulling into the side arm of the T and backing out going in the opposite direction.

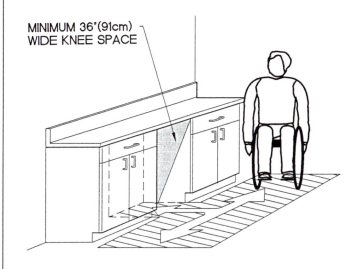

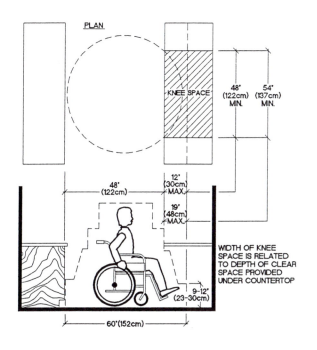

Figure 11 -   Clear floor space with enlarged toespace.

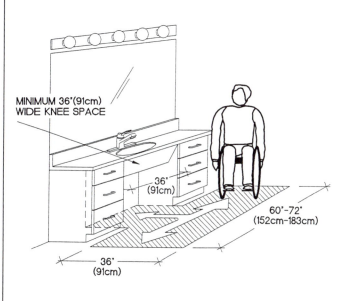

Figure 12 -   Optional turning space - T-Turn.

By making a knee space a minimum 36"
(91cm) wide, it can be one leg of the T. This
is useful information as it allows for flexibility, and wheelchair accessibility without
greatly enlarging spaces.

HEIGHTS AND REACH RANGES

The average person who remains seated to
maneuver in the kitchen or bathroom has a
forward reach range of 15" - 48" (38cm -
122cm) off the floor. If there is an obstruction
greater than 20" (51cm) deep, like a counter,
the upper limit drops to 44" (112cm). From a
seated position reaching to the side, the
range is 15" - 54" (38cm - 137cm). If the obstruction is greater than 10" (25cm) deep, the
upper limit drops to 46" (117cm).

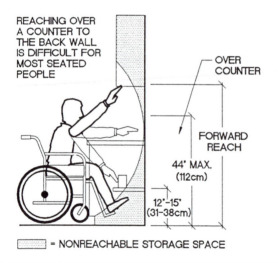

Figure 13 -   Reach Range Guidelines - Seated
Person.

The person who uses crutches, a walker or
in some way needs to use his arms or hands
to maintain balance has a slightly different
reach range. This person will have trouble
reaching very low or very high.

The lower end of this forward reach range
is 15" - 24" (38cm - 61cm) off the floor, depending on a person's ability to bend (back
or knee). The upper limit is 69" - 72" (175cm -
183cm), depending on the depth of any obstruction.

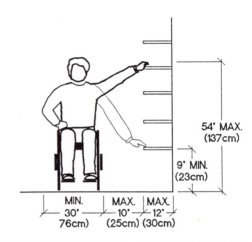

Figure 14 -   Reach Range Guidelines - Seated
Person.

Combining these reach ranges with the
functional limits previously established for individuals 5' 3" - 5' 7" (160cm - 170cm) (24"
(61cm) without bending - 69" (175cm) over a
25" (64cm) deep counter, a universal reach
range of 15" - 48" (38cm - 122cm) is suggested as a guide.

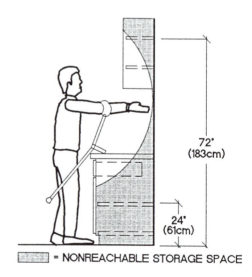

Figure 15 -   Reach Range Guidelines -
Standing, Mobility-Impaired Person.

Information on reach range will impact
how you design storage spaces and counter
heights. Configuration of cabinetry and acces-
sorization for storage will have an impact on
how well the area within the universal reach
range is utilized as well.

	Seated User	Standing, Mobility Impaired Person	Standing Person 5'3" - 5'7" (160cm-170cm)	Universal
Lower Limit - bending	15" (38cm)	15" (38cm)	15" (38cm)	15" (38cm)
Lower Limit - no bending	————	24" (61cm)	24" (61cm)	24" (61cm)
Upper Limit	48" (122cm)	72" (183cm)	79 1/2" (202cm)	48" (122cm)

SPACE PLANNING CONSIDERATIONS

Doors

Because the bathroom is a private area, a door is an important consideration. In a private or master bathroom suite, one option might be to eliminate unnecessary doors. In a powder room or a shared bathroom, a door is usually a necessity and its impact on maneuvering space must be addressed.

Although the importance of a door is predominately related to the bathroom, you may be asked to place a door in the kitchen area. In order to maintain universal access to, and use of a kitchen or bathroom with a door application, a designer must look at the door swing, the clear space on either side of the door, and the approach to the door.

The first consideration is the clear opening at the door, a minimum 32" (81cm), which is the opening minus the thickness of the door stop, the thickness of the door and the space between the door and frame at the hinge side. This requires a 36" (91cm) standard door. It is possible to increase the clear opening at a door by changing to a hinge that allows the door to move out of the door opening.

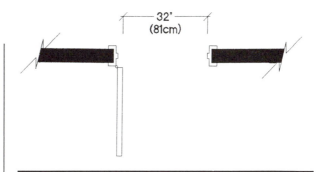

Figure 16 -   Clear opening at the door.

Clear Floor Space at Doors

The clear floor space required at a door varies with approach and swing or style of door. Basically, a larger clear floor space must be allowed on the pull side of the door beyond the latch to allow space to operate the door and move out of the door swing. A narrower clear floor space will be needed on the push side of the door, depending on approach.

The goal of the clearance requirements set down in the codes **(ANSI, UFAS, ADA)** is to allow a person using a mobility aid to approach the door, operate the latch and maneuver through the door. Based on the direction of approach, the maneuvering space will vary. These requirements are called out for commercial buildings, but they will also be of assistance in planning a residential space.

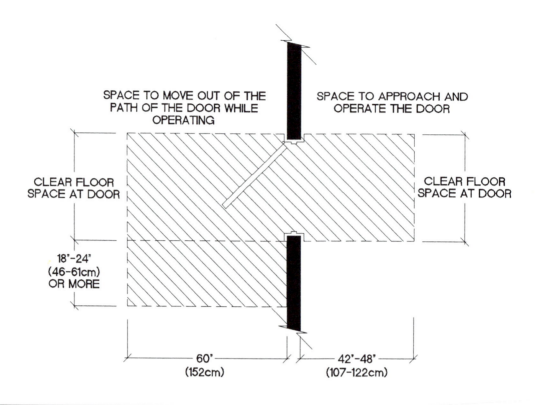

SPACE TO MOVE OUT OF THE
PATH OF THE DOOR WHILE
OPERATING

SPACE TO APPROACH AND
OPERATE THE DOOR

CLEAR FLOOR
SPACE AT DOOR

CLEAR FLOOR
SPACE AT DOOR

18"-24"
(46-61cm)
OR MORE

60"
(152cm)

42"-48"
(107-122cm)

Figure 17 - General minimum clear floor space at doors varies based on approach.

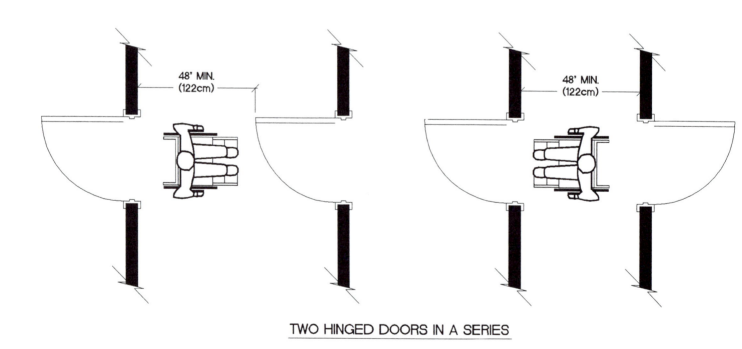

48" MIN.
(122cm)

48" MIN.
(122cm)

TWO HINGED DOORS IN A SERIES

Figure 18 - Clear floor spaces at doors in commercial buildings.

Because requirements for clear floor spaces at doors will impact hallway widths and space within the kitchen or bathroom, they must be examined together.

The actual passage width needed for a person in a wheelchair to make a 90° turn into an opening 32" (81cm) wide is 42" (107cm). Given that often the hall width is less flexible, solutions might involve widening the door or recessing the room entry.

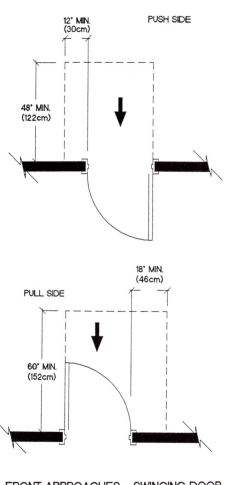

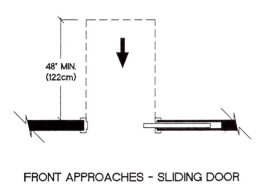

FRONT APPROACHES - SLIDING DOOR

HINGE-SIDE APPROACHES - SWINGING DOOR

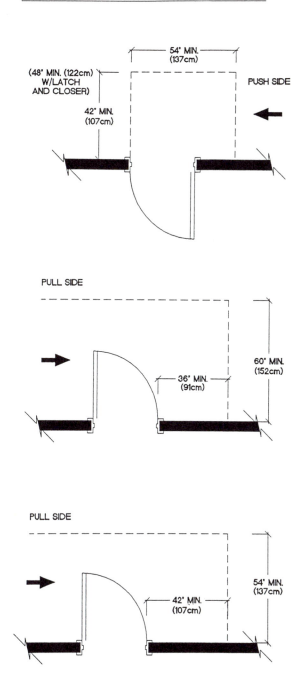

Figure 19 - Clear floor spaces at doors.

Figure 20 - Clear floor spaces at doors.

As in other aspects of universal design, the threshold should not be higher than 1/2" (1.27cm) (beveled) or 1/4" (.64cm) (square), and the door handle should be a lever or a type that will allow use without firm grasp. Automatic door controls or door closers may be a solution.

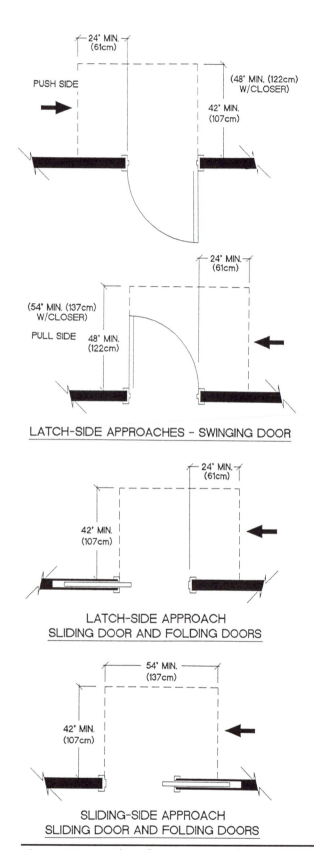

LATCH-SIDE APPROACHES - SWINGING DOOR

LATCH-SIDE APPROACH
SLIDING DOOR AND FOLDING DOORS

SLIDING-SIDE APPROACH
SLIDING DOOR AND FOLDING DOORS

Figure 21 -   Clear floor spaces at doors.

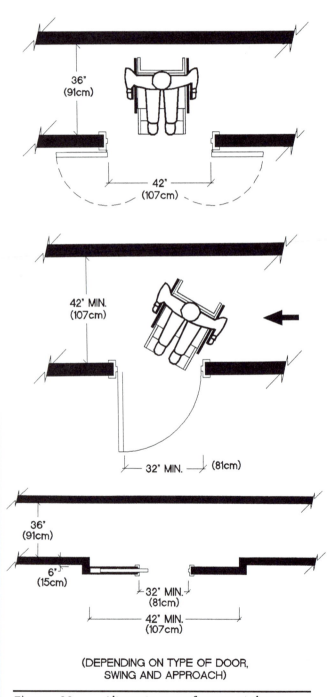

(DEPENDING ON TYPE OF DOOR,
SWING AND APPROACH)

Figure 22 -   Alternate use of space at doors.

Space Planning for Signals and Controls

Controls must be planned within the universal reach range of 15" - 48" (38cm - 122cm) for ease of use. Because of the difficulty a seated user will have in reaching part of the backsplash, controls should be located closer to the front of the work area when possible. Allow space for redundant cuing signals or home control alarm signals when appropriate. Actual design of controls in relation to grip and dexterity should be taken into consideration.

Space Planning for Way-Finding

Contrast in *way-finding* is a fundamental technique which should be used for people with visual impairments. Texture and color planned and applied in a continuous flow through the work area will allow for uninterrupted movement thru the space. Concentrate work areas through the use of a smaller overall space.

Space Planning for Visible and Accessible Storage

Maximize the amount of storage in the universal reach range of 15" - 48" (38cm - 122cm). Carefully consider the maneuvering space required to access the storage. Be especially attentive to the users line of sight, cabinet and appliance door swings and the amount of clear floor space needed for each work area. Cabinetry, accessories and their location will have a great impact on the effectiveness of storage.

A WORD OF CAUTION

We are moving from a *"Peter Pan"* world, where everyone was to have been the same-size, lifestyle, ability and age, to a world that encourages diversity. Not just for the mobility-impaired individual, but for all users of these two very important spaces. Our changing kitchen and bathroom design guidelines reflect this shift in attitudes.

Do not mistake universal design as a new form of *"one size fits all"*, and do not mistake the guidelines explained in this chapter as optimum for everyone. These guidelines, based mainly on **ANSI, UFAS** and the **Accessible Housing Design Files** are minimums. Each client and each space must be considered separately as always. Again, use these guidelines as minimums and as a basis from which to expand creatively.

The planning of clear floor spaces for maneuvering and use of kitchen and bathroom work spaces is complex. It is impacted by space requirements for mobility aids and strengths and abilities of the people using the kitchen and bathroom spaces. *Appendix 7, Bathroom Fixture Transfer Techniques, will assist the designer in understanding the exact goals of these space allotments, enabling the designer to choose optimally within the constraints of each job.*

A complete understanding of the required clear floor spaces and the reasons behind the requirements gives you the opportunity to make optimum choices when balancing these considerations with the other parameters of the job. Several points are worth reiterating here.

- These allowances are minimums. Understanding the reason for these allowances and your clients needs in terms of maneuvering will help you to determine where you might be more generous and where your client's interests will be best met by sticking to the minimum. In particular, people using scooters and kitchens and bathrooms where there will be multiple users will benefit from more generous spaces.

- Whenever possible, measure your client's space requirements, as mobility aids are unique.

- Keep in mind that these spaces can and will overlap in a kitchen or bathroom and do not greatly increase the overall size of the space.

c h a p t e r 3

40 Design Guidelines© *Of Kitchen Planning*

Universal kitchen design requires an understanding and consideration of the broad range of human abilities as well as the other parameters of a design project. It is intended that a kitchen designed around these guidelines will be functional, safe and universal. It is also likely that when the guidelines are applied along with the other constraints of a particular situation, some things will be compromised.

Because every guideline cannot be followed every time and no design can be all things to all people, judgements must frequently be made to achieve an optimum balance.

- The window made to be easily opened by arthritic hands may also provide easy access to an intruder.

- The microwave oven placed easily within the reach of a seated adult may also be within the reach of a toddler.

In 1992, the **National Kitchen & Bath Association** and the **University of Illinois Small Homes Council**, introduced new standards based on an extensive research project conducted by the Association in conjunction with the University of Minnesota.

In 1995, NKBA teamed up with universal design experts to re-examine the basic assumptions of design for the idealized, able-bodied, non-elderly adult. The result was an increased appreciation for diversity, flexibility and adaptability in design, and the basis for the new 40 Guidelines© of Kitchen Planning.

Ultimately, universal kitchen design requires judgement by the designer and these guidelines are provided to be the basis for that judgement.

SECTION I: Traffic and Workflow
Guideline 1 to Guideline 5

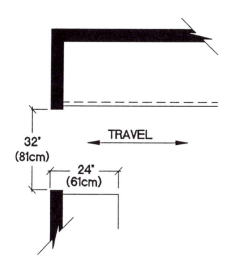

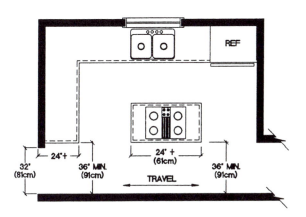

Figure 23 -   **Guideline 1a** - Doorways should be at least 32" (81cm) wide and not more than 24" (61cm) deep in the direction of travel.

Figure 24 -   **Guideline 1b** - Walkways (passages between vertical objects greater than 24" (61cm) deep in the direction of travel, where not more than one is a work counter or appliance) should be at least 36" (91cm) wide.

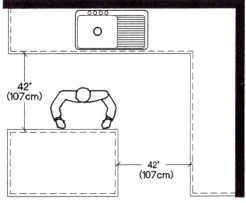

ONE-COOK KITCHEN WORK AISLE

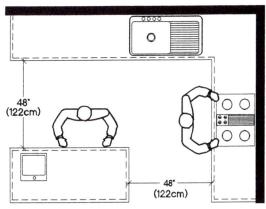

TWO-COOK KITCHEN WORK AISLE

Figure 25 -   **Guideline 1c** - Work aisles (passages between vertical objects, both of which are work counters or appliances) should be at least 42" (107cm) wide in one-cook kitchens, at least 48" (122cm) wide in multiple-cook kitchens.

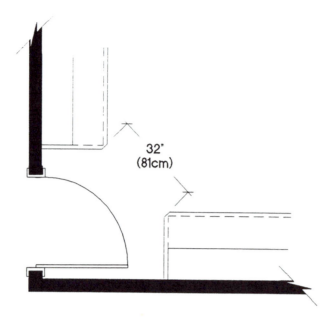

Figure 26 - **Guideline 1a - Clarification** - When two counters flank a doorway entry, the minimum 32" (81cm) wide clearance should be allowed from the point of one counter to the closest point of the opposite counter.

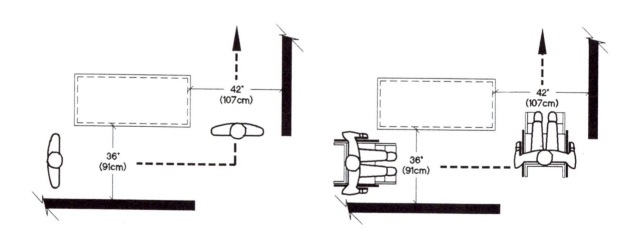

Figure 27 - **Guideline 1b - Clarification** - If there are perpendicular walkways, one should be a minimum of 42" (107cm) wide.

   The 36" (91cm) width of a walkway allows a person using a wheelchair to pass. However, in order to turn when two walkways intersect at right angles, one of the walkways must be a minimum of 42" (107cm) wide.

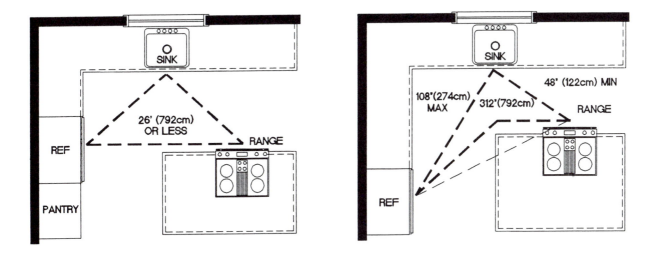

Figure 28 - **Guideline 2** - The work triangle should total 26' (792cm) or less, with no single leg of the triangle shorter than 4' (122cm) nor longer than 9' (274cm). The work triangle should not intersect an island or peninsula by more than 12" (30cm). (The triangle is the shortest walking distance between the refrigerator, primary food preparation sink and primary cooking surface, measured from the center front of each appliance.)

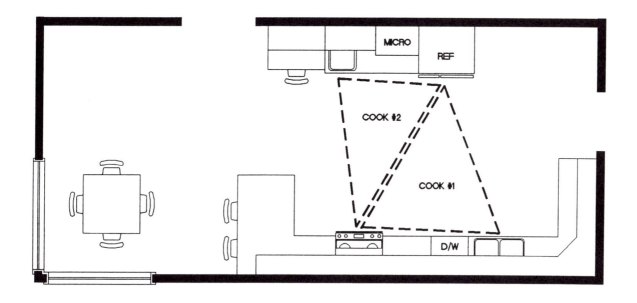

Figure 29 - **Guideline 2 - Clarification** - If two or more people cook simultaneously, a work triangle should be placed for each cook. One leg of the primary and secondary triangles may be shared, but the two should not cross one another. Appliances may be shared or separate.

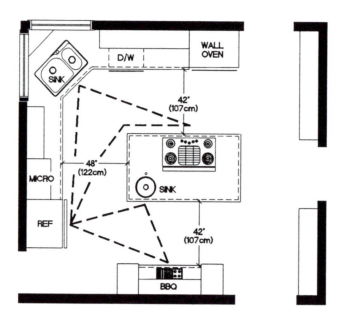

Figure 30 - **Guideline 2 Example 1** - A square room can work for two people if a sink is added at the back of an island which also features the primary cook's cooktop. One cook moves from the refrigerator to the island sink, to the BBQ center; the second cook, from the refrigerator to the primary sink to the cooking surface.

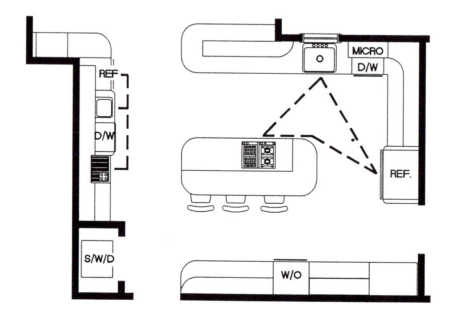

Figure 31 - **Guideline 2 Example 2** - In a large, expansive kitchen created for two cooks, two very separate cooking areas are created. There is very little interaction between the cooks unless they are both working at the counter to the left of the sink. The primary cook works from the refrigerator to the sink to the cooktop. Note the microwave placement close to the sink. The secondary cook has access to his own grill, second microwave, sink and under cabinet refrigerator. Two dishwashers complete the separate work environment.

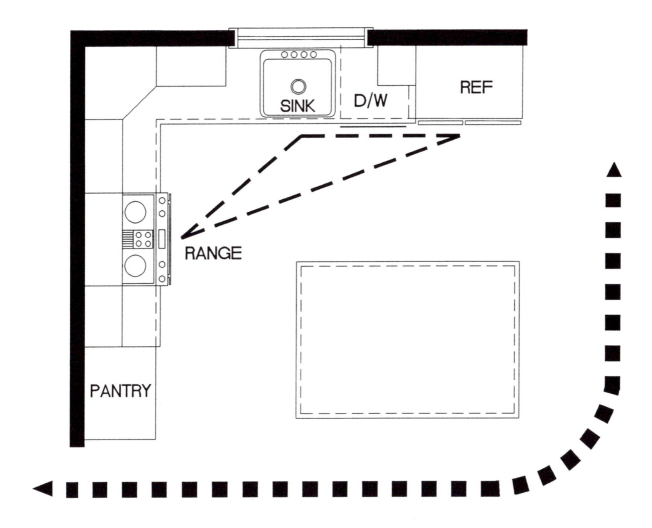

Figure 32 - **Guideline 3** - No major traffic patterns should cross through the work triangle.

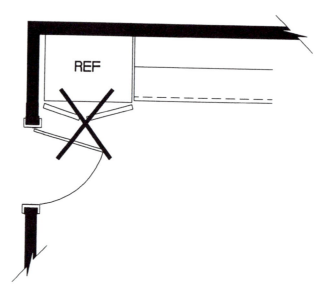

Figure 33 -   **Guideline 4** - No entry, appliance or cabinet doors should interfere with one another.

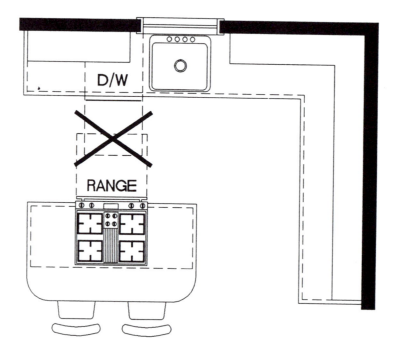

Figure 34 -   **Guideline 4 Example** - In an island configuration, an appliance or cabinet door on an island should not conflict with an appliance or cabinet door opposite it.

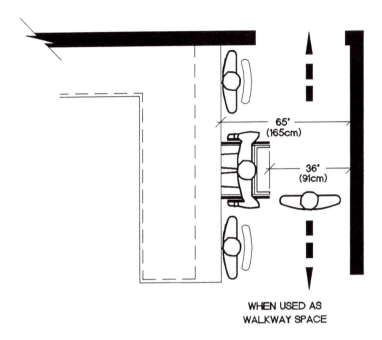

WHEN USED AS
WALKWAY SPACE

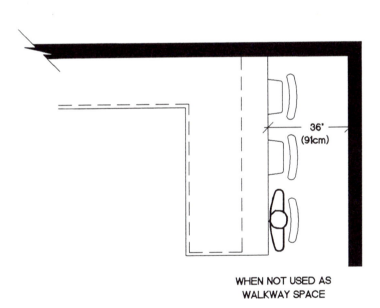

WHEN NOT USED AS
WALKWAY SPACE

Figure 35 -   **Guideline 5** - In a seating area, 36" (91cm) of clearance should be allowed from the counter/table edge to any wall/obstruction behind it if no traffic will pass behind a seated diner. If there is a walkway behind the seating area, 65" (165cm) of clearance, total, including the walkway, should be allowed between the counter/table edge and any wall or obstruction.

   The 65" (165cm) walkway clearance required for a seating area allows room for passage by or behind the person using a wheelchair.

SECTION II: Cabinets and Storage
Guideline 6 to Guideline 12

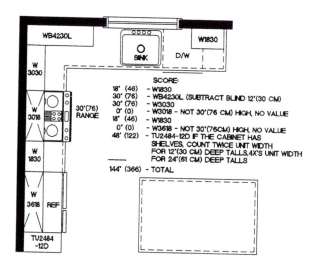

Figure 36 - **Guideline 6** - Wall Cabinet Frontage, Small Kitchens - equal or less than 150 sq. ft. (14 sq.m) - allow at least 144" (366cm) of wall cabinet frontage, with cabinets at least 12" (30cm) deep, and a minimum of 30" (76cm) high (or equivalent) which feature adjustable shelving. Difficult to reach cabinets above the hood, oven or refrigerator do not count unless devices are installed within the case to improve accessibility.

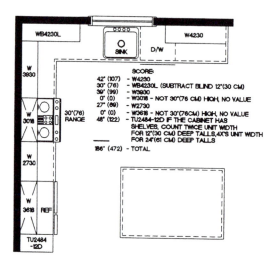

Figure 37 - **Guideline 6** - Wall Cabinet Frontage, Large Kitchens - over 150 sq. ft. (14 sq.m) - allow at least 186" (472cm) of wall cabinet frontage, with cabinets at least 12" (30cm) deep, and a minimum of 30" (76cm) high (or equivalent) which feature adjustable shelving. Difficult to reach cabinets above the hood, oven or refrigerator do not count unless devices are installed within the case to improve accessibility.

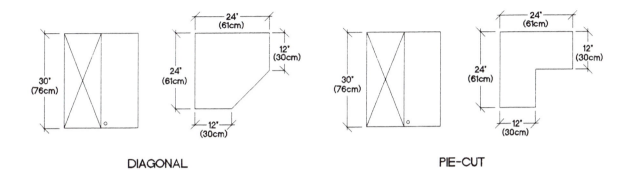

DIAGONAL   PIE-CUT

WALL CABINETS

Figure 38 -   **Guideline 6 - Clarification** - In Small and Large Kitchens, diagonal or pie cut wall cabinets count as a total of 24" (61cm).

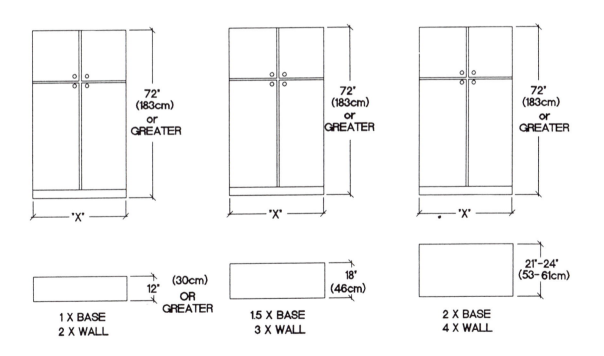

Figure 39 -   **Guideline 6 - Clarification** - Tall cabinets 72" (183cm) or taller can count as either base or wall cabinet storage, but not both.
The calculation is as follows:
12" (30cm) deep tall units = 1 x the base lineal footage, 2 x the wall lineal footage
18" (46cm) deep tall units = 1.5 x the base lineal footage, 3 x the wall lineal footage
21" to 24" (53cm - 61cm) deep tall units = 2 x the base lineal footage, 4 x the wall lineal footage

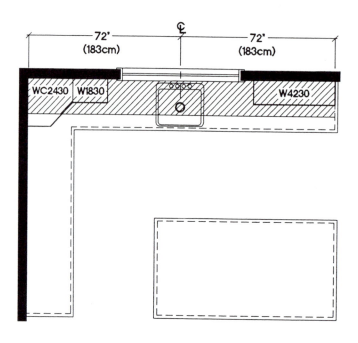

Figure 40 -   **Guideline 7** - At least 60" (152cm) of wall cabinet frontage, with cabinets at least 12" (30cm) deep, a minimum of 30" (76cm) high (or equivalent), should be included within 72" (183cm) of the primary sink centerline.

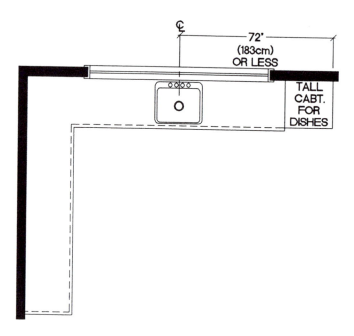

Figure 41 -   **Guideline 7 - Clarification** - A tall cabinet can be substituted for the required wall cabinets if it is placed within 72" (183cm) of the sink centerline.

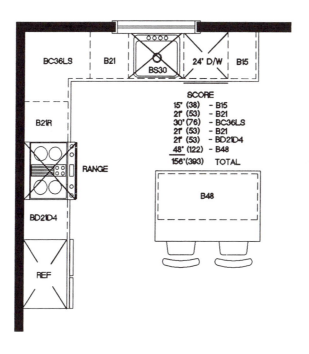

Figure 42 - **Guideline 8** - Base Cabinet Frontage, Small Kitchens - equal or less than 150 sq. ft. (14 sq.m) - allow at least 156" (393cm) of base cabinet frontage, with cabinets at least 21" (53cm) deep (or equivalent). The blind portion of a blind corner box does not count.

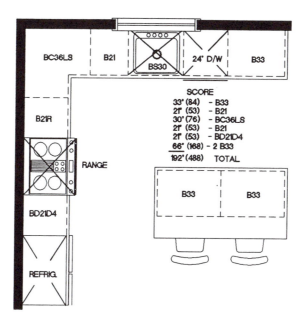

Figure 43 - **Guideline 8** - Base Cabinet Frontage, Large Kitchens - over 150 sq. ft. (14 sq.m) - require at least 192" (488cm) of base cabinet frontage, with cabinets at least 21" (53cm) deep (or equivalent). The blind portion of a blind corner box does not count.

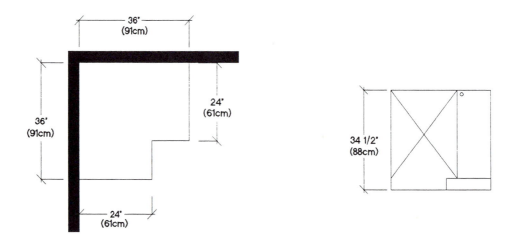

Figure 44 -   **Guideline 8 - Clarification** - In both Small and Large kitchens, pie cut/lazy susan base cabinets count as a total of 30" (72cm).

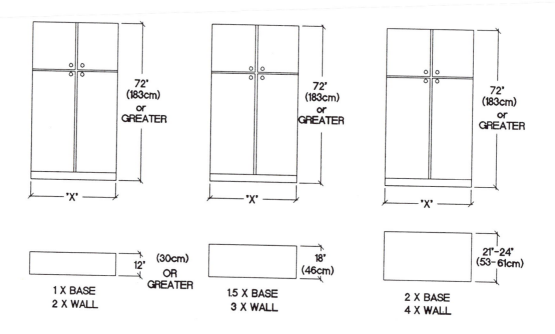

Figure 45 -   **Guideline 8 - Clarification** - Tall cabinets 72" (183cm) or taller can count as either base or wall cabinet storage, but not both.
The calculation is as follows:
12" (30cm) deep tall units = 1 x the base lineal footage, 2 x the wall lineal footage
18" (46cm) deep tall units = 1.5 x the base lineal footage, 3 x the wall lineal footage
21" to 24" (53cm to 61cm) deep tall units = 2 x the base lineal footage, 4 x the wall lineal footage

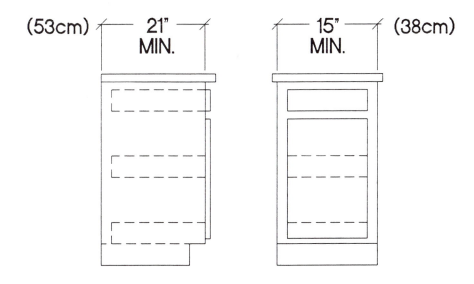

Figure 46 -   **Guideline 9** - Drawer/Roll-out Shelf Frontage - Small Kitchens - equal or less than 150 sq. ft.(14 sq.m) - allow at least 120" (305cm) of drawer or roll-out shelf frontage. Large Kitchens - over 150 sq. ft. (14 sq.m) - allow at least 165" (419cm) of drawer or roll-out shelf frontage. Multiply cabinet width by number of drawers/roll-outs to determine frontage. Drawer/roll-out cabinets must be at least 15" (38cm) wide and 21" (53cm) deep to be counted.

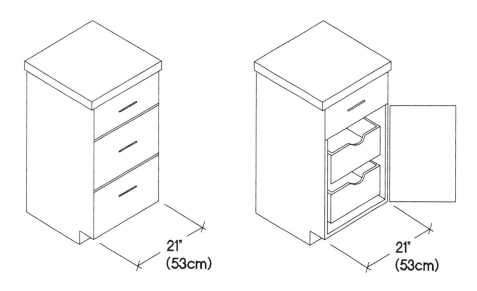

Figure 47 -   **Guideline 9 Example 1** - A 21" (53cm) wide three drawer base would count as 63" (160cm) toward the drawer total. A 21" (53cm) wide single drawer base with one drawer and two sliding shelves would also count as 63" (160cm) towards the total drawer measurement.

Figure 48 -   **Guideline 9 Example 2** - In this example, drawers flank the range.

Figure 49 -   **Guideline 9 Example 3** - Drawers can be placed close to the sink so that items used at the sink or stored near the dishwasher are close at hand.

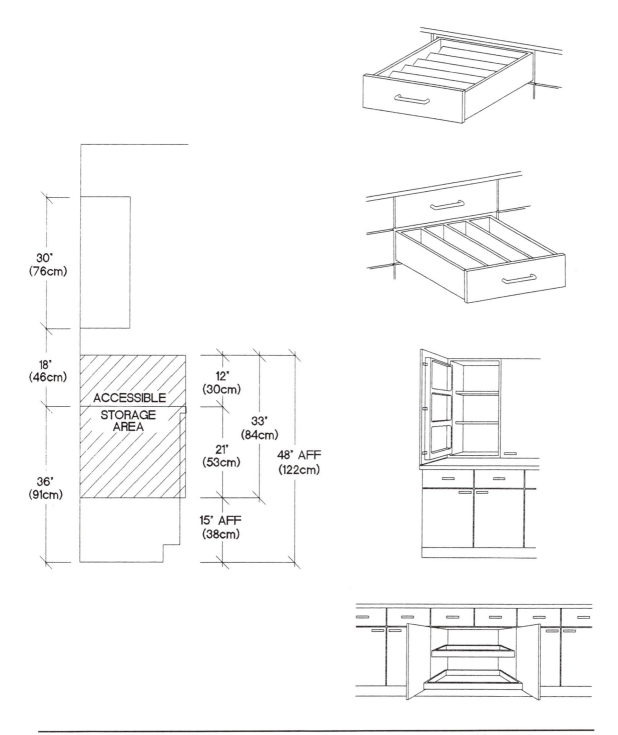

Figure 50 - **Guideline 10** - At least five storage/organizing items, located between 15" - 48" (38cm - 122cm) above the finished floor (or extending into that area), should be included in the kitchen to improve functionality and accessibility. These items may include, but are not limited to: lowered wall cabinets, raised base cabinets, tall cabinets, appliances garages, bins/racks, swing-out pantries, interior vertical dividers, specialized drawers/shelves etc. Full-extension drawers/roll-out shelves greater than the 120" (305cm) minimum for small kitchens or 165" (419cm) for larger kitchens may also be included.

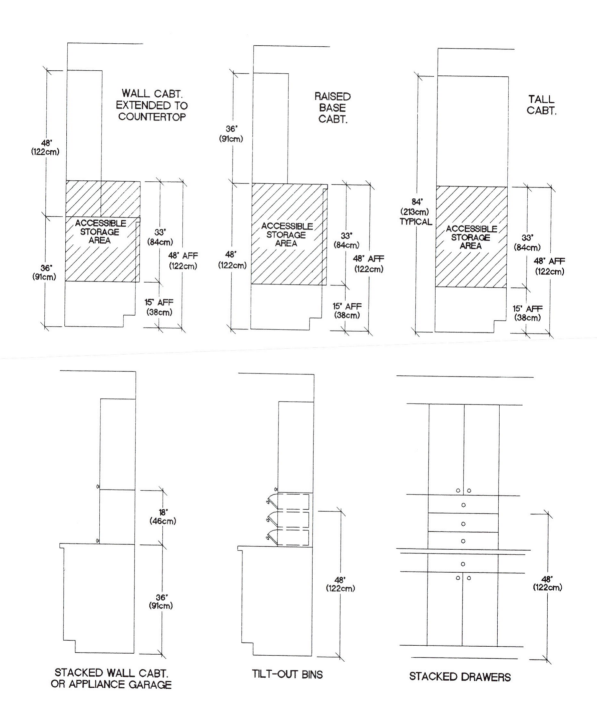

Figure 51 - **Guideline 10 Examples** - Each of these applications puts storage within the 15" - 48" (38cm - 122cm) range.

Figure 52 - **Guideline 10 Examples** - The goal of this guideline is to increase the amount of accessible storage within the universal reach range of 15" - 48" (38cm - 122cm).

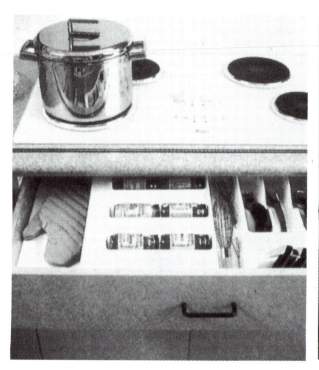

Figure 53 -   **Guideline 10 Examples** - The goal of this guideline is to increase the amount of accessible storage within the universal reach range of 15" - 48" (38cm - 122cm).

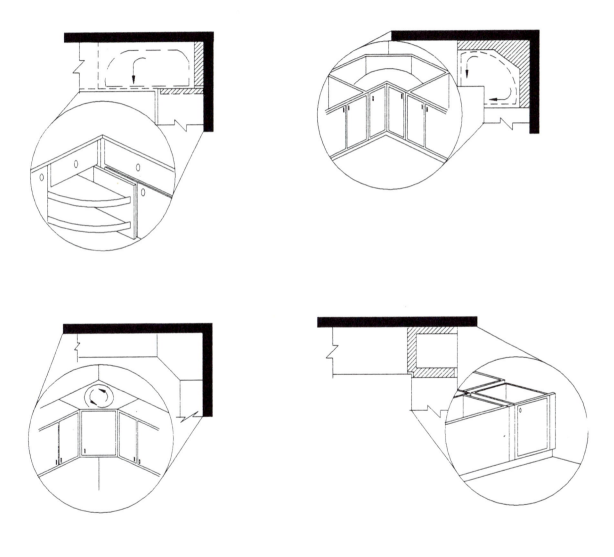

Figure 54 -   **Guideline 11** - For a kitchen with usable corner areas in the plan, at least one functional corner storage unit should be included.

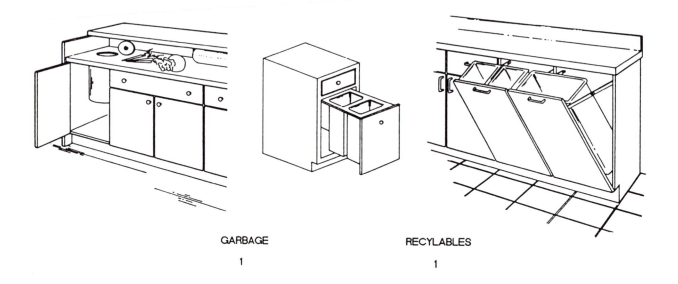

GARBAGE
1

RECYLABLES
1

Figure 55 - **Guideline 12** - At least two waste receptacles should be included in the plan; one for garbage and one for recyclables, or other recycling facilities should be planned.

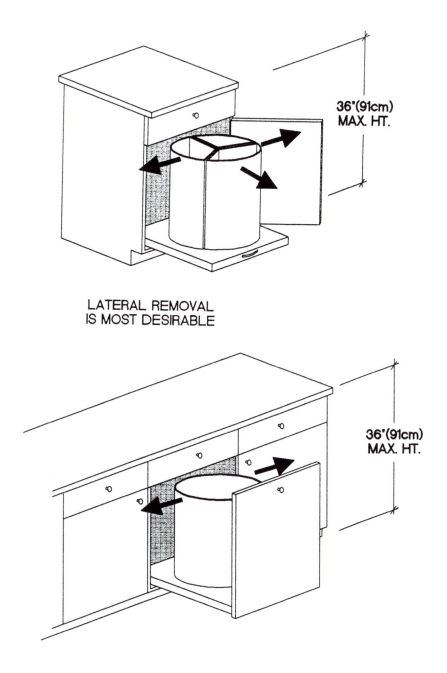

LATERAL REMOVAL
IS MOST DESIRABLE

36"(91cm)
MAX. HT.

36"(91cm)
MAX. HT.

Figure 56 -   **Guideline 12 - Clarification** - The top edge of a waste receptacle should be no higher than 36" (91cm). The receptacle should be easily accessible and should be removable without raising the receptacle bottom higher than the unit's physical height. Lateral removal of the receptacle which does not require lifting is most desirable.

Many recycling and waste receptacles, such as those in deep drawers or tilt out cabinets require lifting them above the cabinet to empty them. Because this can be difficult for a person of shorter stature or a person with limited strength or mobility, it is more desirable to choose a receptacle that slides out or requires minimum lifting.

SECTION III Appliance Placement and Use/Clearance Space
Guideline 13 to Guideline 21

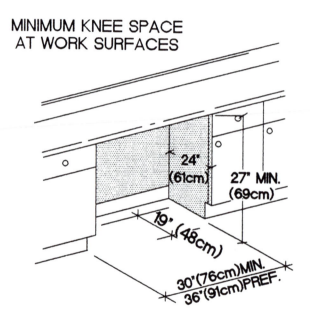

MINIMUM KNEE SPACE
AT WORK SURFACES

24"
(61cm)

27" MIN.
(69cm)

19" (48cm)

30"(76cm)MIN.
36"(91cm)PREF.

Figure 57 -   **Guideline 13** - Knee space (which may be open or adaptable) should be planned below or adjacent to sinks, cooktops, ranges, dishwashers, refrigerators and ovens whenever possible. Knee space should be a minimum of 30" (76cm) wide by 27" (69cm) high by 19" (48cm) deep under the counter. The 27" (69cm) height at the front of the knee space may decrease progressively as depth increases.

The actual counter height at a knee space will vary. For a person in a wheelchair, the preferred height is 30" (76cm), but it may be as high as 34" (86cm). For a person with limited endurance or balance, a 36" (91cm) high counter may be comfortable if a stool is provided that is compatible with that counter height. The height of the armrest on a wheelchair or the depth of an appliance will also influence the counter height required for clearance.

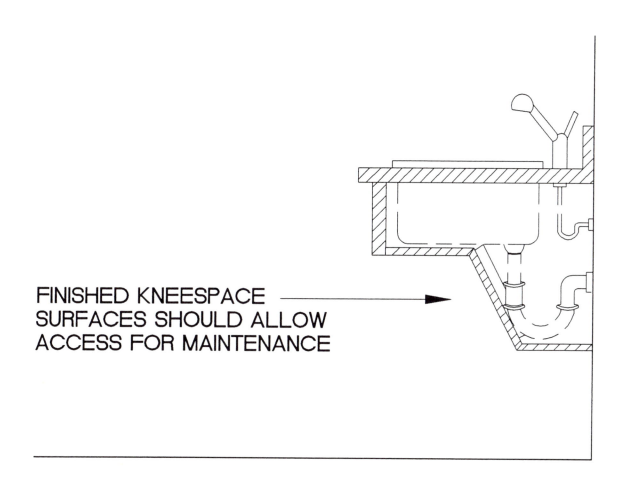

FINISHED KNEESPACE
SURFACES SHOULD ALLOW
ACCESS FOR MAINTENANCE

Figure 58 -   **Guideline 13 - Clarification** - Surfaces in the knee space area should be finished for safety and aesthetic purposes.

A protective and decorative panel should be part of the design of a knee space. A seated user should be protected from rough surfaces, hot elements, and the working parts of the appliance or fixture. In addition, the appliance, fixture, or plumbing should be protected from repeated impact. Finally, aesthetics dictate the use of a covering to coordinate with the look of the space.

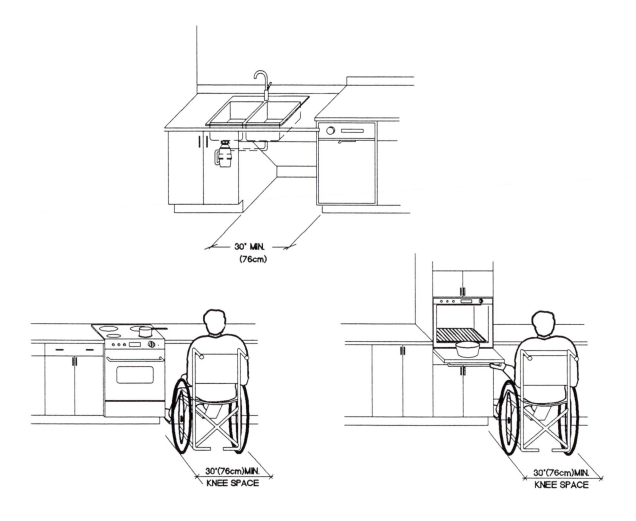

Figure 59 - **Guideline 13 Examples** - Knee space provided at appliances makes them universally accessible. Surfaces in the knee space area should be finished for safety and aesthetic purposes.

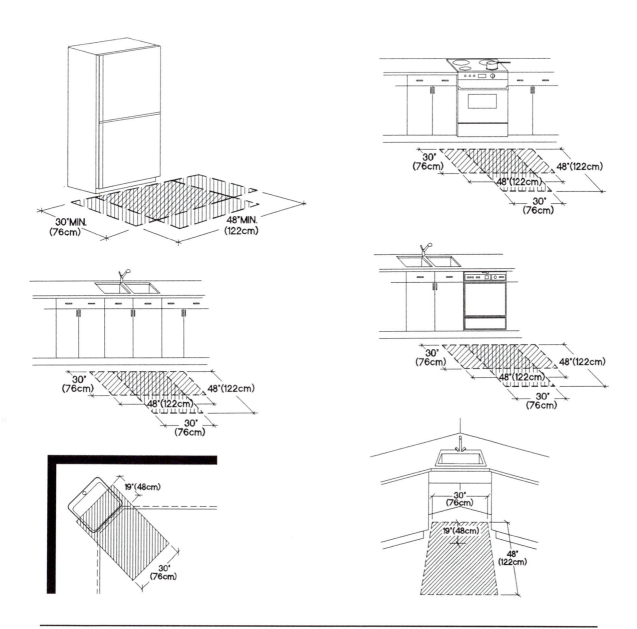

Figure 60 - **Guideline 14** - A clear floor space of 30" x 48" (76cm x 122cm) should be provided at the sink, dishwasher, cooktop, oven and refrigerator. (Measure from face of cabinet or appliance if toe kick is less than 9" (23cm) high.)

If you are working with a standard height toekick, calculate the clear floor space from the face of the cabinetry. If the toekick is raised to 9" (23cm) or higher, you may include the depth of the toekick when figuring clear floor space. The reason is that a 9" - 12" (23cm - 30cm) toekick allows clearance for the footrest on most wheelchairs.

When a sink or cooktop is designed in an angled corner, there must be the minimum 30" x 48" (76cm x 122cm) clear floor space access. Note the corner sink drawing that incorporates knee space where the actual angled countertop edge is less than 30" (76cm) but the distance between the two cabinets is greater. The 30" x 48" (76cm x 122cm) clear floor space may however include the knee space below, which begins 19" (48cm) in from the front edge of the counter as measured at the floor.

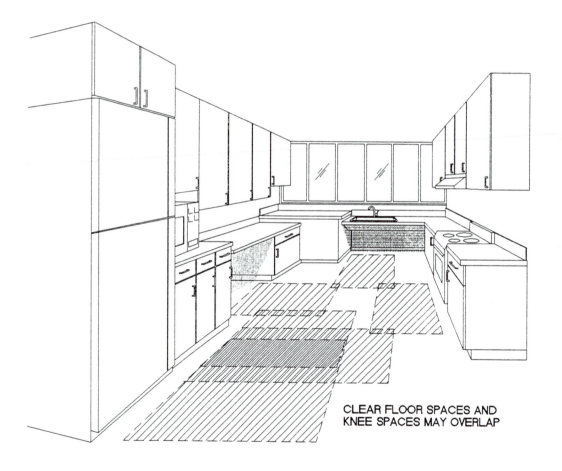

CLEAR FLOOR SPACES AND
KNEE SPACES MAY OVERLAP

Figure 61 - **Guideline 14 - Clarification** - These spaces may overlap and up to 19" (48cm) of knee space (beneath an appliance, counter, cabinet, etc.) may be part of the total 30" (76cm) and/or 48" (122cm) dimension.

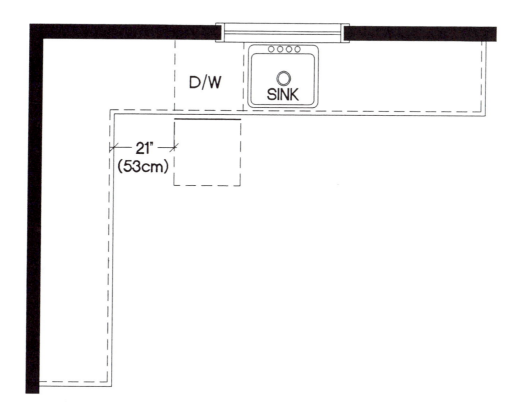

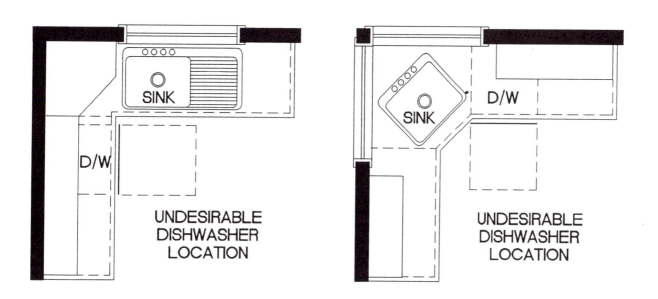

UNDESIRABLE
DISHWASHER
LOCATION

UNDESIRABLE
DISHWASHER
LOCATION

Figure 62 - **Guideline 15** - A minimum of 21" (53cm) clear floor space should be allowed between the edge of the dishwasher and counters, appliances and/or cabinets which are placed at a right angle to the dishwasher.

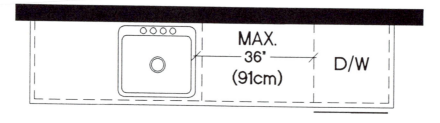

Figure 63 -   **Guideline 16** - The edge of the primary dishwasher should be within 36" (91cm) of the edge of one sink.

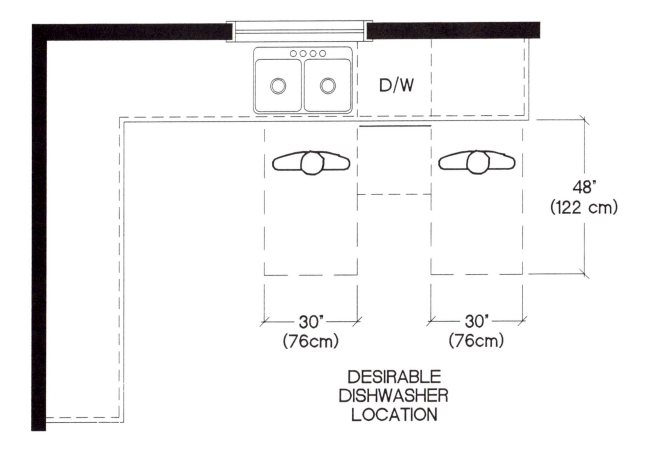

Figure 64 - **Guideline 16 - Clarification** - The dishwasher should be reachable by more than one person at a time to accommodate other cooks, kitchen clean-up helpers and/or other family members.

A 30" x 48" (76cm x 122cm) clear floor space on both sides of the dishwasher will allow a person access to the dishwasher from either side.

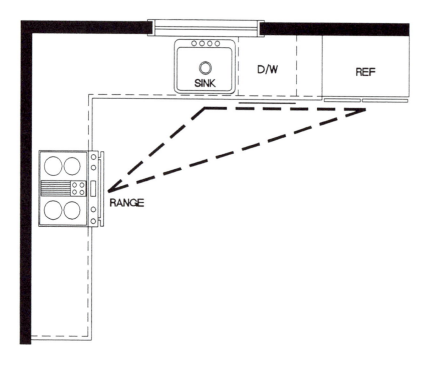

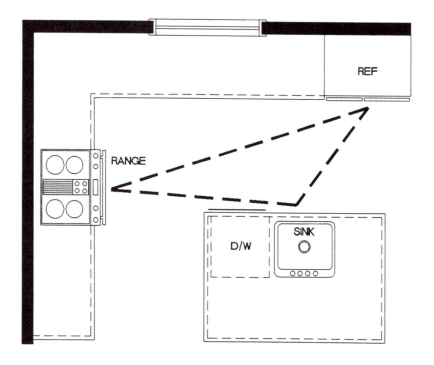

Figure 65 -   **Guideline 17** - If the kitchen has only one sink, it should be located between or across from the cooking surface, preparation area or refrigerator.

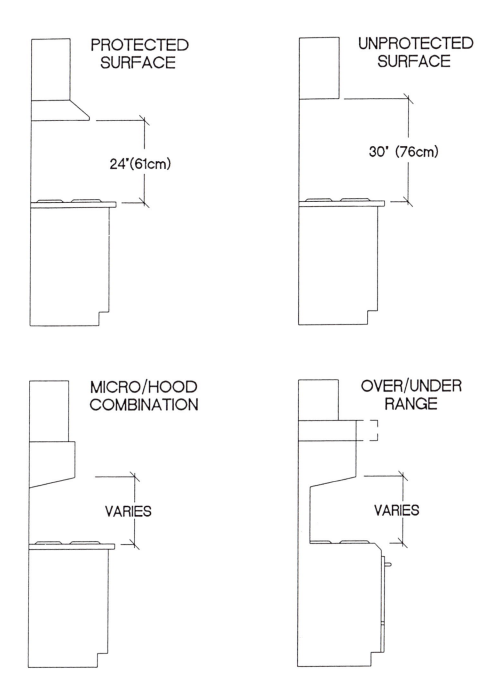

Figure 66 - **Guideline 18** - There should be at least 24" (61cm) of clearance between the cooking surface and a protected surface above, or at least 30" (76cm) of clearance between the cooking surface and an unprotected surface above. (If the protected surface is a microwave hood combination, manufacturer's specifications may dictate a clearance less than 24" (61cm).

While manufacturer specifications may call for less clearance with a microwave/hood or an oven over a cooking surface, safety and access relating to an upper oven or back burners should be considered.

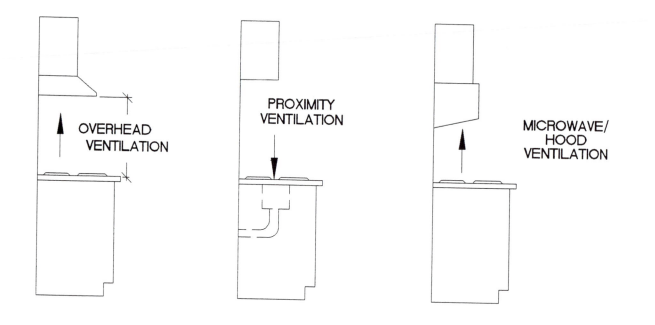

Figure 67 -   **Guideline 19** - All major appliances used for surface cooking should have a ventilation system, with a fan rated at 150 CFM minimum.

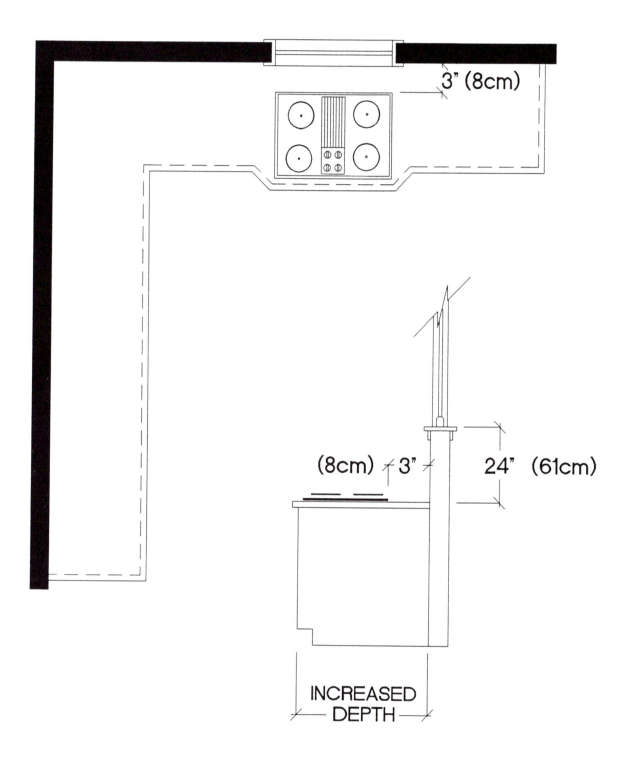

Figure 68 - **Guideline 20** - The cooking surface should not be placed below an operable window unless the window is 3" (8cm) or more behind the appliance and more than 24" (61cm) above it. Windows, operable or inoperable, above a cooking surface should not be dressed with flammable window treatments.

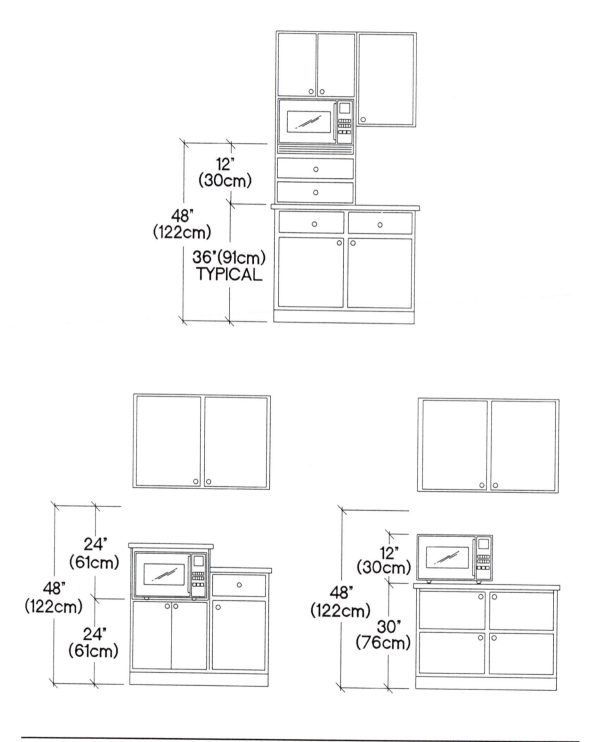

Figure 69 -   **Guideline 21** - Microwave ovens should be placed so that the bottom of the appliance is 24" to 48" (61cm to 122cm) above the floor.

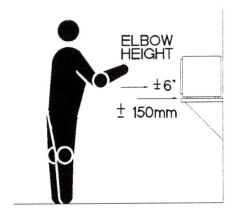
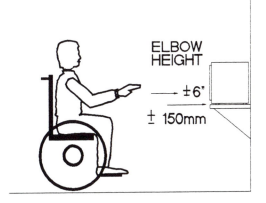

CONVENIENT MICROWAVE
HEIGHT

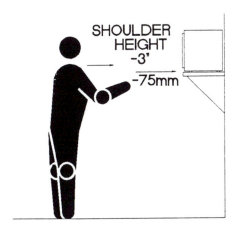
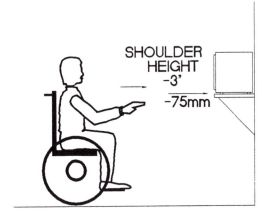

SAFE MICROWAVE
HEIGHT

Figure 70 - **Guideline 21 - Clarification** - The final placement recommendation should be based on the user's physical abilities, which may require placement outside of the preferred 24" to 48" (61cm to 122cm) range.

Appliances designed with a microwave/hood or oven over a range will not meet this guideline but may be a necessary choice. When designing for a seated user, it may be desirable to go below the 24" (61cm) guideline. If this is the case, safety for toddlers becomes an issue and must be addressed.

SECTION IV Counter Surface and Landing Space
Guideline 22 to Guideline 34

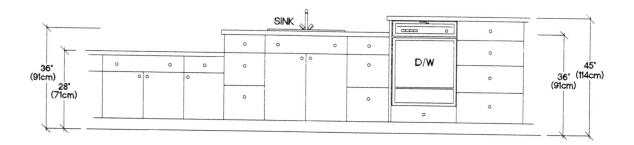

Figure 71 -   **Guideline 22** - At least two work-counter heights should be offered in the kitchen, with one 28" - 36" (71cm - 91cm) above the finished floor and the other 36" - 45" (91cm - 114cm) above the finished floor.

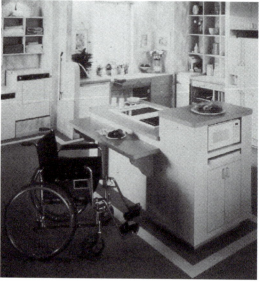

Figure 72 -   **Guideline 22 - Example** - Varying counter heights will create work spaces for various tasks and for cooks of varying stature, including seated cooks.

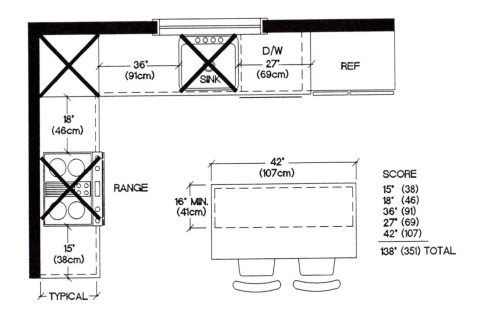

Figure 73 -   **Guideline 23** - Countertop Frontage, Small kitchens - equal or less than 150 sq.ft. (14 sq.m) - allow at least 132" (335cm) of usable countertop frontage.

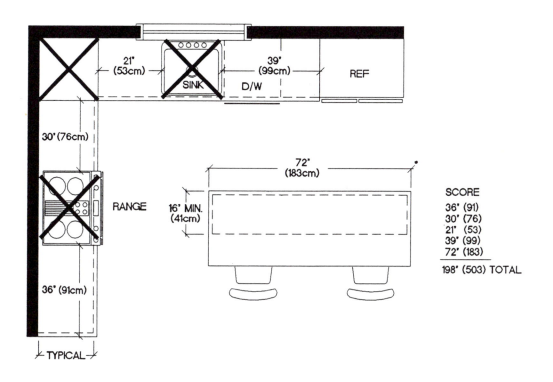

Figure 74 -   **Guideline 23** - Countertop Frontage, Large kitchens - over 150 sq.ft. (14 sq.m) - allow at least 198" (503cm) of usable countertop frontage.

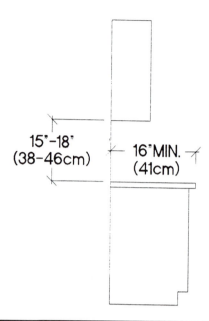

Figure 75   **Guideline 23** - Countertop Frontage - Counters must be a minimum of 16" (41cm) deep, and wall cabinets must be at least 15" (38cm) above their surface for counter to be included in total frontage measurement. (Measure only countertop frontage, do not count corner space.)

The minimum 15" (38cm) of clearance between a work surface and a wall cabinet relates to appliance storage and line of sight. However, there are times when dropping the wall cabinets lower, even onto the counter, will provide needed storage in the universal reach range.

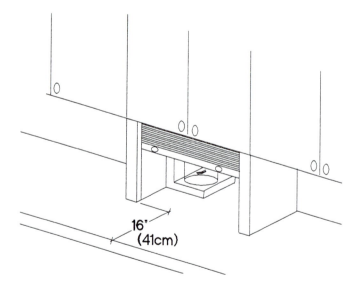

Figure 76 -   **Guideline 23 - Clarification** - If an appliance garage/storage cabinet extends to the counter, there must be 16" (41cm) or more of clear space in front of this cabinet for the area to be counted as usable countertop frontage.

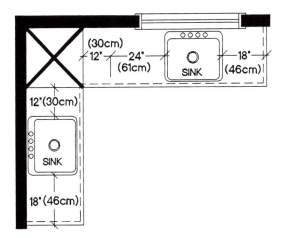

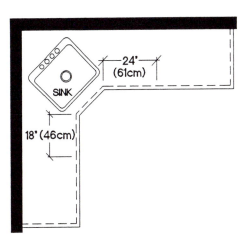

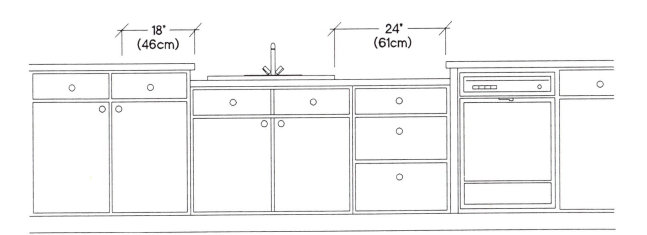

Figure 77 -   **Guideline 24** - There should be at least 24" (61cm) of countertop frontage to
one side of the primary sink, and 18" (46cm) on the other side (including corner sink applications) with the 24" (61cm) counter frontage at the same counter height as the sink. The countertop frontage may be a continuous surface, or the total of two angled countertop sections.
(Measure only countertop frontage, do not count corner space.) *For further instruction on these
requirements see Guideline 31.*

Whenever possible, the counter space on both sides of the sink should be at the
same height.

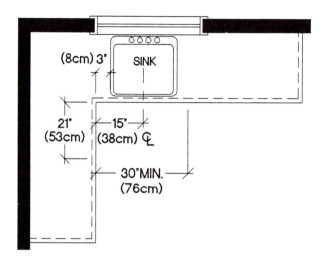

Figure 78 -   **Guideline 24 Clarification** - The minimum allowable space from a corner to the edge of the primary sink is 3" (8cm); it should also be a minimum of 15" (38cm) from that corner to the sink centerline.

The minimum 15" (38cm) to centerline allows 30" x 48" (76cm x 122cm) clear floor space to be planned centered on the sink.

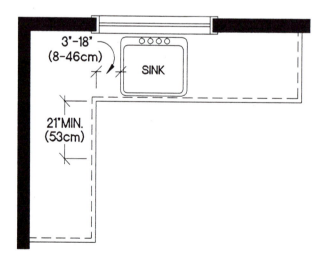

Figure 79 -   **Guideline 24 Clarification** - If there is anything less than 18" (46cm) of frontage from the edge of the primary sink to a corner, 21" (53cm) of clear counter (measure frontage) should be allowed on the return.

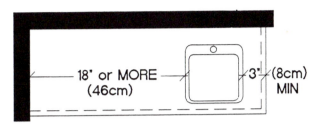

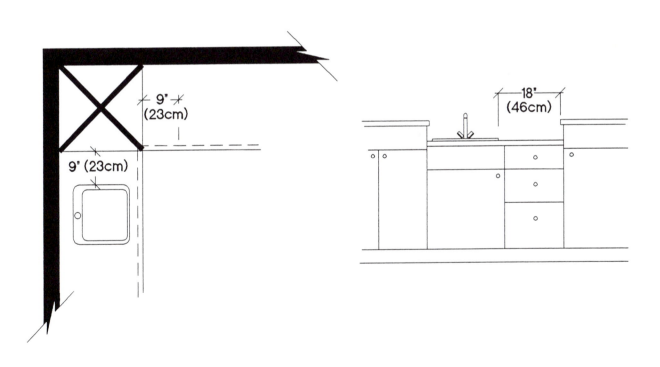

Figure 80 - **Guideline 25** - At least 3" (8cm) of countertop frontage should be provided on one side of secondary sinks, and 18" (46cm) on the other side (including corner sink applications) with the 18" (46cm) counter frontage at the same counter height as the sink. The countertop frontage may be a continuous surface, or the total of two angled countertop sections. (Measure only countertop frontage, do not count corner space.) *For further instruction on these requirements see Guideline 31.*

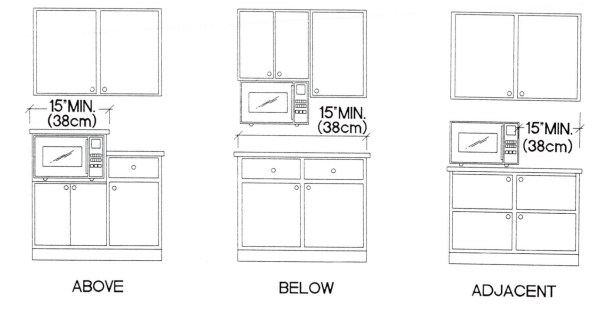

ABOVE   BELOW   ADJACENT

Figure 81 -   **Guideline 26** - At least 15" (38cm) of landing space, a minimum of 16" (41cm) deep, should be planned above, below or adjacent to a microwave oven. *For further instruction on these requirements see Guideline 31.*

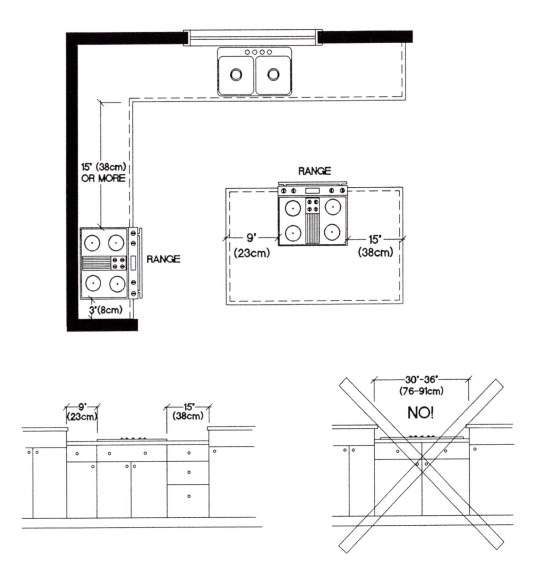

Figure 82 - **Guideline 27** - In an open-ended kitchen configuration, at least 9" (23cm) of counter space should be allowed on one side of the cooking surface and 15" (38cm) on the other, at the same counter height as the appliance. For an enclosed configuration, at least 3" (8cm) of clearance space should be planned at an end wall protected by flame-retardant surfacing material and 15" (38cm) should be allowed on the other side of the appliance, at the same counter height as the appliance. *For further instruction on these requirements see Guideline 31.*

Maintaining the minimum counter area adjacent to a cooktop at the same height as the cooktop improves safety and accessibility. In case of emergency/fire, the cook should be able to slide a pot right off the burner onto adjacent counter without lifting or lowering. A person with limited strength, grip, or balance will use this technique on a regular basis and in this case, adjacent spaces should be heat resistant.

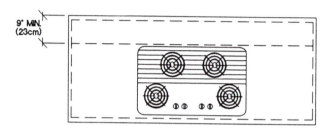

Figure 83 -   **Guideline 27 - Clarification** - For safety reasons, countertop should also extend a minimum of 9" (23cm) behind the cooking surface, at the same counter height as the appliance, in any instance where there is not an abutting wall/backsplash.

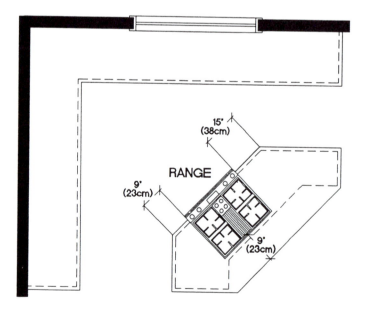

Figure 84 -   **Guideline 27 - Clarification** - In an outside angle installation of cooking surfaces, there should be at least 9" (23cm) of straight counter space on one side and 15" (38cm) of straight counter space on the other side, at the same counter height as the appliance.

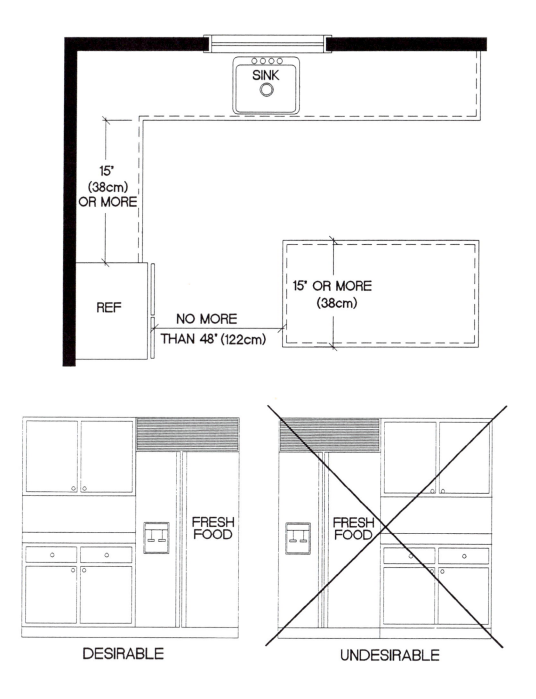

Fgiure 85 - **Guideline 28** - The plan should allow at least 15" (38cm) of counter space on the handle side of the refrigerator or on either side of a side-by-side refrigerator or, at least 15" (38cm) of landing space which is no more than 48" (122cm) across from the refrigerator. (Measure the 48" (122cm) distance from the center front of the refrigerator to the countertop opposite it.) *For further instruction on these requirements see Guideline 31.*

When side-by-side refrigerators are specified, it is preferable to design the space so that the countertop can be easily accessed by an individual using the fresh food section.

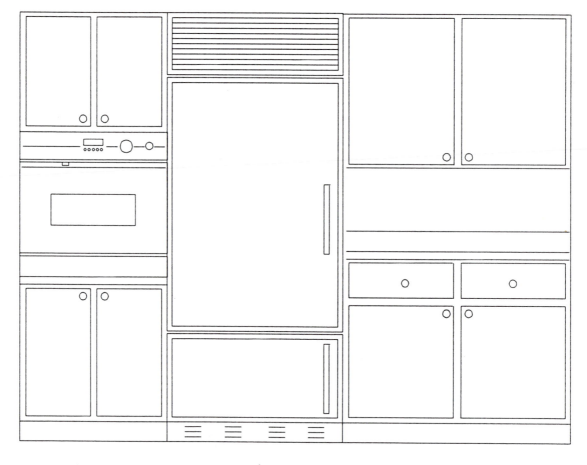

ACCEPTABLE OVEN / REFRIGERATOR PLACEMENT

Figure 86 - **Guideline 28 - Clarification** - Although not ideal, it is acceptable to place an oven adjacent to a refrigerator. For convenience, the refrigerator should be the appliance placed next to available countertop. If there is no safe landing area across from the oven, this arrangement may be reversed.

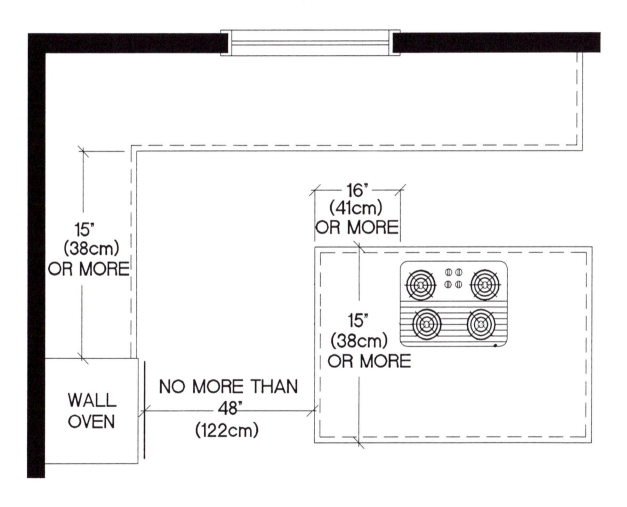

Figure 87 - **Guideline 29** - There should be at least 15" (38cm) of landing space which is at least 16"(41cm) deep next to or above the oven if the appliance door opens into a primary traffic pattern. At least 15" x 16" (38cm x 41cm) of landing space which is no more than 48" (122cm) across from the oven is acceptable if the appliance does not open into a traffic area. (Measure the 48" (122cm) distance from the center front of the oven to the countertop opposite it.) *For further instruction on these requirements see Guideline 31.*

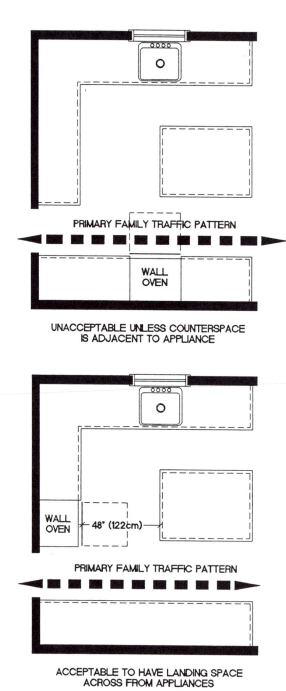

PRIMARY FAMILY TRAFFIC PATTERN

WALL
OVEN

UNACCEPTABLE UNLESS COUNTERSPACE
IS ADJACENT TO APPLIANCE

WALL
OVEN |← 48" (122cm) →|

PRIMARY FAMILY TRAFFIC PATTERN

ACCEPTABLE TO HAVE LANDING SPACE
ACROSS FROM APPLIANCES

Figure 88 -   **Guideline 29 Examples** - In the top example, the oven opens directly into a major traffic pattern leading from the utility area to the family room. This is a dangerous installation which should be avoided unless there is landing space on either side of the oven. In the bottom example, the oven is located within the cook's primary work space, away from the family traffic pattern. Therefore, a landing area can be directly opposite it.

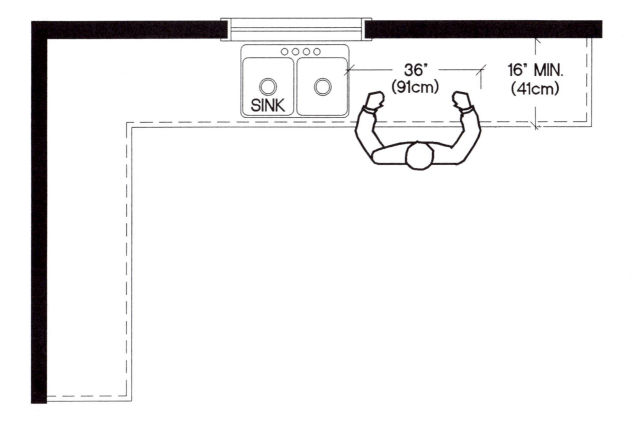

Figure 89 - **Guideline 30** - At least 36" (91cm) of continuous countertop which is at least 16" (41cm) deep should be planned for the preparation center. The preparation center should be immediately adjacent to a water source. *For further instruction on these requirements see Guideline 31.*

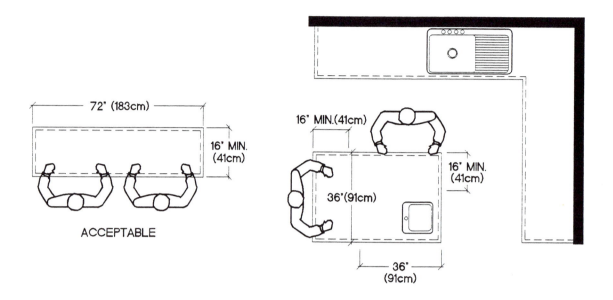

Figure 90 -   **Guideline 30 - Clarification** - If two or more people work in the kitchen simultaneously, each will need a minimum 36" (91cm) wide by 16" (41cm) deep preparation center of their own. If two people will stand adjacent to one another, a 72" (183cm) wide by 16" (41cm) deep space should be planned.

Try to orient the two people so that conversation can be continued during cooking and/or clean up process.

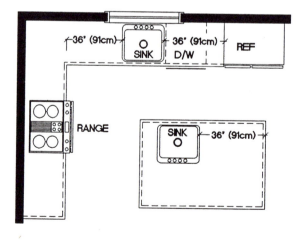

Figure 91 -   **Guideline 30 - Clarification** - The preparation center can be placed between the primary sink and the cooking surface, between the refrigerator and the primary sink, or adjacent to a secondary sink on an island or other cabinet section.

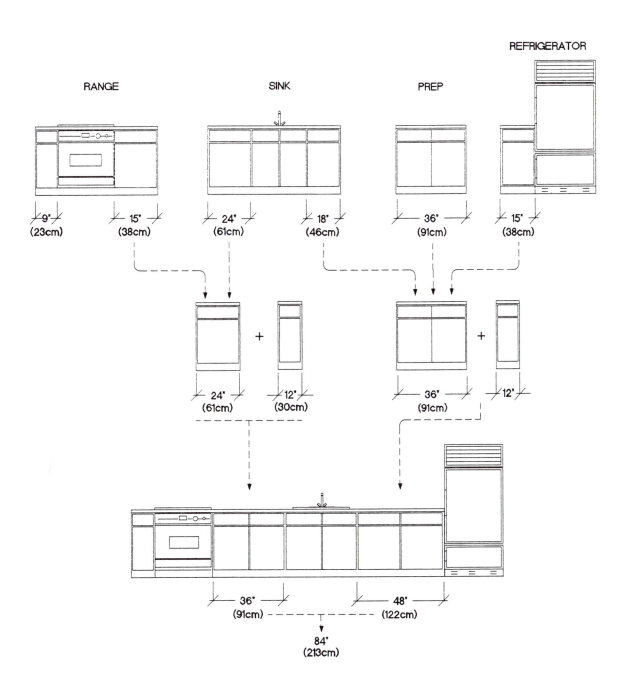

Figure 92 -   **Guideline 31** - If two work centers are adjacent to one another, determine a new minimum counter frontage requirement for the two adjoining spaces by taking the longest of the two required counter lengths and adding 12" (30cm).

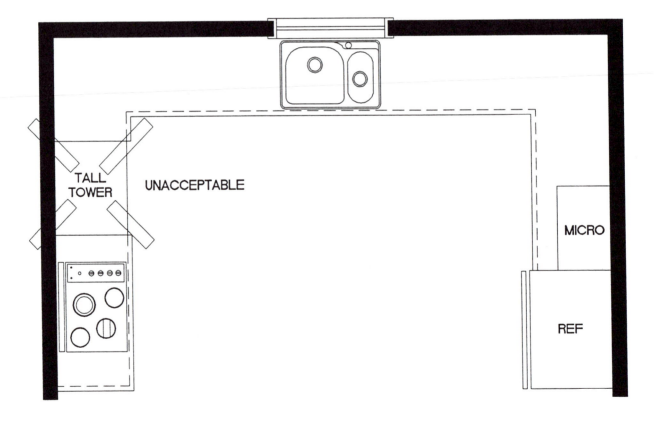

Figure 93 - **Guideline 32** - No two primary work centers (the primary sink, refrigerator, preparation or cooktop/range center) should be separated by a full-height, full-depth tall tower, such as an oven cabinet, pantry cabinet or refrigerator.

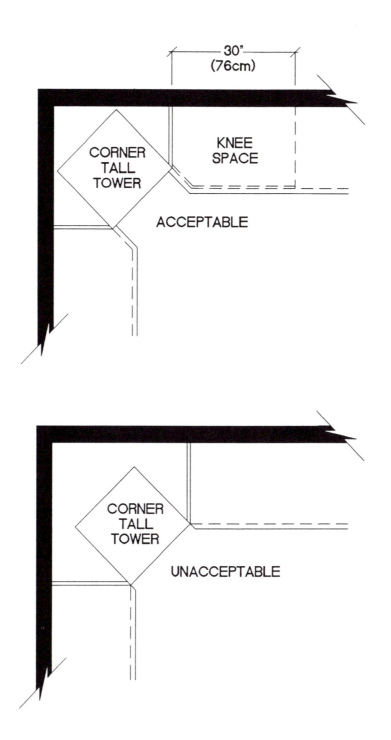

Figure 94 - **Guideline 32 - Clarification** - A corner-recessed tall tower between primary work centers is acceptable if knee space is planned to one side of the tower.

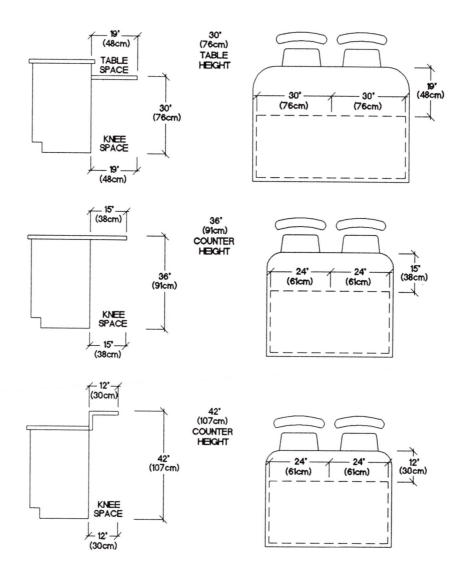

Figure 95 -   **Guideline 33** - Kitchen seating areas require the following minimum clearances:

30" (76cm) high tables/counters:
                        allow a 30" (76cm) wide x 19" (48cm) deep counter/table space
                        for each seated diner, and at least 19" (48cm) of clear knee
                        space
36" (91cm) high counters:
                        allow a 24" (61cm) wide by 15" (38cm) deep counter space for
                        each seated diner, and at least 15" (38cm) of clear knee space
42" (107cm) high counters:
                        allow a 24" (61cm) wide by 12" (30cm) deep counter space for
                        each seated diner, and 12" (30cm) of clear knee space

    Given that a 30" (76cm) high table or counter will work for a person in a wheel-chair, the width of the allowance for each seated diner has been increased to allow for diners using wheelchairs.

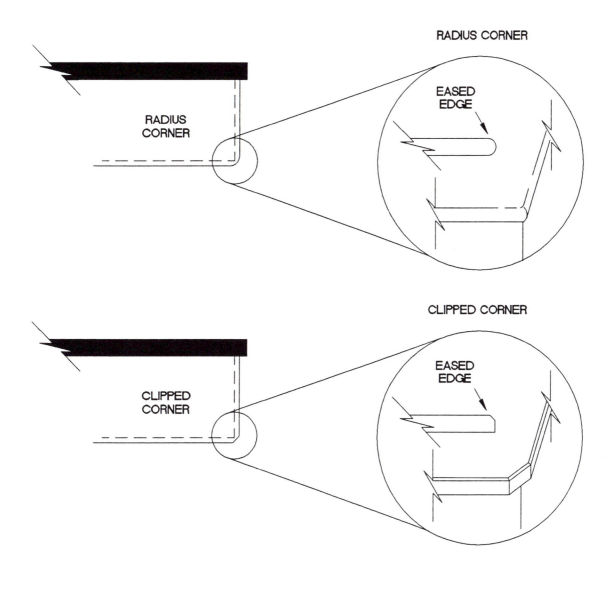

Figure 96 -   **Guideline 34** - Use clipped or radius corners for open countertops. Countertop edges should be eased to eliminate sharp edges.

SECTION V: Room, Appliance and Equipment Controls
Guideline 35 to Guideline 40

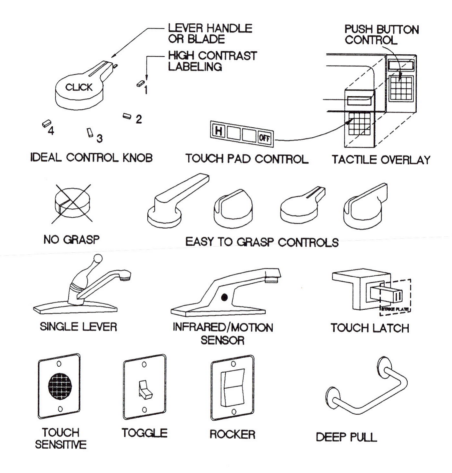

Figure 97 - **Guideline 35** - Controls, handles and door/drawer pulls should be operable with one hand, require only a minimal amount of strength for operation, and should not require tight grasping, pinching or twisting of the wrist. (Includes handles/knobs/pulls on entry and exit doors, appliances, cabinets, drawers and plumbing fixtures, as well as light and thermostat controls, switches, intercoms, and other room controls.)

Controls that meet this guideline expand their use to include people with limited strength, dexterity and grasping abilities. A simple test is to try operating the controls with a closed fist.

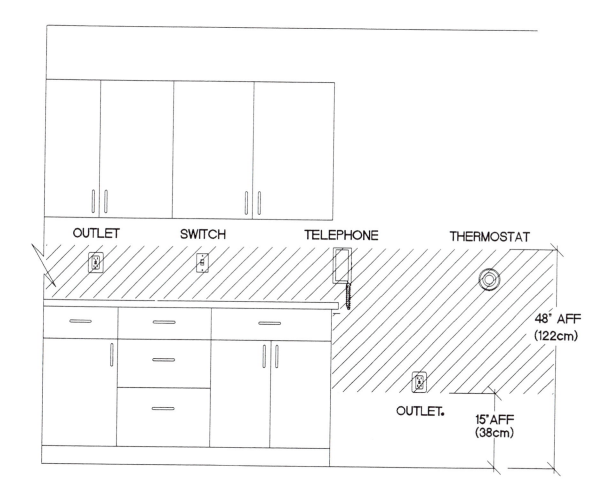

OUTLET   SWITCH   TELEPHONE   THERMOSTAT

48" AFF
(122cm)

OUTLET.

15" AFF
(38cm)

Figure 98 -   **Guideline 36** - Wall-mounted room controls (i.e.: wall receptacles, switches, thermostats, telephones, intercoms etc.) should be 15" to 48"(38cm to 122cm) above the finished floor. The switch plate can extend beyond that dimension, but the control itself should be within it.

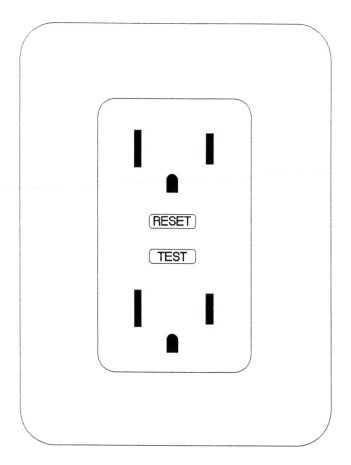

Figure 99 -   **Guideline 37** - Ground fault circuit interrupters should be specified on all receptacles within the kitchen.

GFCI are a safety feature throughout the kitchen, including protection when foreign objects are accidentally inserted in an outlet, as well as, when an outlet is close to water.

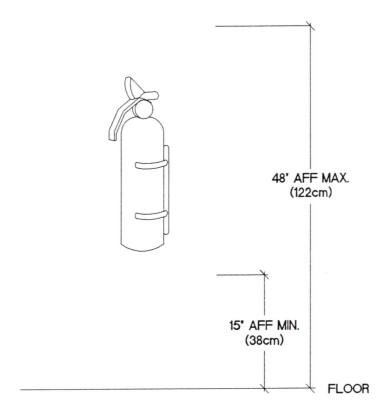

48" AFF MAX.
(122cm)

15" AFF MIN.
(38cm)

FLOOR

Figure 100 - **Guideline 38** - A fire extinguisher should be visibly located in the kitchen, away from cooking equipment and 15" to 48" (38cm to 122cm) above the floor. Smoke alarms should be included near the kitchen.

A fire extinguisher that can be seen and reached easily expands access to most people.

Figure 101 -   **Guideline 39** - Window/skylight area should equal at least 10% of the total
square footage of the separate kitchen, or a total living space which includes a kitchen.

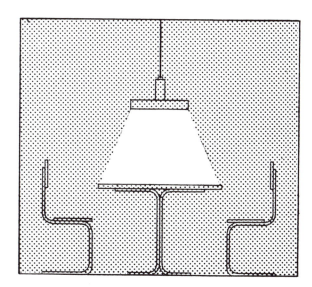

Figure 102 - **Guideline 40** - Every work surface in the kitchen should be well-illuminated by appropriate task and/or general lighting.

chapter 4

Countertops and Cabinets

As always, countertops and cabinetry must be designed to allow storage and use within the reach of the client. Items should be stored as close to their first place of use as possible and counters designed to allow for both work and transfer.

These principles require careful consideration of design and materials. In universal design, this simply means expanding on the consideration given to these two key elements of the kitchen.

COUNTERTOPS

Height, area and materials used are the main universal design concerns in planning countertops. It is also important to consider the installation of countertops, particularly where there are overhangs or knee spaces.

Heights

The standard 36" (91cm) high kitchen countertop is comfortable for most standing users, but not for those who are shorter than average, taller than average, or for those who prefer to work while seated. The solution is not to throw out 36" (91cm) high countertops, but to supplement them with additional counters at other desired heights.

- For seated users, **ANSI** recommends 28" - 34" (71cm - 86cm) high counters. If you start with 27" - 29" (69cm - 74cm) high knee space (as per ANSI), add 1 1/2" (4cm) for an apron panel to hide support for the counter over a knee space, and 1 1/2" (4cm) for the thickness of the counter, this places the counter height at 30" - 32" (76cm - 81cm) which is comfortable and workable for most seated users.

- Standard table height of 30" (76cm) is the most preferred lowered countertop height and works well for a person in standard seating. This height counter is also recommended for a baking or chopping center for the average height cook.

- If the person is using a wheelchair, the armrest height will determine the optimum knee space and counter height.

- The next height would be the standard 36" (91cm) counter, good for most standing users and for spaces adjacent to ranges or dishwashers in standard installations.

- The last common height would be 42" - 45" (107cm - 114cm), for taller users, for dishwashers in raised applications, snack bars and visual or safety barriers.

Recommended Countertop Heights in Universal Kitchens

- 28" - 32" (71cm - 81cm) for seated users, table, baking or chopping center, users of shorter stature.

- 36" (91cm) for general use by standing users.

- 42" - 45" (107cm - 114cm) for users of taller stature, for counters over raised standard dishwashers, for snack bars/visual dividers/safety barriers.

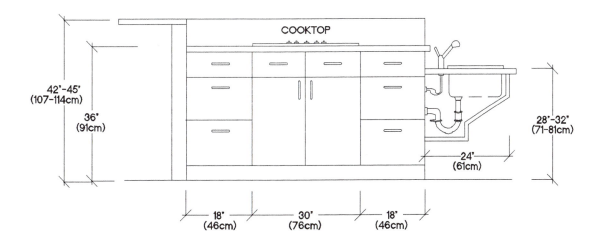

Figure 103 - Universal counter heights.

Adjustable Height Countertops

In addition to the three functional recommended ranges, countertop heights may be designed to be adaptable or adjustable. This can be done with a motorized system, mechanical system or manually adjustable system.

Motorized Adjustable

Motor-driven adjustable-height countertops accommodate standing and seated users of varying statures with a simple push of a button to adjust the height. This requires the use of flexible or slip-joint plumbing if a sink is involved and wiring in flexible conduit for cooktops or sinks, so the designer must check all local codes.

These units do add cost, but their cost may be offset by the flexibility and independence they create.

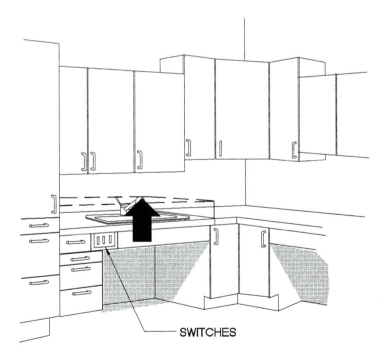

SWITCHES

Figure 104 -   Motorized adjustable countertop.

Mechanically Adjustable

Countertops that adjust in height mechanically also allow for a variety of users. This system requires that the person adjusting the countertop have the strength and dexterity to operate the mechanical actuator or lever handle. When mechanically adjustable devices support and involve electrical and plumbing systems, great care and flexibility must be used in the planning and design process. Mechanically adjustable devices offer moderately priced solutions when there is a need for adjustable countertops.

When planning for adjustable countertops always take the extra effort to consider the full extension of travel distance of the countertop in its extended position. You will want to be sure that adjacent countertop overhangs are eliminated allowing for the up and down movement of the adjustable countertop.

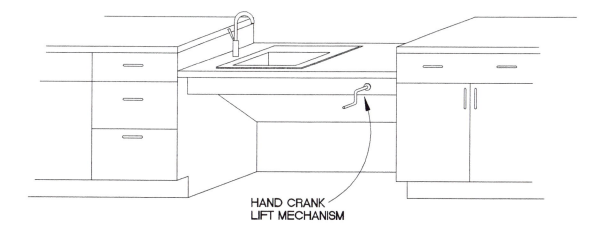

HAND CRANK
LIFT MECHANISM

Figure 105 - Mechanically adjustable countertop.

Manually Adjustable

Manually adjustable counter segments can be installed to meet the changing needs over the life of a kitchen. They are intended to be adaptable, to be adjusted in a short time with no renovation costs as users needs change, but not intended for daily or frequent adjustment.

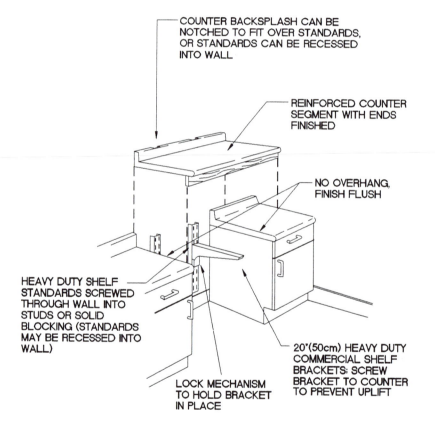

COUNTER BACKSPLASH CAN BE NOTCHED TO FIT OVER STANDARDS, OR STANDARDS CAN BE RECESSED INTO WALL

REINFORCED COUNTER SEGMENT WITH ENDS FINISHED

NO OVERHANG, FINISH FLUSH

HEAVY DUTY SHELF STANDARDS SCREWED THROUGH WALL INTO STUDS OR SOLID BLOCKING (STANDARDS MAY BE RECESSED INTO WALL)

LOCK MECHANISM TO HOLD BRACKET IN PLACE

20"(50cm) HEAVY DUTY COMMERCIAL SHELF BRACKETS; SCREW BRACKET TO COUNTER TO PREVENT UPLIFT

Figure 106 -   Manually adjustable countertop.

Amount of Counter Space

When planning counters at varying heights that include sinks, cooktops, refrigerators, ovens or dishwashers, the designer must consider the adjacent spaces. In an effort to provide continuous counter space at these various heights, flexibility is the key to keeping countertop work surfaces close at hand.

Pull-out Work Surfaces

Pull-out work surfaces at varying heights will add flexibility to the countertops in most kitchens.

If an appliance or fixture in a lowered counter has limited adjacent counter, a pull-out work surface or a rolling cart with a surface at the same height might help to provide the needed transfer and working space.

The preferred choice would always be continuous adjacent counter. In considering the parameters of a kitchen and the needs of the clients, the designer may need to consider these alternatives.

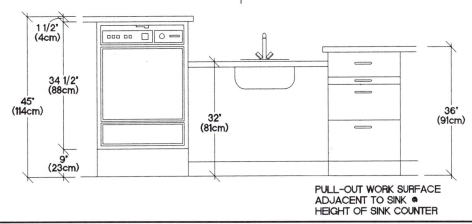

Figure 107 -   A pull-out work surface adjacent to the sink is seen just below the height of the sink counter.

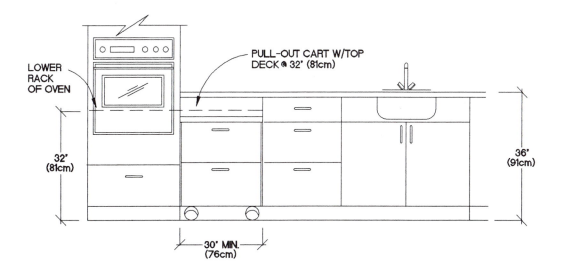

Figure 108 -   A pull-out cart with the top deck at 32" (81cm) creates a knee space and provides for transfer from the oven.

SURFACING MATERIALS

Universal design expands the considerations that go into choosing surfacing materials for the counters in a kitchen. For an extensive examination of the materials available, refer to the **NKBA® Kitchen Industry Technical Manuals.**

Universal design principles require counters that are easy-care, resilient, sometimes heat-resistant and flexible to allow for tactile or visual contrast.

- **Resilient:** when something is dropped on this, there is some forgiveness before breaking.

- **Heat Resistant:** equipment may be placed on this directly from the oven or cooktop.

- **Flexible Fabrication:** allows for contrast in touch, shape and color.

- **Easy-care:** wipes clean with water, no maintenance.

- **Durable:** if damaged, this can be repaired, does not need to be replaced.

Reference the following table for material attributes and characteristics.

Material	Resilient	Heat Resistant	Flexible Fabrication	Easy Care	Durable
Butcher Block	X		X		X
Tile		X	X	to some degree	X
Laminate	to some degree		X	X	
Solid Surface	to some degree		X	X	X
Stone		X	to some degree	X (more so in dark colors)	X
Stainless Steel		X	to some degree	X	X

Butcher Block

The benefits of butcher block in the universal kitchen include its resilience, its application as a cutting surface and its flexibility in fabrication.

If something is dropped on a butcher block counter there is more chance that neither the surface nor the item will be damaged. The ability to cut right on the surface eliminates the need for access to an additional cutting board.

Edges, corners, curbs and contrast can be cut into the surface in fabricating. Using this as a surface away from water sources helps to cut down on maintenance concerns.

Tile

Tile can be a cost effective way to provide heat-resistant surfaces in the kitchen. By choosing machine-cut tiles that are smooth and straight, grout is minimized as is maintenance.

The variety of colors and edge treatments available provide opportunities for both tactile and visual contrast as well as some spill protection.

Laminates

Laminates provide easy-care, economical counters. Common fabrication techniques allow for a variety of treatments to create eased or clipped edges and corners. Color is limitless to provide contrast as desired.

Solid Surface

Solid surface materials provide ease of maintenance and tremendous flexibility in design and fabrication. There is no limit to the contrasting patterns and creative edge treatments that can be designed.

Integral sinks add to the ease of maintenance and the nature of the material lends itself to adjustable height segments of counter. This material is particularly durable in that it is somewhat resistant to heat and cutting,

and although it is not intended as a cutting or heat resistant surface, damage can usually be repaired.

Stone

Stone counters are heat resistant and therefore a good transfer area from ovens or cooktops. Careful fabrication will allow for a variety of edge or curb treatments. Smooth finished darker tones of more dense stone are the most durable.

Stainless Steel

Stainless steel surfaces are heat resistant and tremendously durable. They can be fabricated with a variety of edge treatments and can add dramatic contrast in the proper setting.

COUNTERTOP FABRICATION

In a universal kitchen, the countertops provide *way-finding* assistant and support for the user. Along with choosing heights and materials, there are several important considerations on fabricating and installing universal counters.

- Whenever possible, the counter surfaces near the oven and cooktop should be heat resistant to allow for transfer of hot items with the least amount of grasping or lifting necessary, especially helpful to a person with limited grip or strength.

- Color contrast at or near the counter edge will help a person with visual impairments to see the edge.

- A change in texture, such as a slightly raised edge or curb, will provide further tactile indication of the counter edge and help contain spills.

- Contrasting colors in the counter surface will assist the visually impaired in working with light and dark foods - measuring flour on a dark counter or coffee on a light counter.

- Edge treatments should include clipped or rounded corners and eased edges so that there are no sharp points.

COUNTERTOP INSTALLATION

When installing counters, universal design principles require careful consideration to the structural integrity of each counter.

- Knowing that decorative edge railings may be used for support requires that they be installed to support a minimum of 250 pounds (113 kilograms).

- Where an overhang or a knee space is provided, the edge of the counter should be capable of supporting the weight.

Blocking and brackets

In all these situations, blocking should be installed in the wall, before it is covered with drywall. The blocking should be extended to include the minimum and maximum heights that might be chosen for the counters (28" - 45" (71cm - 114cm) is a good guide). Commercial shelf brackets may be used to support a counter intended for adaptable height.

Be sure support brackets are secured in place with locking fasteners. Another option would be to use movable wood support strips or a frame that could be secured to the back wall and cabinetry on either side.

Fixed counters over knee spaces and motorized adjustable-height counters will require equivalent support.

It is important to note that the thickness of a standard countertop plus the thickness of the apron to conceal these support systems will typically be 3" (8cm), more than the 2" (5cm) that **ANSI** and **UFAS** specify. Also, whatever the bracing system, the counter must be securely fastened to allow the user to rely on it for support.

The best solution will usually be a combination of materials, height and fabrication techniques to meet the needs of the client and fall within the parameters of budget, space and appearance.

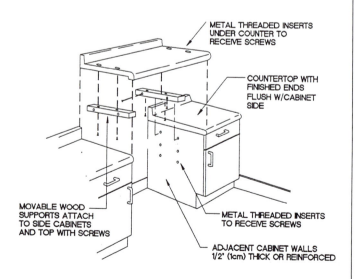

METAL THREADED INSERTS UNDER COUNTER TO RECEIVE SCREWS

COUNTERTOP WITH FINISHED ENDS FLUSH W/CABINET SIDE

MOVABLE WOOD SUPPORTS ATTACH TO SIDE CABINETS AND TOP WITH SCREWS

METAL THREADED INSERTS TO RECEIVE SCREWS

ADJACENT CABINET WALLS 1/2" (1cm) THICK OR REINFORCED

Figure 109 -   Movable wood support strips.

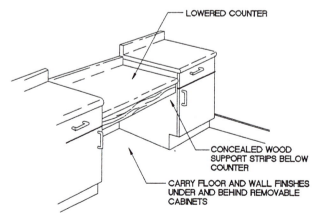

LOWERED COUNTER

CONCEALED WOOD SUPPORT STRIPS BELOW COUNTER

CARRY FLOOR AND WALL FINISHES UNDER AND BEHIND REMOVABLE CABINETS

Figure 110 -   Movable wood support strips.

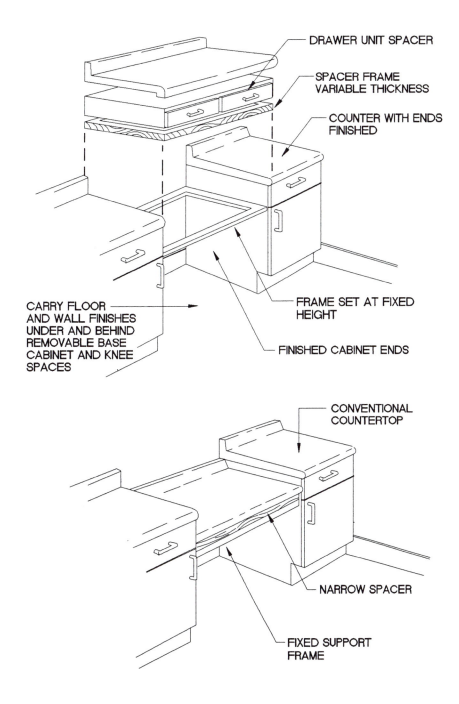

DRAWER UNIT SPACER

SPACER FRAME
VARIABLE THICKNESS

COUNTER WITH ENDS
FINISHED

FRAME SET AT FIXED
HEIGHT

FINISHED CABINET ENDS

CARRY FLOOR
AND WALL FINISHES
UNDER AND BEHIND
REMOVABLE BASE
CABINET AND KNEE
SPACES

CONVENTIONAL
COUNTERTOP

NARROW SPACER

FIXED SUPPORT
FRAME

Figure 111 - Fixed frame with spacers.

CABINETRY

Considering the reach range parameters and the addition of varying heights of counters and knee spaces, storage becomes a key issue in the universal kitchen. In considering cabinetry, design and location of storage, construction and hardware have particular importance in the universal kitchen.

Design and Location of Storage

The main goal is to put the maximum amount of storage in the universal reach range of 15" - 48" (38cm - 122cm) and to make all storage as safe and easy to access as possible. Another goal is to make stored items easy to see. As always, storing items near the point of their first use is a good guide.

Wall Cabinets and Accessory Options

As designers, a creative approach to how we use wall cabinetry will maximize the storage in the traditional backsplash area. Consider dropping cabinet applications lower on the wall even to the point where they rest on standard height or raised countertops. You may also want to consider:

- Some glass door cabinets with lighted interiors, especially helpful for people with decreased memory.

- Open shelves, which eliminate the hazard of open doors for people with visual impairments.

- Lowering wall cabinets via a motorized system or via a mechanical system. These systems include a safety-stop mechanism to halt motion when they come in contact with an obstacle.

- That counter space under the wall cabinet provides storage in the universal range. Whether open or closed as with an appliance garage, this area should not be overlooked.

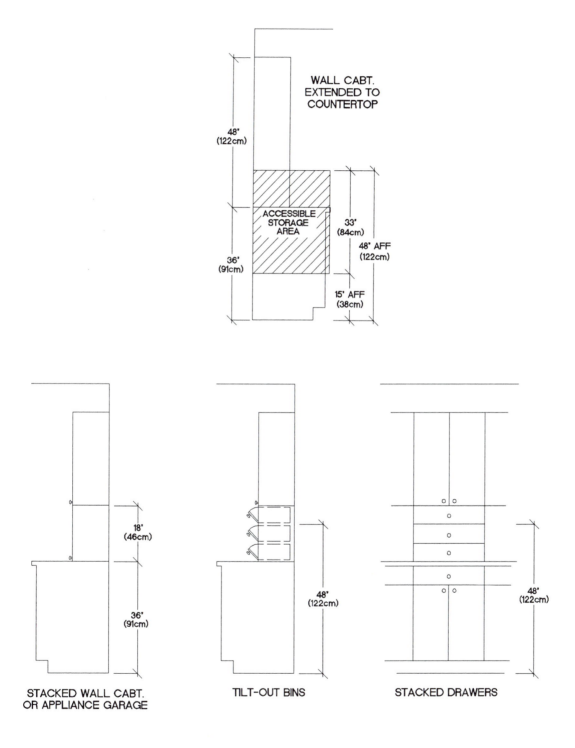

WALL CABT.
EXTENDED TO
COUNTERTOP

48"
(122cm)

ACCESSIBLE
STORAGE
AREA

33"
(84cm)

48" AFF
(122cm)

36"
(91cm)

15" AFF
(38cm)

18"
(46cm)

36"
(91cm)

48"
(122cm)

48"
(122cm)

STACKED WALL CABT.
OR APPLIANCE GARAGE

TILT-OUT BINS

STACKED DRAWERS

Figure 112 -   Wall cabinetry brought into the backsplash area.

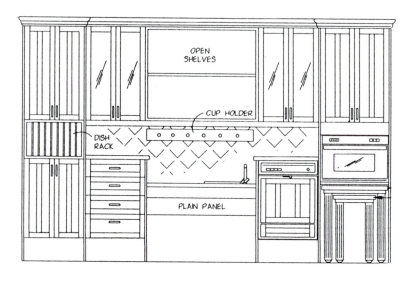

Figure 113 -   Glass doors and open shelving help to locate items readily.

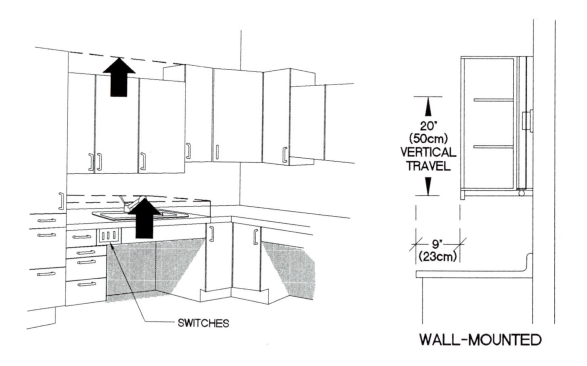

Figure 114 -   Motor driven adjustable cabinetry.

Figure 115 -   Mechanical system to lower wall cabinet storage.

SWING-UP CABINET
DOOR HARDWARE
INCREASES
HEADROOM AND
SAFETY FOR SOME
STANDING
USERS

Figure 116 -   Consider using wall cabinet with tambour doors or a wall cabinet with swing-up doors.

Base Cabinets and Accessory Options

Like wall cabinets, base cabinetry can also be used more creatively. Consider raising base cabinets higher when it makes sense to do so. This technique moves storage into the traditional backsplash area. Raising the base cabinet will also increase the toe space height while placing items stored at the bottom of the base cabinet closer to the universal reach range.

Base cabinetry enhanced with storage accessories typical to every kitchen planned by a designer, further brings items into reach, cutting down on bending. Many accessories are available from cabinet manufacturers or as after market additions.

You may also want to consider:

• Drawers to replace doors whenever practical, eliminating the need to get around the open door, particularly helpful to people with mobility or visual impairments.

• Full-extension slides, on deep drawers, consider lowering the sides for easier viewing and reaching.

• Using wall cabinets for shallow-depth base cabinetry, good for storage of items traditionally stored above reach-in wall cabinets.

• Recycle accessories and bins that do not require lifting above their own physical height for removal and can slide in/out of cabinetry.

• Corners as optimum knee space locations as this storage is frequently less than ideal.

• Pull-out work surfaces between the first and second drawer can often be the ideal height for a seated user.

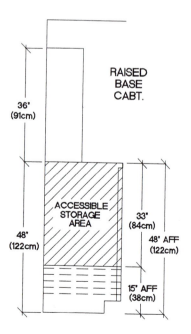

Figure 117 -   Base cabinetry raised into backsplash area.

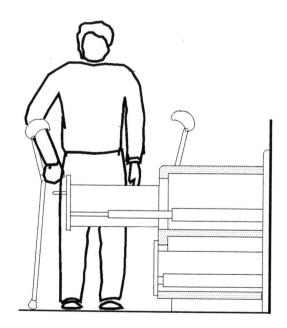

Figure 118 -   Base cabinets with drawers on full-extension slides.

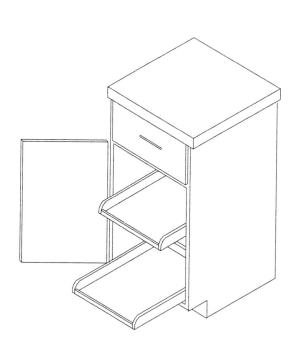

Figure 119 -   Base cabinets with roll-out shelves.

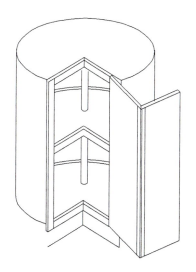

Figure 121 -   Corner susan.

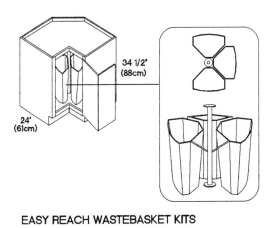

EASY REACH WASTEBASKET KITS

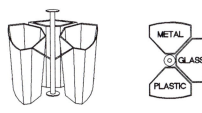

Figure 120 -   Base cabinets with recycle bins.

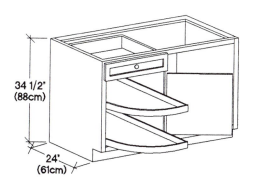

Figure 122 -   Blind corner swing-out shelf.

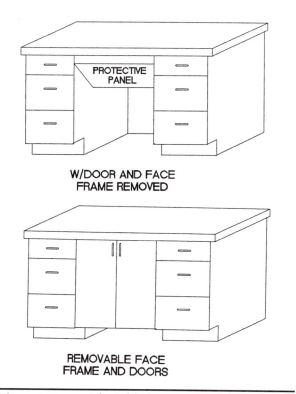

W/DOOR AND FACE FRAME REMOVED

REMOVABLE FACE FRAME AND DOORS

Figure 123 -   Adaptable knee space.

A great addition to the base cabinetry in the universal kitchen is a rolling cart. The space occupied by the cart becomes knee space by rolling the cart out. In addition, the cart provides storage and a safe and convenient method for transporting items around the kitchen.

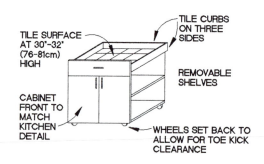

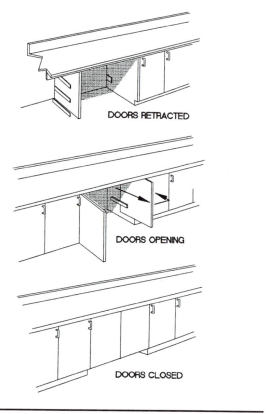

Figure 124 -   Knee space with retractable doors.

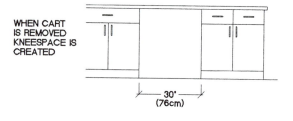

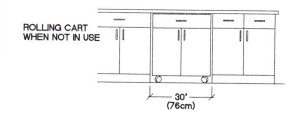

Figure 125 -   Rolling cart.

Tall Cabinets and Accessory Options

Full-height cabinet storage makes the greatest use of storage in the universal reach range if it is thoughtfully planned. Like base and wall cabinets, creativity and the application of accessory items can enhance their use.

• In some instances, drawers may be configured as high as 60" (152cm) above the floor. These drawers should be on full-extension slides, with the sides cut down and hardware for the upper draw

ers should be placed closer to the bottom of the drawer head.

• In other cases, drawers may go from the toekick to 30" (76cm) high, with a pull-out surface at that point and doors and rollouts above.

• A knee space can be created in a 30" (76cm) wide tall cabinet. When removed, a rolling cart at the lower section becomes a work surface when the upper cabinet doors are open.

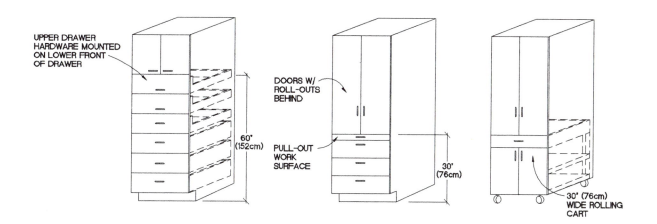

Figure 126 -   Tall cabinets options.

CONSTRUCTION AND HARDWARE

Several options in construction and hardware selection have impact on universal design.

A benefit of frameless construction is its total accessibility to the interior of the cabinet. The same is also true with much of today's framed construction. Raising toekicks to 9" - 12" (23cm - 30cm) high provides clearance for wheelchair footrests and other walking aids. This option is available on most custom lines and some stock lines as well.

Hinging

A variety of options are available for moving doors out of the way.

- Hinging that allows doors to swing completely open to 180° is helpful. In addition, a hinge is available that folds the doors back against themselves and flat against adjacent cabinets, making the doors less obstructive.

- Doors can also be hinged to be retractable, but this option takes up as much as 6" (15cm) on a side, which translates to needing 42" (107cm) for a 30" (76cm) knee space.

- Doors mounted on removable face frames can be used for adapting to knee space by removal of the door and frames.

- Tambour doors or doors that slide or open upward on wall cabinets also eliminate the concern for moving safely around them.

Hardware

Decorative hardware should be easy to use and should not require strength or dexterity to operate. Pulls should be choosen in place of knobs. Touch latches eliminate the need for any grasp or strength.

Material Selection

Finally, material selection should consider durability and forgiveness in terms of finish. High-gloss or finishes that create glare should be avoided. Beyond this, selection of cabinetry is not impacted by universal design. For a more general study of cabinetry, refer to **NKBA® Kitchen Industry Technical Manuals.**

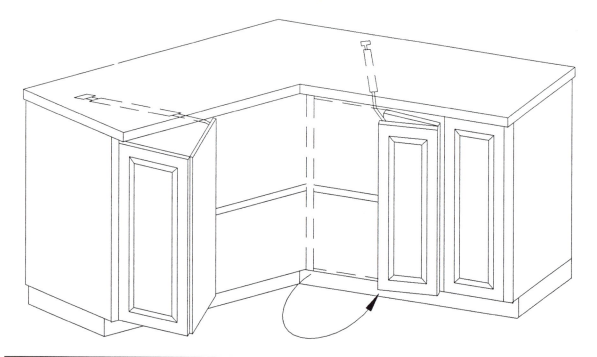

Figure 127 -   Bi-fold hinge system.

c h a p t e r 5

Kitchen Appliances

Universal design principles will impact both the selection process and the design for installation of appliances. As manufacturers are becoming aware of these principles, new features are appearing to make appliances more accessible. In addition, you as the designer must plan for accessibility when creating the work centers around appliances, including installations that sometimes break with tradition.

REFRIGERATOR/FREEZER

Side-by-Side

A side-by-side refrigerator/freezer provides the greatest amount of both types of storage within the universal reach range of 15" - 48" (38cm - 122cm). This style also has narrower doors, which are easier to get around. The fact that the doors open to both sides blocking adjacent counter space can be compensated for planning a rolling cart for transfer of items out of the refrigerator or freezer.

Top-Mount Freezer

Top-mount freezer models put most freezer storage outside the reach of a seated or shorter person. However, if the bottom of the freezer is no higher than 48" (122cm), these models are an option. For all but seated or shorter people they work well as there is some storage of both types within reach without requiring bending.

Bottom-Mount Freezer

Bottom-mount freezer models work well for most people, particularly if the freezer storage is designed to rollout for access.

Separate Refrigerator/Freezer

Choosing separate units for refrigerator and freezer is another option. It provides greater storage within the universal reach range, but may sometimes be limited by available space or budget constraints.

Features

There are several features that are helpful in terms of universal design for the refrigerator/freezer.

- Ice and water dispensers in the door are a good idea, particularly for people who have limited grip or use their hands to aid in balance or mobility. (Some dispensers require a fair amount of pressure to operate).

- Some feature models incorporate a quick access refreshment door that can be used as a shelf.

- The thickness of the door handle and the space between the handle and the door make grasping and opening the door easier.

- A guide to use for handles is a thickness of 1 1/2" (4cm) and a space of 1 1/2" (4cm) - standard for grab bars.

- A non-slip material on the door handles will also help. This handle design will allow a person with limited strength or grasp to more easily grip the handle. In addition, a towel or strap can be run through the space to give better leverage.

- Controls that are set closer to the front will be easier to reach and to read. The light inside the unit should also be brought towards the front for better visibility and for ease in changing the bulb.

- Storage in refrigerators is becoming more accessible with roll-out, spill-proof (solid shelves and deeper door storage, better for viewing and reaching.

- Shallower units will be easier to reach into. Doors that swing a full 180° allow for greater access.

Planning for a Refrigerator

In designing the space around a refrigerator, remember the need for clear floor space, for adjacent work surfaces at a variety of heights, and for knee space Exercise caution in choosing decorative raised panels so that they do not impede grip. If there is to be storage over a refrigerator, it is more accessible when it is the full depth of the refrigerator as opposed to being set back. Consider accessorizing the over-refrigerator cabinet with tray dividers or other accessory options such as a pull-out rack.

MICROWAVE OVENS

Microwave ovens with either side-hinged or bottom hinged doors can work well in the universal kitchen, the key being the placement of the appliance and the adjacent spaces. The goals are to put the oven and its contents within reach and sight of the people who will use it and to eliminate lifting and carrying, particularly of hot items, to the greatest extent possible.

- The ideal location for the microwave is with the bottom of the oven 24" - 48" (61cm - 122cm) off the floor, as this allows people of various heights to see and reach into the oven.

- If a bottom-hinged (drop-down) door is used, consider a model that allows the door to be a resting place.

- Counter space directly below or adjacent to the oven can allow foods to be slid to the point of next use, and a knee space will allow for seated use.

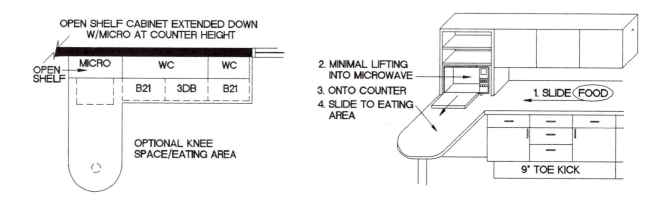

Figure 128 -   Possible location - microwave with drop-down door.

• A microwave with a side-hinged door
might be installed at counter height in
an angled corner cabinet, creating continuous counter space for transfer and
sliding and making good use of the corner.

Figure 129 -   Microwave - angled corner installation.

• Another option would be to install the
microwave at countertop height parallel
with the wall, providing a transfer space
in front of the door and the desired continuous counter space.

• If a knee space is provided, it should be
below and to the handle side of the oven.

• If the depth of the microwave leaves a
counter space in front of it less than 10"
(25cm), a pull-out shelf directly below
the oven or a rolling cart might be used.

The microwave oven is by nature, a universal appliance in that most people can use it
safely and easily and, it eliminates steps in
food preparation. However, there are features
that will make one model more universal
than another.

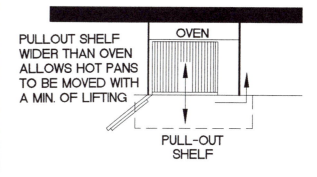

Figure 130 -   Pull-out shelf.

Microwave Oven Controls

When selecting a microwave oven, location and design of the controls are key considerations.

• The microwave should be placed so that
controls are within the universal reach
range and not obstructed.

• Having each button relate to only one
function is best.

• High contrast and raised indicators will
simplify use for a person with visual impairments.

• Tactile overlays are commonly available
upon request from the manufacturer.

• Clear visual and audible indications of
use are helpful.

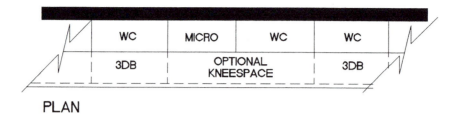

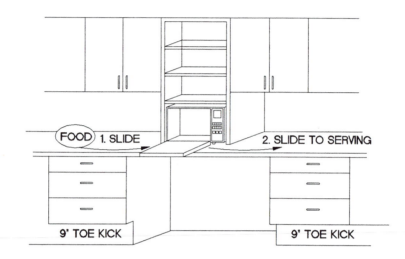

Figure 131 -   Microwave parallel to wall.

COOKTOPS

Cooktops are a good choice for universal design because of their flexibility. There are features to look for and spacial design considerations that will make a cooktop more universal.

- Smooth surface cooktops make transfer onto and off of heat easier, requiring no lifting. In addition, these surfaces are easier to clean.

- It is important that there be clear indicators as to whether a unit is on or off, hot or cool, both audio and visual. Halogen units light up when in use and induction units provide the desired audio and visual indicators as well as an automatic shut-off if not used properly.

- There should be a minimum edge thickness to the cooktop and to burners so

that pots may be slid safely on and off the cooktop.

- Burner configuration should be such that a user does not have to reach directly over one burner to reach another. This can be accomplished with staggered burners or parallel burners. Thickness of the cooktop will impact flexibility in counter height with the thinner cooktops being preferred.

Cooktop Controls

- As with ranges, controls on cooktops should be near the front and placed so that one does not have to reach across or over the burners to operate the cooktop.

- High contrast blade or touch pad controls with both visual and audible indicators of function are recommended.

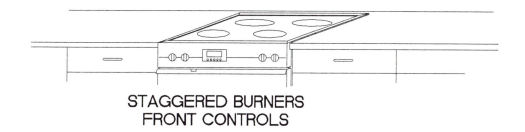

STAGGERED BURNERS
FRONT CONTROLS

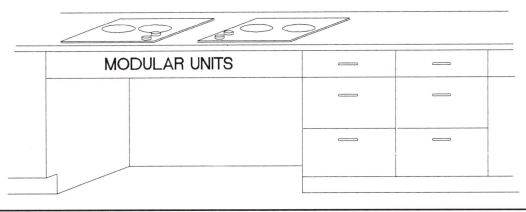

MODULAR UNITS

Figure 132 -   Cooktop placement and controls.

Planning for the Cooktop

Designing a universal space that incorporates the cooktop begins with counter height.

A cooktop may be installed in a fixed counter at a height lower than 36" (91cm) - optimum is 30" - 34" (76cm - 86cm) with a 27" (69cm) minimum height knee space - for use by seated cooks.

If a knee space is provided, it should be the minimum 30" (76cm) wide and 19" (48cm) deep. When possible, the deeper knee space is preferred, but using 19" (48cm) as a guide provides space for a downdraft venting system.

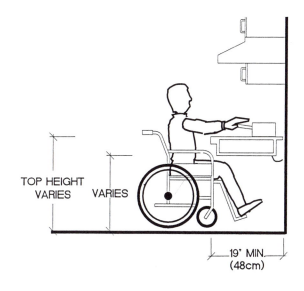

TOP HEIGHT
VARIES   VARIES

19" MIN.
(48cm)

Figure 133 -   Cooktop for seated user.

Adjustable Installations

Cooktops can also be installed in manually or motorized adjustable-height counters. These installations require flexible conduit for power and venting. The motorized concept is great for a kitchen with cooks of various heights. The underside of the cooktop may heat up or have sharp edges. For safety and appearance, a protective panel should be installed. Whether fixed or adjustable, adjacent counter for transfer should be at the same level as the cooktop. Having a sink particularly with a pull-out spray faucet, near the cooking surface allows for filling pots without moving them and for the shortest transfer of hot pots to the sink for draining.

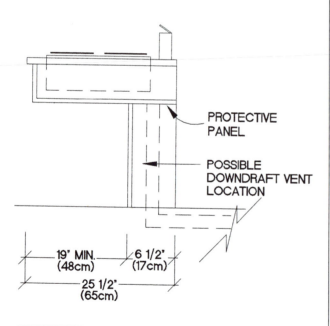

PROTECTIVE PANEL

POSSIBLE DOWNDRAFT VENT LOCATION

19" MIN. (48cm)   6 1/2" (17cm)

25 1/2" (65cm)

Figure 134 -   Cooktop with downdraft venting.

WALL OVENS

Wall ovens are easier to use for more people because they minimize the amount of bending, lifting and carrying of hot items. There are certain features that will make an oven more universal and there are points to consider in designing the space around it.

Doors

- Oven doors can be an obstacle in access to the oven. Doors that swing to the side are better for many people because they allow the cook to move closer to the oven and cut down on the transfer distance, but either style will work well.

- Doors should be hinged and handled to open and close with a minimum amount of strength.

- Drop-down doors should be designed as a resting place for foods coming out of the oven.

Interiors

Interiors of ovens are improving in terms of accessibility.

- Lighting should be toward the front of the oven for better function and ease of maintenance.

- Racks should slide in and out easily and should be designed to support the weight of the food and the pan in the extended position.

- Self-cleaning creates an ease of use that benefits everyone.

Oven Controls

- Oven controls must be within the universal reach range, which usually means installing the oven somewhat lower than the traditional placement.

- Controls should be easy to read and operate, with high contrast and redundant cuing or cues that are audible, tactile and visual.

- Touch pads with large digital readouts are good.

Planning for the Oven

- The first consideration in designing space for the oven is height.

- Ovens with side-swing doors should be installed at counter height, preferably

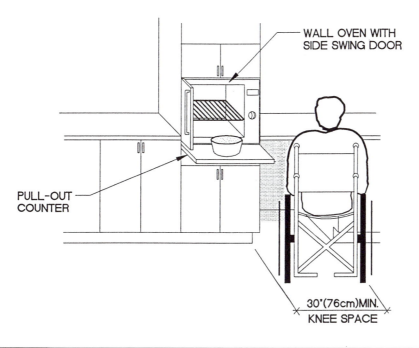

Figure 135 - Wall oven with adjacent knee space.

with pull-out shelf immediately below and an adjacent knee space.

- Another way to accomplish this would be with a rolling cart that pulls out to create the knee space and moves into place directly below the oven.

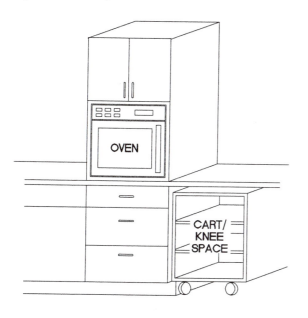

Figure 136 - Wall oven with cart/knee space.

- Ovens with drop-down doors will be installed lower, so that one oven rack is at the height of the adjacent counter with a knee space to one side.

- When a knee space cannot be provided, a pull-out surface under or to one side of the oven will help, but keep in mind that a seated user will have difficulty reaching into the oven this way.

- Pay attention to the heights of the controls created by oven placement. If placing the oven at counter height puts the oven controls above the universal reach range of 48" (122cm), then it would be more realistic to drop the height.

- Other design considerations for the area around a wall oven include heat resistant transfer surfaces and storage. Transfer surfaces will be adjacent counters, pull-out surfaces or rolling carts. Near the oven and cooktop, a rolling cart with a heat resistant surface provides a safe way to transport hot foods to the table. Storage should account for the size and weight of cooking equipment.

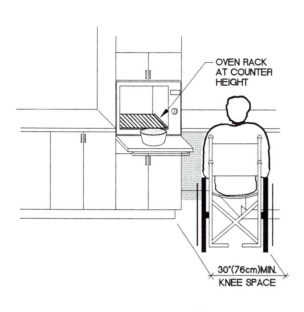

Figure 137 - Oven rack at height of adjacent counter.

RANGES

By their nature, ranges do not lend themselves to universal design in that they place the cooking surface at 36" (91cm) above the floor and ovens at a lower height than is preferred. This cooking surface height works well for many people, but it is a problem for those who cannot always see into cooking pots or may have trouble reaching safely to back burners.

In addition, the lower oven requires bending and lifting of hot items. These concerns are increased for a seated user because a knee space can not be created under the cooking surface to improve reach.

In spite of these inherent drawbacks, ranges are economical in terms of cost and space and should not be ruled out as an option. There are considerations in the features of the range and the design of the adjacent spaces that will help to minimize the drawbacks.

- The cooking surface on a range should have characteristics similar to those described for cooktops.

- Ovens in ranges should have features similar to those given for wall ovens.

- Units with ovens or microwaves above the rangetop create concerns of safety and function for many users in terms of viewing and reaching.

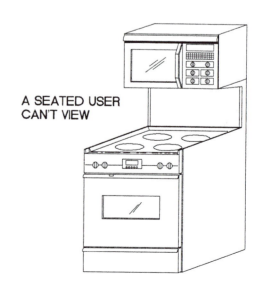

Figure 138 - Hazards of oven/microwave over range.

Range Controls

The most preferred locations for controls are at the front and the second choice, at the side, with the objective to eliminate the need to reach across or over the burners in order to use them.

- High contrast touch pad or blade controls are best, as are clear visual and audible indicators relating to function.

- It is best to avoid rear controls and to have ventilation controls within the universal reach range. This may mean a vent control on the range or in the adjacent cabinet at countertop height, or at least on the front lower panel of the hood.

Figure 140 - Hazards of rear controls.

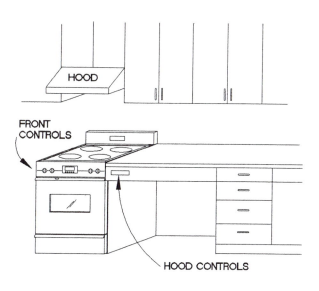

Figure 139 - Range with vent control in adjacent panel.

Planning for the Range

When planning the cooking center around the range, first consider a mirror angled off the back wall over the cooktop to allow people of any height to see into cooking pots. Ovens in ranges can be made more accessible by careful planning of adjacent spaces. The minimum clear transfer space of 9" (23cm) to one side and 15" (38cm) on the other side of the range is important. Preferable, the transfer area will be wider and a knee space will be incorporated. The knee space allows a seated user to reach burners and to use the oven with one hand. When planning for a particular individual, the knee space should be on the side that allows that person to use his/her stronger side.

The wider adjacent space also allows a standing mobility-impaired person to avoid the danger of using the range for support to reach into the oven.

Figure 141 -   Adjacent clear floor space allows cook to stand to one side, not using range for support.

• A pull-out surface at a height near the oven-rack height can create a temporary resting place away from the oven heat, as could a rolling cart. The addition of a countertop toaster oven or convection oven may be a good alternative for a standing mobility-impaired person.

VENTILATION

Along with the range or cooktop and wall oven, the ventilation system must be chosen. The mechanical and design requirements for cooking ventilation remain the same for the universal kitchen as for any other. For a review of the related mechanics, refer to the **NKBA® Kitchen Industry Technical Manuals.**

• **Keep safety in mind** with regard to size and shape of the hood. Radiused corners, size and location should be chosen so as not to obstruct the cook.

• Both downdraft and overhead ventilation systems will work in the universal kitchen, provided they are quiet and have switches within the universal reach range - 48" (122cm) maximum height.

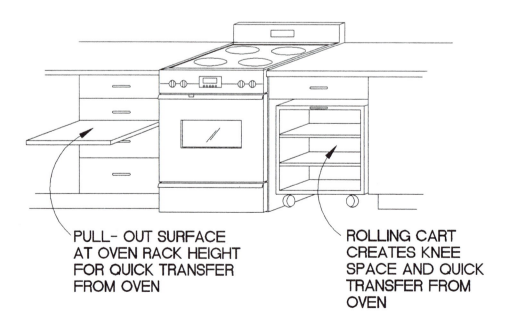

PULL- OUT SURFACE
AT OVEN RACK HEIGHT
FOR QUICK TRANSFER
FROM OVEN

ROLLING CART
CREATES KNEE
SPACE AND QUICK
TRANSFER FROM
OVEN

Figure 142 -   Pull-out at oven shelf height.

- An overhead system can be wired to a switch in an adjacent base cabinet.

- Additional sound protection is important as background noise of this type is particularly deafening to people with certain hearing impairments. Consult the manufacturer when considering this.

- There are venting systems available that include a fire extinguisher that can be automatically activated by a cooktop fire.

- Reasonable maintenance can be provided if the filters of the ventilation system can be cleaned in the dishwasher and the lights can be replaced easily.

DISHWASHERS

Dishwashers, like ranges, have traditionally created a set counter height of 36" (91cm). Unlike ranges, dishwashers can be installed in less traditional ways. To make them more universal in use, dishwashers must have certain features and attention to design of their space.

- The door of a dishwasher, like the drop-down oven door, should be evaluated for its ease of operation.

- The loading/rack system of the dishwasher should also be tested, lift-out baskets for smaller items make emptying easier, and flexibility in loading patterns is also a help.

Planning for the Dishwasher

To design the area that includes the dishwasher, look first at the height.

- The traditional installation creates a continuous counter height with a sink at 36" (91cm). This height works well for many people but requires that any standing user bend to access the bottom rack.

- Another option might be to mount the dishwasher at a high elevation and to plan a sink with work space in an adjustable or lowered counter. This option creates a clean-up center that is accessible to more types of users.

- Either way, a knee space adjacent to the dishwasher will allow access to a seated user. Manufacturer's recommendations should be followed in this installation.

Dishwasher Controls

- Controls should be touch pad or blade design rather than smooth round knobs. The correlation between the control and the function should be simple and clear, i.e.. one button for each function or clear click stops for each function on a dial.

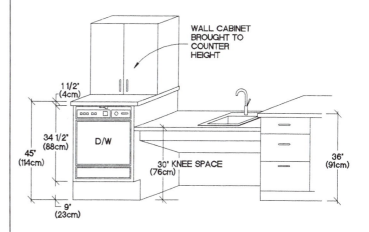

Figure 143 -   Dishwasher in raised position.

DISPOSER

Before a disposer is added to a universal kitchen, serious considerations should be given to safety precautions.

• While there are advantages and disadvantages to both batch-feed and continuous-feed garbage disposers, the continuous-feed type is more universal in its operation.

• The operating switch of the disposer should be located away from any other switches and be clearly marked, perhaps by a different color or a different type of switch to eliminate the possibility of confusing it with another switch.

Location and housing of the disposer will be discussed in conjunction with sinks.

CONTROLS AND OPERATION OF APPLIANCES

Controls and operating systems are universal when they are straight-forward and easy to use by a variety of people.

While technology brings many wonderful features to appliances, the system used to operate these appliances must be clear and simple or they will go unused.

Ease of Use

• Controls must be easy to operate, and they must provide a clear variety of types of feedback for use by people with different abilities.

• To identify a universal control, consider the strength and grasp required to use it and the amount and type of information it gives. One good rule to follow is one function per control.

• The **ANSI** and **UFAS** performance specifications indicate that a control must be operable with one hand and not require gripping or twisting of more than 5 pounds (2 kilograms) of force to operate. Controls that require dual motion, as in pressing down and turning are difficult for many people to use.

• Control styles that work best are levers, which are not so common on appliances, but are available as after market add-ons in some assistive-device catalogs.

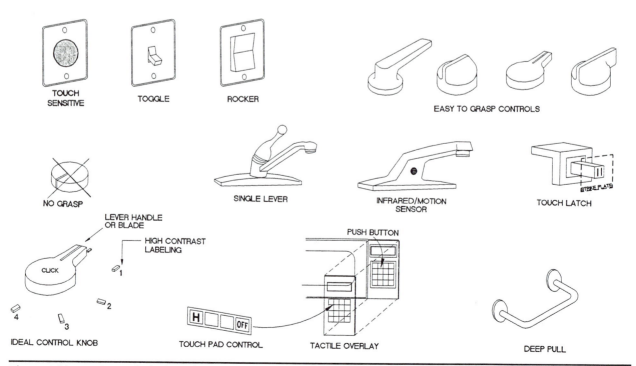

Figure 144 -   Control choices for strength and grasp.

- The least functional style is the smooth round knob which is becoming less common on appliances.

- Blade handles work better than smooth round knobs, particularly if they are asymmetrical.

- A good test for ease of use is to try to operate the control with a closed fist. If it can be operated with a closed fist and little effort, it probably meets code and will be easy to use from a strength and grasp standpoint.

- Along with lever handles and asymmetrical shapes, the touch controls, growing in popularity, pass this test.

Control Feedback Cuing

The next test for controls relates to feedback.

- Redundant and high-contrast cuing is helpful for people with visual or hearing impairments or for those who need extra reminders of what is happening. A microwave oven that flashes a light and sounds an alert when the cooking is through is an example of this.

- A lever handle that clicks into high, medium, low and off indicates function by sound, by lever position and by the feel of the control clicking into position is another example. Particularly if the calibration is marked with high contrast and raised markings.

Implementing Cuing

There are some easy ways to add redundant cuing when an appliance does not have it.

- High contrast or tactile indicators can be added to the existing control at frequently used settings - labeling tape at 350°F (177°C) on the oven or medium on the cooktop.

- Tactile cuing can be added to touch pad controls at frequently used settings - a stick on button (such as the spacers used on inside corners of cabinets,

doors and drawers) on the microwave at high or off.

- Devices are available through assistive-technology suppliers that will augment the cuing in a given appliance - such as a light that will flash or a tone that will sound when an appliance is on or left on beyond a certain time, or an automatic timer to shut an appliance off at a certain time of day or evening.

- Happily, as manufacturers become aware of these needs, they are changing control design. Add-on tactile panel overlays for visually impaired people are available from several appliance manufacturers, and one day they may be a part of all touch pad controls, making them truly universal.

- The growing use of *"voice response"* in appliance controls would also increase the numbers of people who could use the appliance.

- Operating systems must be simple and straight-forward, easy to understand, use and remember. Technology has made it possible to do things with appliances we could never do before, making them more universal. The level of understanding required to program some of these appliances will negate the benefits. Systems that are tremendously complex on the inside must translate to clear and self-evident operating systems for universal application.

The best test for appliance controls is by use of the client. Consider ease of use and comfort level. When this is not possible, these suggestions can serve as a guide.

APPLIANCE SAFETY

In making appliances and kitchens more accessible to more people, there is a need for thorough consideration of the safety implications.

- The 30" (76cm) high cooktop with touch pad controls that is accessible to the seated user is also within reach of the toddler who's using it edge as a grip for balance.

- The front controls on the range allow everyone to use them.
- The continuous-feed disposer switch, if activated by mistake, will still grind whatever may be in it.

These concerns should not preclude designing kitchens with accessible appliances, but they must be addressed. One major safety concern centers around appliance misuse by those of us too young to understand and those of us who are aging or for other reasons becoming forgetful or confused.

- One feature becoming more common in appliances is control lockout. By pressing a code, you can make the appliance inoperable until the release code is pressed in.
- Another way of accomplishing this is to wire the appliance or outlet for the appliance to a separate switch or circuit breaker to allow power to be shut off to the appliance when desired.
- The appliance features previously discussed relating to redundant cuing, high contrast indicators and clear operating systems will help cut down on forgetfulness and confusion.
- Whole house or room control systems are available to allow the cook to double check on the status of the appliance, even from a remote location.

Another major concern relates to the risk of spilling hot foods, particularly as it relates to the wheelchair or seated user in a knee space at a cooktop.

- Creating a countertop curb will help somewhat.
- As discussed in cooktop selection, front controls, a smooth surface (flush with the countertop) and a sink nearby will cut down this risk.
- Consultation with a physical or occupational therapist may provide added precautions.

Fire in the kitchen relates directly to use of the cooking appliances and is of particular concern when the user cannot move quickly.

- Hoods with automatic extinguishing and fire extinguishers that are close to the user and "*easy to understand and operate*" help to address this concern.
- Smoke alarms with dual cuing and direct and easy exits are also important.

There are as many safety concerns as there are situations. When working with a particular client, look at who will use this space and discuss the pros and cons of each design decision or appliance feature, focusing on safety concerns and possible solutions. Reference the chart below for a few examples. Once responsible decisions have been made, it is necessary, as always, to be careful in the kitchen.

Design or Appliance Feature	Safety Concerns	Possible Solutions
Lowered Cooktop	child can reach	control lockout or use appliance circuit breaker
Front Controls	child can reach	control lockout, cover controls
Lowered Microwave Oven	child can reach	control lockout, or plug into switched outlet

c h a p t e r 6

Kitchen Fixtures and Equipment

The main fixture in the kitchen is the sink. Selection of the best sink and design of the space around the sink are closely related and must be considered together.

SINKS

Depth and drain location are unique in the universal kitchen, based on counter height and knee space requirements. In general, the sink will be shallower than traditional, 5" - 6 1/2" (13cm - 17cm) instead of 7" (18cm) or more, and the drains will be placed toward the rear of the sink.

Sink Materials/Types

Materials chosen should be slow to transfer heat and/or sound and be well-insulated. The underside of the sink should be smooth and insulated to protect the legs of a seated user.

- Stainless steel sinks are the most readily available sinks that meet these requirements. They are economical and easy to maintain, and several manufacturers are now insulating them against sound and heat transfer. There are several series of stainless steel sinks that can be ordered with depth and drain location to be called out by the designer.

- Sinks of solid surface material are more expensive, but they transfer less heat and sound.

- Porcelain sinks for the kitchen are generally deeper than the needed maximum 6 1/2" (17cm). There are a few, however, that are suitable for universal kitchens. One model is 6 1/2" (17cm) deep and has an insulating panel for residential use, and another is 5 1/2" (13cm) deep with a pop-up drain control at the front of the sink.

Planning for a Sink

Designing the space to incorporate the sink(s) in the kitchen will impact which sink might be chosen.

- The first critical determinant is the desired counter and knee space height. Based on ANSI standards, the knee space will be a minimum of 27" (69cm) high, the counter a maximum of 6 1/2" (17cm) deep.

- Individually the knee space must be high enough to clear a wheelchair arm, and for many people 29" (74cm) is required.

- For most seated users, 32" (81cm) is the preferred counter height. This combination would leave only 3" (8cm) for the sink depth which is obviously not enough.

• When working with a client, measure their specific needs. If not, work to get the maximum knee space with the minimum counter height.

Design/Installation Techniques

There are some design and installation techniques that will help you reach optimum use of the space.

MINIMUM KNEE SPACE AT SINKS

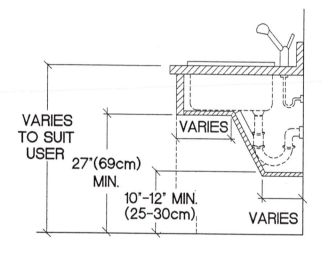

Figure 145 -   Knee space at sinks.

• Consider an apron panel below counter height just high enough to conceal the support system. A second panel angles back and down towards the wall from the apron to allow for the creation of the knee space.

• Setting the sink back slightly may help to increase the knee space. Be careful not to move the sink back beyond a comfortable reach and consider installing faucet/controls to left or right of the sink for easier access.

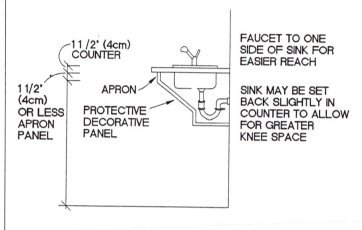

Figure 146 -   Getting optimum knee space and counter height - one option.

• Base the location on the preference and strength of your client. Pipes can also be wrapped or shrouded, but you must still pay attention to the underside of the sink.

• Another option, particularly appealing for sinks for more than one cook, is the motorized adjustable-height counter and sink. This requires flexible plumbing lines and some creative work with custom decorative panels, but results in a totally flexible, easy-to-operate system that truly works for everyone.

• When there will be more than one sink in the kitchen, another design option is to plan one area for a sink at a lowered height of 30" - 34" (76cm - 86cm) with provisions for a knee space and one area for a sink at the standard height of 36" (91cm). While this planning does not account for the taller cook, most people will be comfortable at one of the two sinks.

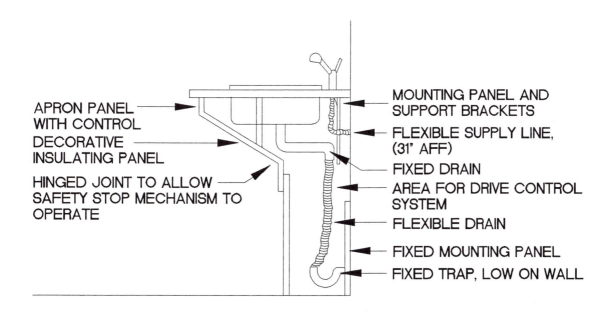

APRON PANEL WITH CONTROL

DECORATIVE INSULATING PANEL

HINGED JOINT TO ALLOW SAFETY STOP MECHANISM TO OPERATE

MOUNTING PANEL AND SUPPORT BRACKETS

FLEXIBLE SUPPLY LINE, (31" AFF)

FIXED DRAIN

AREA FOR DRIVE CONTROL SYSTEM

FLEXIBLE DRAIN

FIXED MOUNTING PANEL

FIXED TRAP, LOW ON WALL

Figure 147 - Flexible plumbing lines.

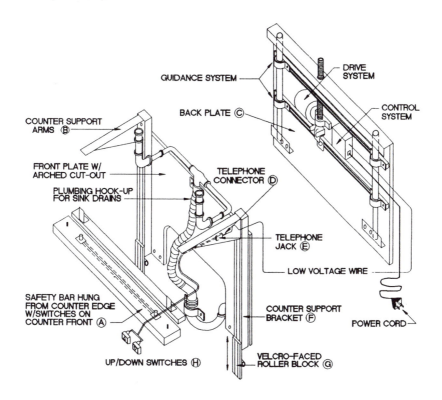

COUNTER SUPPORT ARMS Ⓑ

FRONT PLATE W/ ARCHED CUT-OUT

PLUMBING HOOK-UP FOR SINK DRAINS

SAFETY BAR HUNG FROM COUNTER EDGE W/SWITCHES ON COUNTER FRONT Ⓐ

UP/DOWN SWITCHES Ⓗ

GUIDANCE SYSTEM

BACK PLATE Ⓒ

TELEPHONE CONNECTOR Ⓓ

TELEPHONE JACK Ⓔ

LOW VOLTAGE WIRE

COUNTER SUPPORT BRACKET Ⓕ

VELCRO-FACED ROLLER BLOCK Ⓖ

DRIVE SYSTEM

CONTROL SYSTEM

POWER CORD

Figure 148 - Drive assembly for motorized sink and counter support system.

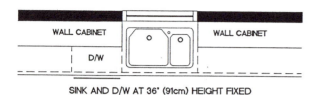

SINK AND D/W AT 36" (91cm) HEIGHT FIXED

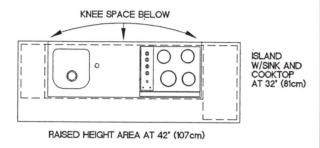

RAISED HEIGHT AREA AT 42" (107cm)

Figure 149 -   Option with more than one sink.

- The space under the sink plays a key role in safety and function of the knee space. The drain pipes and plumbing should be as far to the rear as possible.

- For protection and insulation as well as for appearance, a covering for the underside of the sink and the plumbing should be planned. This covering must be installed so as to be removable for plumbing repair. One option is to create decorative panels to match the cabinetry.

- Another option more common in bathroom lavatories, is the shroud that is available from the sink manufacturer or from outside sources.

- A third option might be to wrap the plumbing and insulation in fabric to blend with the room decor.

- Sinks designed to be adjustable via a motorized system will have a built-in safety mechanism to stop the drive system should it come in contact with an obstruction. Motorized installations require the protective panel installed below it to be hinged.

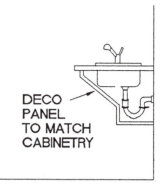

DECO PANEL TO MATCH CABINETRY

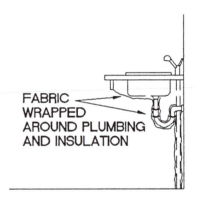

FABRIC WRAPPED AROUND PLUMBING AND INSULATION

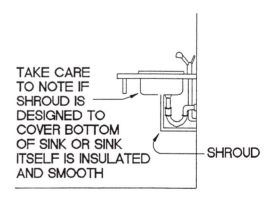

TAKE CARE TO NOTE IF SHROUD IS DESIGNED TO COVER BOTTOM OF SINK OR SINK ITSELF IS INSULATED AND SMOOTH

SHROUD

Figure 150 -   Options for covering pipes.

The shape and configuration of the sink remains a matter of personal preference.

- If a double-bowl sink is preferred, it is important that at least one side be big enough to hold large pots.
- If a disposer is to be used, a double-bowl sink is preferred with the disposer at the smaller sink.

Faucets

- The single-lever faucet is the most universal in design. It allows temperature and flow adjustment with one control, easier for one-handed use or for use when both hands are occupied.
- A retractable spray head is another good feature, particularly near a cooktop, as it allows pots to be filled outside of the sink. This is a benefit in that it requires less lifting of full and heavy pots and it allows the contents of a pot to be cooled down before moving them.

- Handles on faucets should be examined based on the same criteria as controls on appliances.
- A blade handle or a cross handle is preferred over a round knob.
- There are single-lever faucets with loop handles which provide more options in use.
- Separate hot and cold controls can be used, but the single lever provides more ease of use.
- There are systems available today that control temperature and water flow through sensors in the front part of the sink or touch pads on the front apron of the sink area, but these systems are not yet common.

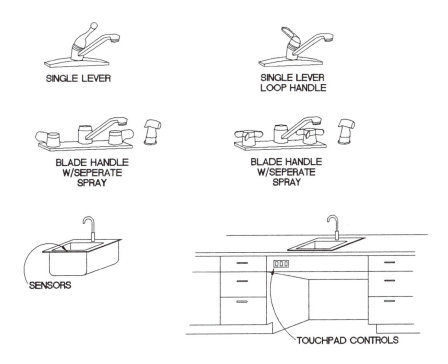

SINGLE LEVER

SINGLE LEVER
LOOP HANDLE

BLADE HANDLE
W/SEPERATE
SPRAY

BLADE HANDLE
W/SEPERATE
SPRAY

SENSORS

TOUCHPAD CONTROLS

Figure 151 - Universal faucet options.

Other Sink Area Accessories

Other accessories to the sink area include:

• water filtering systems

• instant hot water dispensers and

• soap/lotion dispensers.

These items for the most part, are a matter of personal preference.

• Instant hot water dispensers are a good addition to the universal kitchen as they eliminate steps, including eliminating use of the cooktop for some food and beverage preparation.

• Soap dispensers located within reach can also eliminate steps.

Planning for Accessory Items

When desired, these items should be chosen and designed into the space to be easy to operate and not interfere with knee space.

• Water filtering systems and soap dispensers when properly planned, do not tend to create space problems, but must be thought out in detail. Operation is the main issue. No smooth round knobs - levers are preferred.

• Instant hot water dispensers take a minimum of space and can be placed to the back of the sink cavity or the adjacent cabinet and not interfere with the knee space. The lever control is the feature to watch for.

• The garbage disposer must be installed directly below a drain and does impact the knee space. When a disposer is desired, it can be installed under one bowl of the sink, enclosed in a cabinet, and the knee space extended beyond the opposite side of the sink. This layout will provide desired counter adjacent to the sink and allow for easier loading of the dishwasher.

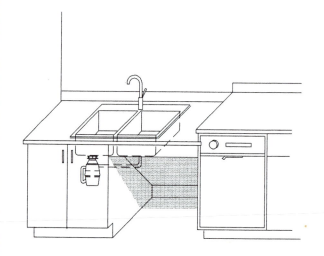

Figure 152 -   Sink with disposer.

Planning for the Sink Area

Designing the space around the sink and the location of the sink in the kitchen requires consideration of the work plan of the kitchen. Adjacent counter space should be included at the same height as the sink. A sink with knee space designed in a corner at a 45° angle to adjacent cabinetry can provide counter space on both sides of the sink in an area that is less than ideal for storage.

Design that includes a counter at sink height between the sink and the dishwasher is helpful for use of the dishwasher by a seated person. When planning a sink in a lowered counter, it may be more functional to move the sink to one end of the lowered counter to provide for the greatest continuous length of work space.

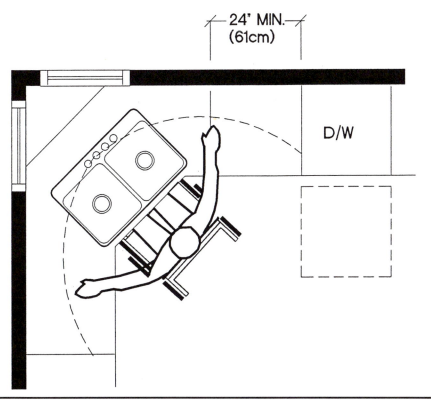

Figure 153 -   Sink in angled corner application.

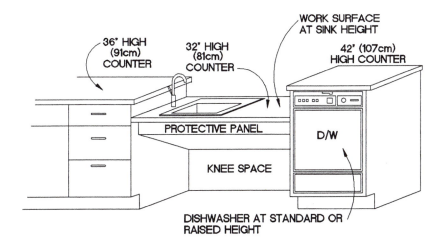

Figure 154 -   Sink moved to one end of counter.

chapter 7

41 Design Guidelines© Of Bathroom Planning

Likewise, universal bathroom design also requires an understanding and consideration of the broad range of human abilities as well as the other parameters of a design project. It is intended that a bathroom designed around these guidelines will be functional, safe and universal. It is also likely that when the Guidelines© are applied, along with the other constraints of a particular situation, some things will be compromised.

Because every guideline cannot be followed everytime and no design can be all things to all people, judgments must frequently be made to achieve an optimum balance.

• The shower control that is easily accessed by a seated person may also be within the reach of a toddler.

• The clear floor space required for transfer from a wheelchair to a toilet may not be feasible given cost and space constraints.

Because there are over 40 million pre-existing homes in the United States alone, designers may often have to work with the typical 5' x 7' (152cm x 213cm) bathroom space. Designers are encouraged to expand this space as necessary to provide universal access. When this is not possible, designers will need to make judgements based on the scope of the project, the space available and the needs and budget of the client. Particularly in these instances, job parameters must be weighted against the guidelines. These guidelines are provided to be the basis for that judgment. The diversities in population which make up our society dictate that these guidelines be revised to more fully incorporate universal design as clarified in the **Uniform Federal Accessibility Standards (UFAS)** and the **American National Standard for Accessible and Usable Buildings and Facilities (ANSI A117.1-1992)**. The dimensions included in these NKBA Guidelines© are based on ANSI and UFAS, but they are not intended to replace them.

To date, most single-family residential projects do not fall under any standard for accessibility, but this is changing. If a particular project is subject to local, state or national laws or codes, the designer must comply with those requirements. These guidelines and the space planning provided here are intended to be useful design standards, supplemental to the applicable codes. Not rules, but guidelines, they will help you in planning bathrooms that are functional and flexible or universal to better meet the needs of today's varied lifestyles.

SECTION I: Clear Floor Spaces and Door Openings
Guideline 1 to Guideline 10

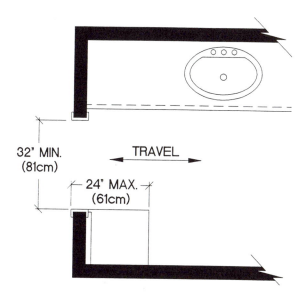

Figure 155 - **Guideline 1a** - The clear space at doorways should be at least 32" (81cm) wide and not more than 24" (61cm) deep in the direction of travel.
  Guideline 1a Clarification - While a designer should always try to meet this goal, physical constraints of a job site may require deviation from the guideline. Be aware that a lesser clearance may not allow for full use by all people.

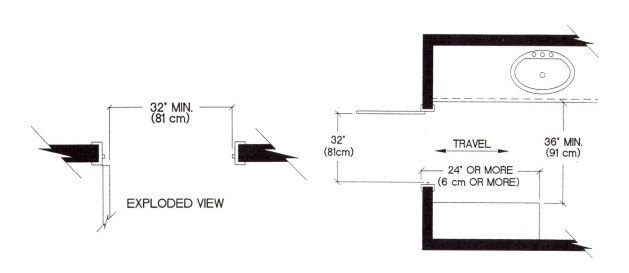

Figure 156 - **Guideline 1b** - The clear space at a doorway must be measured at the narrowest point.

Figure 157 - **Guideline 1c** - Walkways (passages between vertical objects greater than 24" (61cm) deep in the direction of travel), should be a minimum of 36" (91cm) wide.

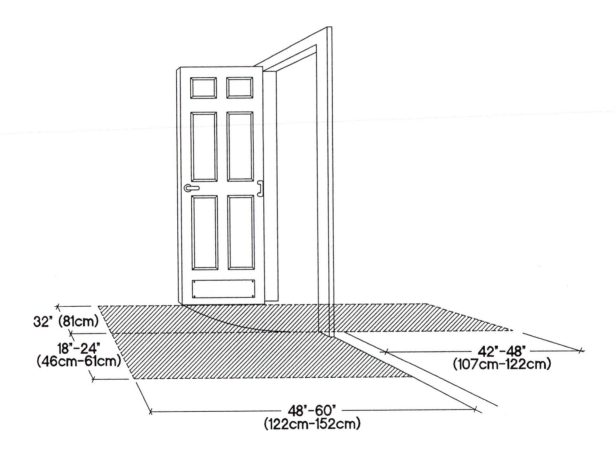

32" (81cm)

18"-24"
(46cm-61cm)

42"-48"
(107cm-122cm)

48"-60"
(122cm-152cm)

Figure 158 -   **Guideline 2** - A clear floor space at least the width of the door on the push side and a larger clear floor space on the pull side should be planned at doors for maneuvering to open, close, and pass through the doorway. The exact amount needed will depend on the type of door and the approach.

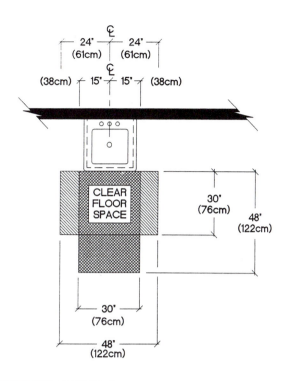

Figure 159 - **Guideline 3** - A minimum clear floor space of 30" x 48" (76cm x 122cm) either parallel or perpendicular should be provided at the lavatory.

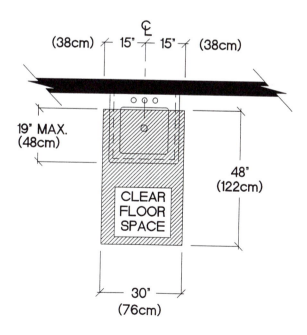

Figure 160 - **Guideline 3 - Clarification** - Up to 19" (48cm) of the 48" (122cm) clear floor space dimension can extend under the lavatory when a knee space is provided.

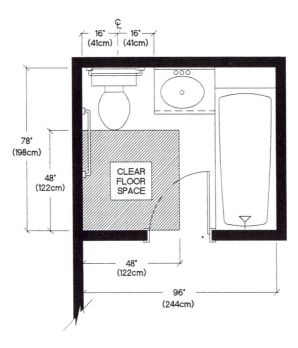

Figure 161 -   **Guideline 4a** - A minimum clear floor space of 48" x 48" (122cm x 122cm) should be provided in front of the toilet. A minimum of 16" (41cm) of that clear floor space must extend to each side of the centerline of the fixture.

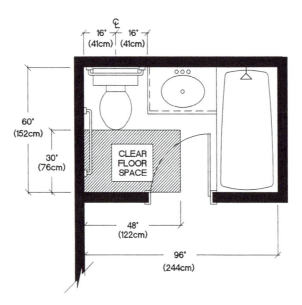

Figure 162 -   **Guideline 4a - Clarification** - While a designer should always try to meet this goal, physical constraints of a job site may require deviation from the guideline. If a 48" x 48" (122cm x 122cm) clear floor space is unavailable, this space may be reduced to 30" x 48" (76cm x 122cm). This compromise may not allow for full use by all people.

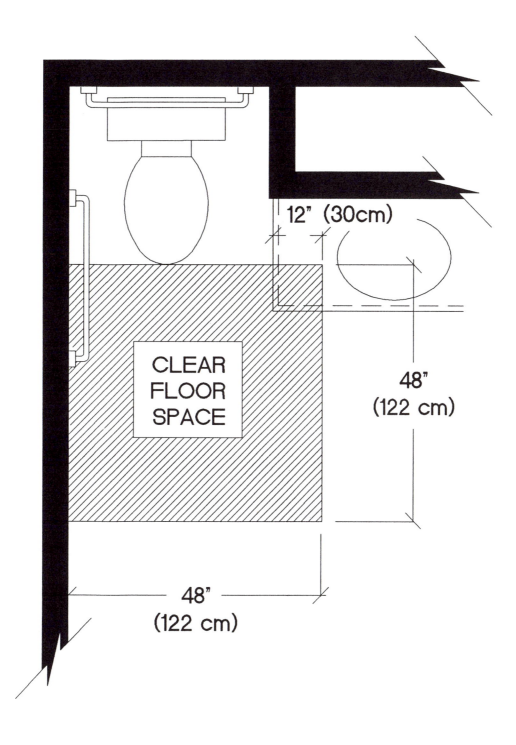

12" (30cm)

CLEAR
FLOOR
SPACE

48"
(122 cm)

48"
(122 cm)

Figure 163 - **Guideline 4b** - Up to 12" (30cm) of the 48" x 48" (122cm x 122cm) clear floor space can extend under the lavatory when total access to a knee space is provided.

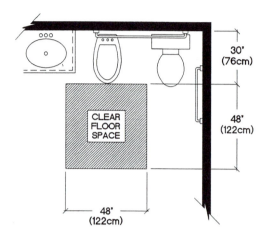

Figure 164 -   **Guideline 5** - A minimum clear floor space of 48" x 48" (122cm x 122cm) from
the front of the bidet should be provided.

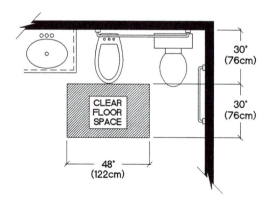

Figure 165 -   **Guideline 5 Clarification 1** - While a designer should always try to meet this
goal, physical constraints of a job site may require deviation from the guideline. If a 48" x 48"
(122cm x 122cm) clear floor space is not available, this space may be reduced to 30" x 48"
(76cm x 122cm). This compromise may not allow for full use by all people.

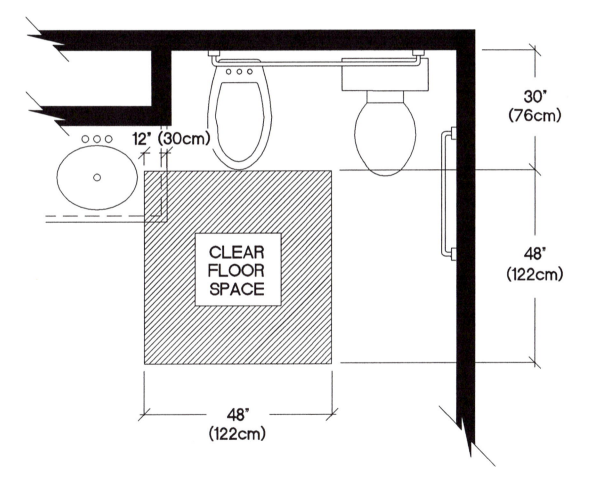

Figure 166 - **Guideline 5 - Clarification 2** - Up to 12" (30cm) of the 48" x 48" (122cm x 122cm) of the clear floor space can extend under the lavatory when total access to a knee space is provided.

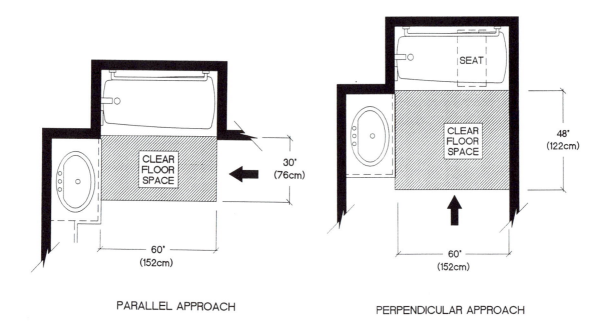

PARALLEL APPROACH   PERPENDICULAR APPROACH

Figure 167 - **Guideline 6a** - The minimum   *Figure 169 -* **Guideline 6b** - The minimum
clear floor space at a bathtub is 60" (152cm)   clear floor space at a bathtub is 60" (152cm)
wide by 30" (76cm) deep for a parallel ap-   wide x 48" (122cm) deep for a perpendicular
proach, even with the length of the bathtub.   approach.

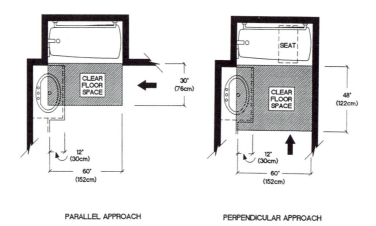

PARALLEL APPROACH   PERPENDICULAR APPROACH

Figure 168 - **Guideline 6a, 6b - Clarification 1** - Up to 12" (30cm) of the 60" (152cm) clear
floor space required for parallel or perpendicular approach can extend under the lavatory when
total access to a kneespace is provided.

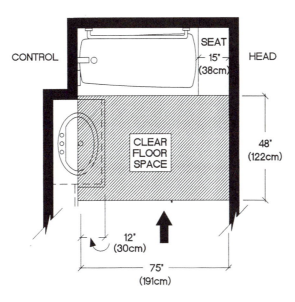

Figure 170 - **Guideline 6a, 6b - Clarification 2** - If a built-in seat is planned, increase the width of the clear floor space by the depth of the seat, a minimum 15" (38cm).

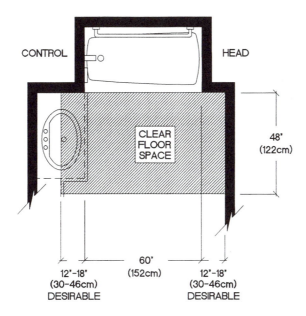

Figure 171 - **Guideline 6a, 6b - Clarification 3** - An additional 12"-18" (30cm-46cm) of clear floor space beyond the control wall is desirable to ease access to controls. The same 12"-18" (30cm-46cm) of clear floor space is desirable beyond the head of the bathtub for maneuvering mobility aids for transfer.

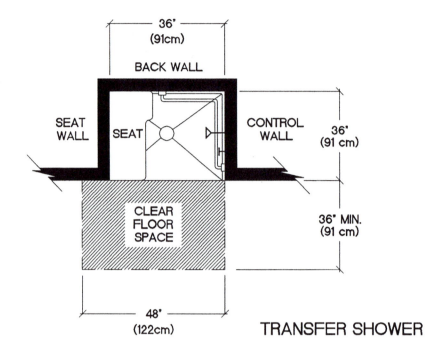

TRANSFER SHOWER

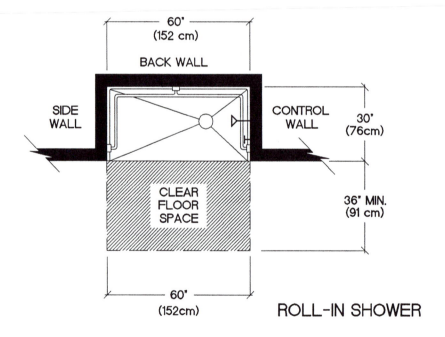

ROLL-IN SHOWER

Figure 172 - **Guideline 7** - The minimum clear floor space at showers less than 60" (152cm) wide should be 36" (91cm) deep by the width of the shower plus 12" (30cm). The 12" (30cm) should extend beyond the seat wall. At a shower that is 60" (152cm) wide or greater, clear floor space should be 36" (91cm) deep by the width of the shower.

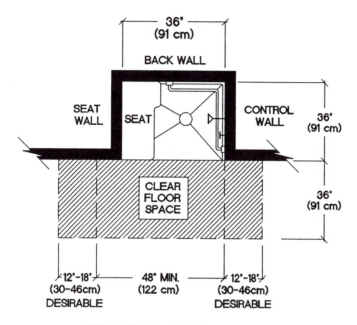

TRANSFER SHOWER

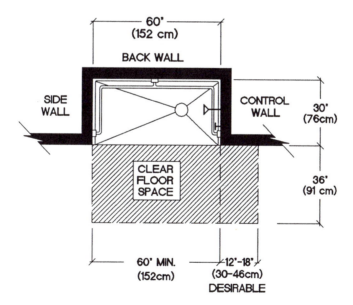

ROLL-IN SHOWER

Figure 173 - **Guideline 7 - Clarification** - An additional 12"-18" (30cm-46cm) of clear floor space beyond the control wall is desirable to ease access to controls. The same 12"-18" (30cm-46cm) of clear floor space is desirable beyond the side wall opposite the control wall for maneuvering aids for transfer.

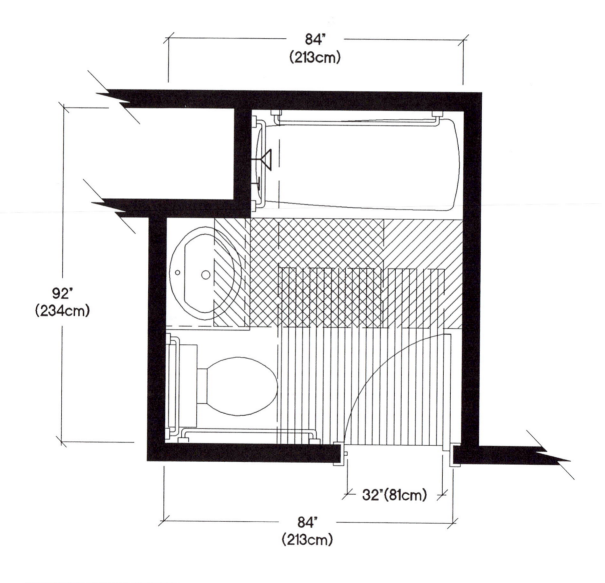

Figure 174 -   **Guideline 8** - Clear floor spaces required at each fixture may overlap.

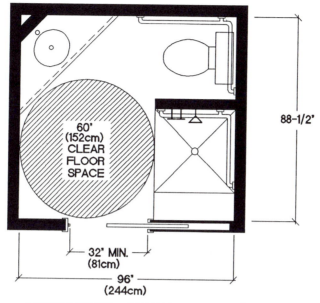

88-1/2"

60"
(152cm)
CLEAR
FLOOR
SPACE

32" MIN.
(81cm)

96"
(244cm)

MINIMUM 60" (152cm) DIAMETER FOR 360° TURNS

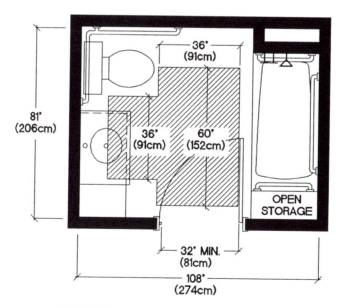

81"
(206cm)

36"
(91cm)

36"
(91cm)

60"
(152cm)

OPEN
STORAGE

32" MIN.
(81cm)

108"
(274cm)

MINIMUM 36" x 36" x 60" (91cm x 91cm x 152cm)
SPACE FOR T-TURNS

Figure 175 - **Guideline 9** - Space for turning (mobility aids) 180° should be planned in the bathroom.

A minimum diameter of 60" (152cm) for 360° turns and/or a minimum T-turn space of 36" (91cm) x 36" (91cm) x 60" (152cm).

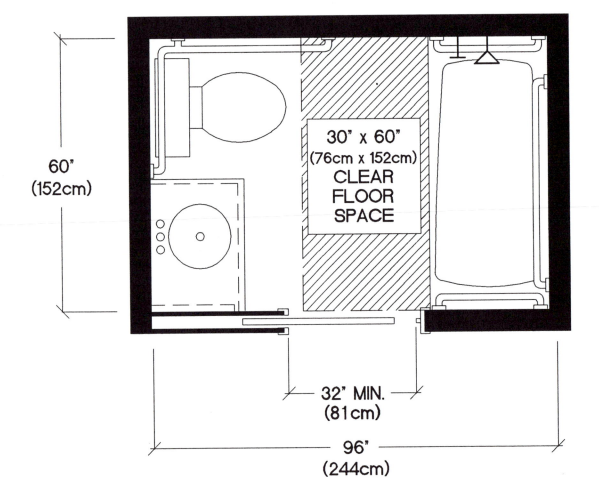

ALTERNATIVE TO TURNING SPACE
30" x 60" (76cm x 152cm) CLEAR FLOOR SPACE

Figure 176 - **Guideline 9 - Clarification** - While a designer should always try to meet this goal, physical constraints of a job site may require deviation from the guideline. When space for a 360° diameter or T-turn is unavailable, a 30" x 60" (76cm x 152cm) clear floor space can be substituted, but this compromise will not allow full access by all users.

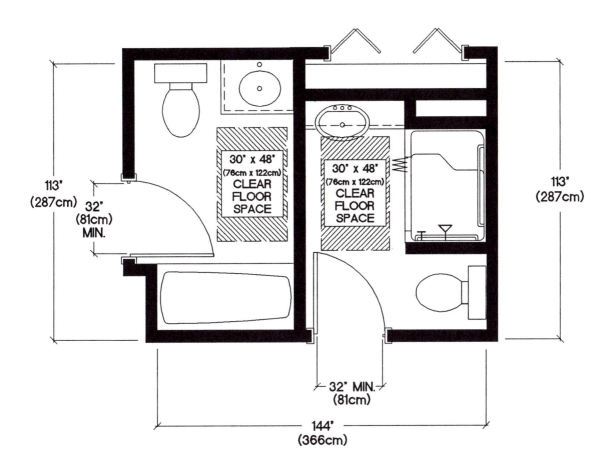

Figure 177 - **Guideline 10 -** A minimum clear floor space of 30" x 48" (76cm-122cm) is required beyond the door swing in a bathroom.

SECTION II: Lavatories
Guideline 11 to Guideline 15

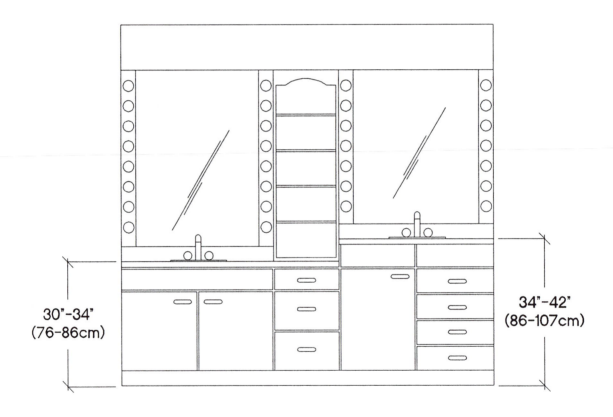

30"-34"
(76-86cm)

34"-42"
(86-107cm)

VARIED VANITY COUNTER HEIGHTS ARE DESIRABLE

Figure 178 - **Guideline 11** - When more than one vanity is included, one may be 30"-34" (76cm-86cm) high and another at 34"-42" (86cm-107cm) high. Vanity height should fit the user(s).

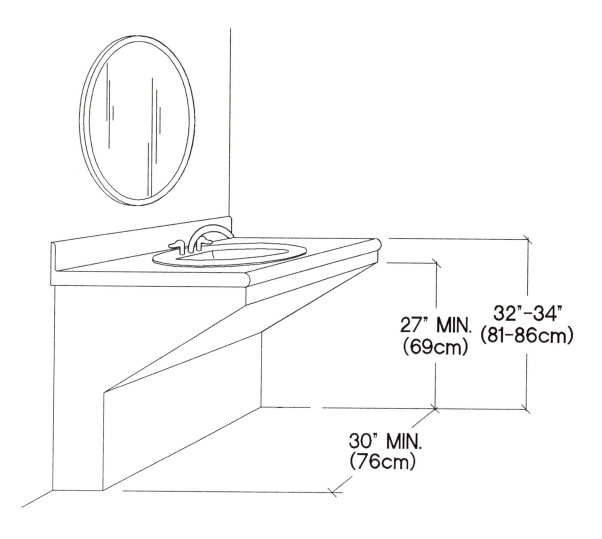

Figure 179 - **Guideline 12** - Kneespace (which may be open or adaptable) should be provided at a lavatory. The kneespace should be a minimum of 27" (69cm) above the floor at the front edge, decreasing progressively as the depth increases, and the recommended width is a minimum of 30" (76cm) wide.

Figure 180 -   **Guideline 13** - The bottom edge of the mirror over the lavatory should be a maximum of 40" (102cm) above the floor or a maximum of 48" (122cm) above the floor if it is tilted.

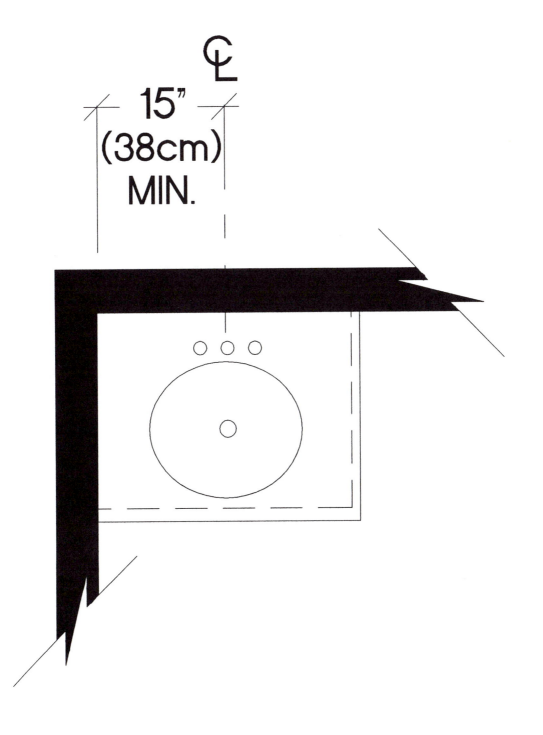

15"
(38cm)
MIN.

Figure 181 - **Guideline 14** - The minimum clearance from the centerline of the lavatory to any side wall is 15" (38cm).

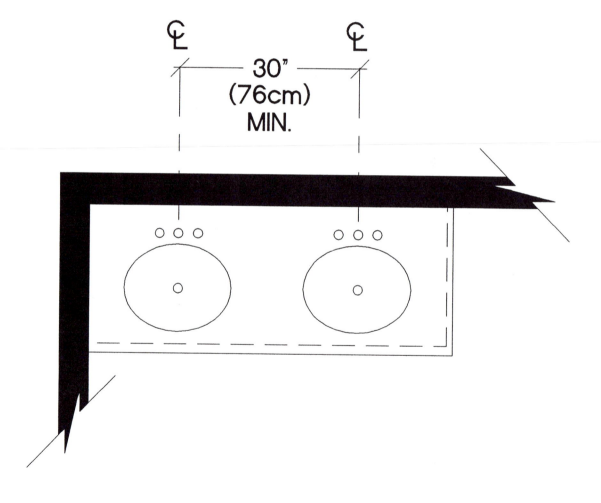

Figure 182 - **Guideline 15** - The minimum clearance between two bowls in the lavatory center is 30" (76cm), centerline to centerline.

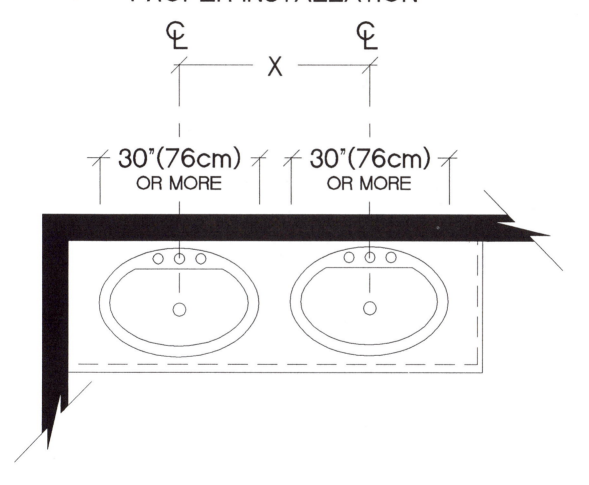

Figure 183 - **Guideline 15 - Clarification** - When using lavatories that are 30" (76cm) wide or greater, the minimum distance of 30" (76cm) between centerlines of the two bowls must be increased to allow proper installation of each lavatory.

SECTION III: Showers and Bathtubs
Guideline 16 to Guideline 22

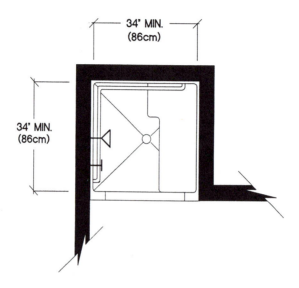

Figure 184 -   **Guideline 16** - In an enclosed shower, the minimum usable interior dimensions are 34" (86cm) x 34" (86cm). These dimensions are measured from wall to wall. Grab bars, controls, movable and folding seats do not diminish the measurement.

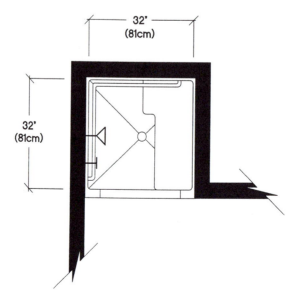

Figure 185 -   **Guideline 16 - Clarification** - While a designer should always try to meet this goal, physical constraints of a job site may require deviation from the guideline. If a 34" x 34" (86cm x 86cm) interior dimension is unavailable, these dimensions may be reduced to 32" x 32" (81cm x 81cm). Be aware that this compromise may not allow for full use by all people.

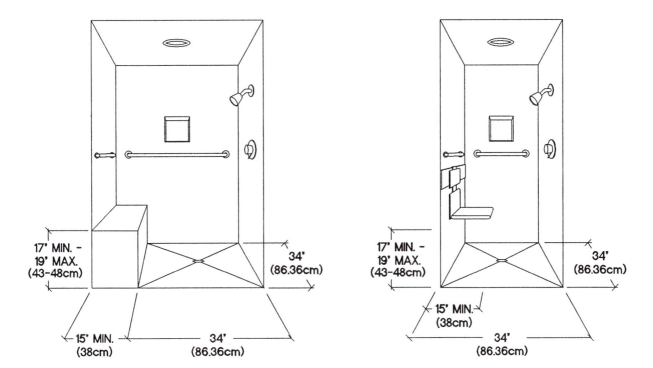

Figure 186 - **Guideline 17** - Showers should include a bench or seat that is 17-19" (43cm-48cm) above the floor and a minimum of 15" (38cm) deep.

Guideline 17 - Clarification 1 - Built-in permanent seats should not encroach upon the minimum 34" x 34" (86cm x 86cm) interior clear floor space of the shower.

Guideline 17 - Clarification 2 - Reinforced wall supports for future placement of hanging and folding seat hardware should be planned at the time of shower installation.

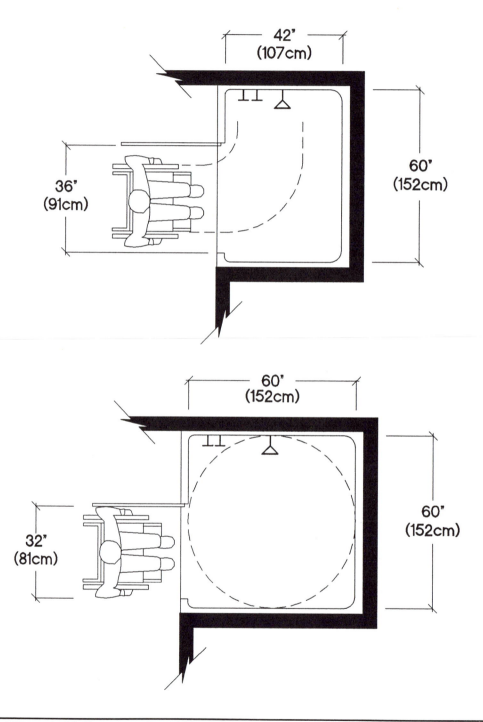

Figure 187 - **Guideline 18** - The width of the door opening must take into consideration the interior space in the shower for entry and maneuvering. When the shower is 60" (152cm) deep, a person can enter straight into the shower and turn after entry, therefore 32" (81cm) is adequate. If the shower is 42" (107cm) deep, the entry must be increased to 36" (91cm) in order to allow for turning space.

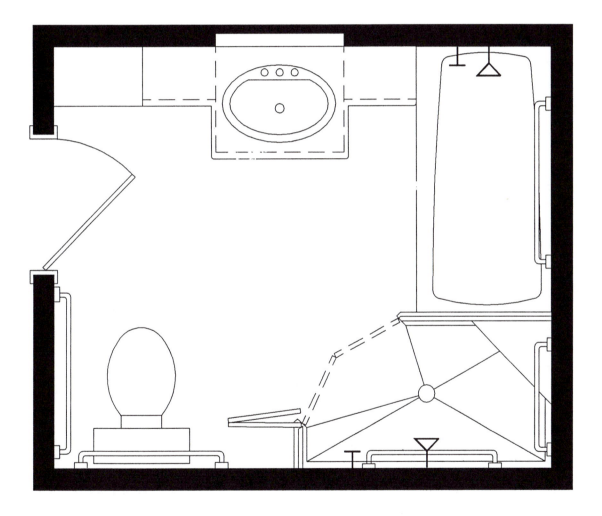

Figure 188 - **Guideline 19** - Shower doors must open into the bathroom.

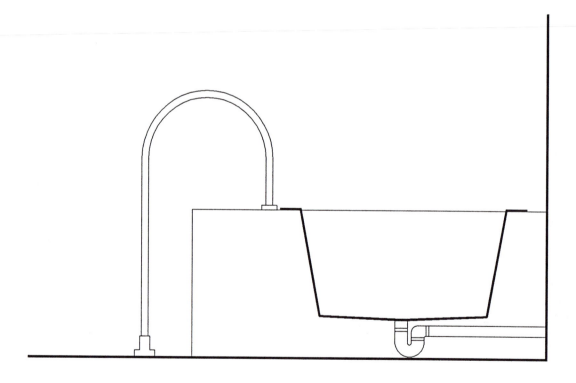

Figure 189 -   **Guideline 20** - Steps should not be planned at the bathtub or shower area.
Safety rails should be installed to facilitate transfer to and from the fixture.

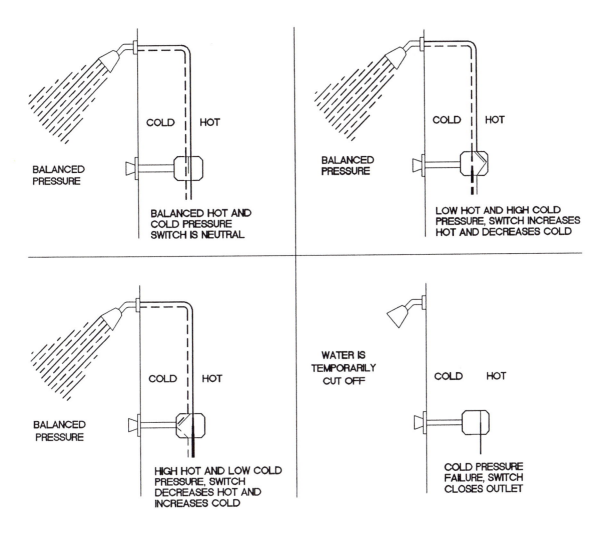

COLD | HOT

BALANCED
PRESSURE

BALANCED HOT AND
COLD PRESSURE
SWITCH IS NEUTRAL

COLD | HOT

BALANCED
PRESSURE

LOW HOT AND HIGH COLD
PRESSURE, SWITCH INCREASES
HOT AND DECREASES COLD

COLD | HOT

BALANCED
PRESSURE

HIGH HOT AND LOW COLD
PRESSURE, SWITCH
DECREASES HOT AND
INCREASES COLD

WATER IS
TEMPORARILY
CUT OFF

COLD HOT

COLD PRESSURE
FAILURE, SWITCH
CLOSES OUTLET

Figure 190 - **Guideline 21** - All showerheads should be equipped with pressure balance/temperature regulator or temperature limiting device.

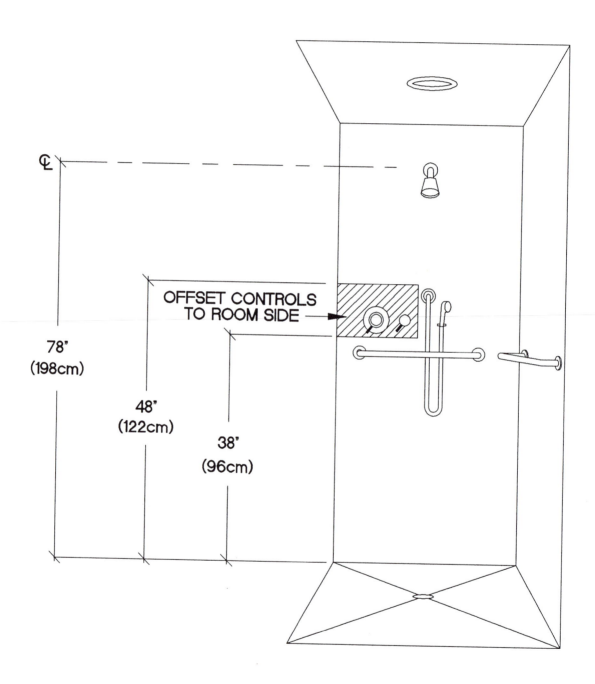

Ȼ

OFFSET CONTROLS
TO ROOM SIDE

78"
(198cm)

48"
(122cm)

38"
(96cm)

Figure 191 -   **Guideline 22a** - Shower controls should be accessible from inside and outside the fixture. Shower controls should be located between 38"-48" (96cm - 122cm) above the floor (placed above the grab bar) and offset toward the room.

Guideline 22a - Clarification - A handheld showerhead may be used in place of or in addition to a fixed showerhead. When mounted, a handheld showerhead should be no higher than 48" (122cm) in its lowest position.

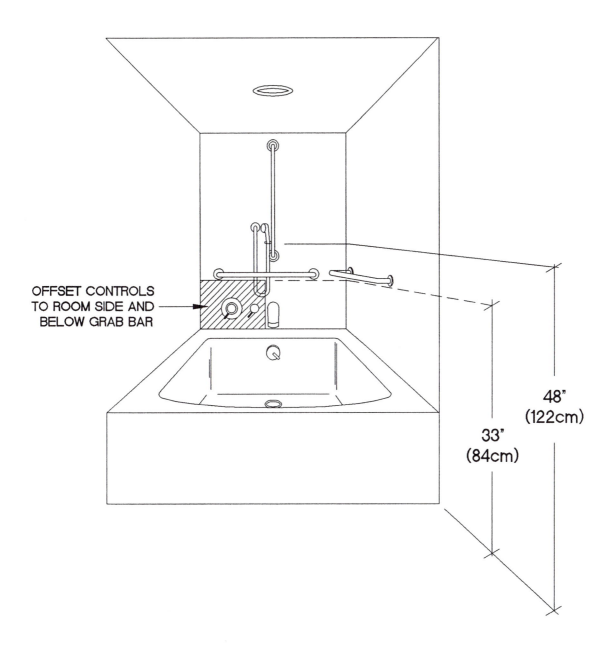

OFFSET CONTROLS
TO ROOM SIDE AND
BELOW GRAB BAR

48"
(122cm)

33"
(84cm)

Figure 192 - **Guideline 22b** - Tub controls should be accessible from inside and outside the fixture. Tub controls should be located between the rim of the bathtub and 33" (84cm) above the floor, placed below the grab bar and offset toward the room.

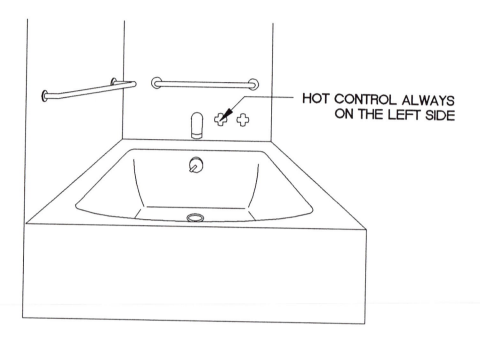

HOT CONTROL ALWAYS
ON THE LEFT SIDE

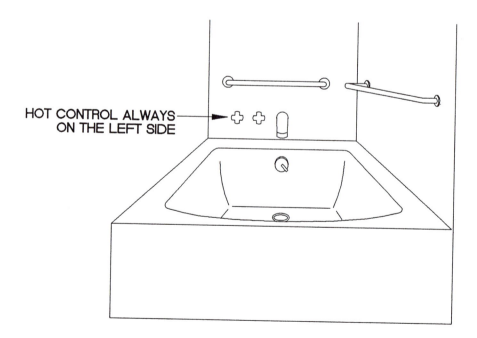

HOT CONTROL ALWAYS
ON THE LEFT SIDE

Figure 193 -   **Guideline 22b - Clarification** - If separate hot and cold controls are used in a bathtub (not permissible in a shower), for safe use the hot control is always on the left as viewed from inside the fixture.

SECTION IV: Toilets and Bidets
Guideline 23 to Guideline 25

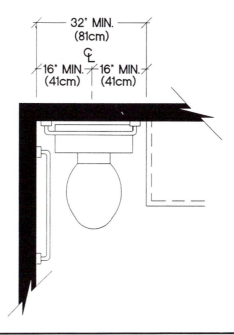

Figure 194 - **Guideline 23a** - A minimum 16" (41cm) clearance should be allowed from the centerline of the toilet or bidet to any obstruction, fixture or equipment (except grab bars) on either side.

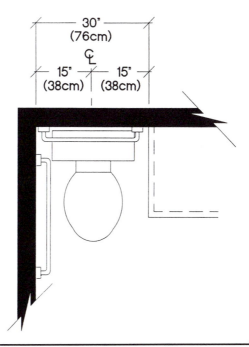

Figure 195 - **Guideline 23a - Clarification** - While a designer should always try to meet this goal, physical constraints of a job site may require deviation from the guideline. If a 32" (81cm) clearance is unavailable, this space may be reduced to 30" (76cm). Be aware that this compromise may not allow for full use by all people.

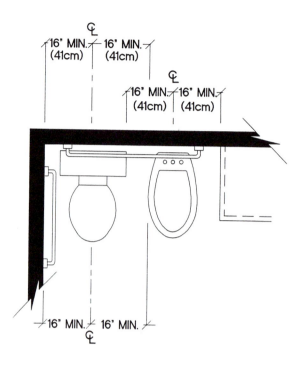

Figure 196 - **Guideline 23b** - When the toilet and bidet are planned adjacent to one another, the 16" minimum (41cm) centerline clearance to all obstructions should be maintained.

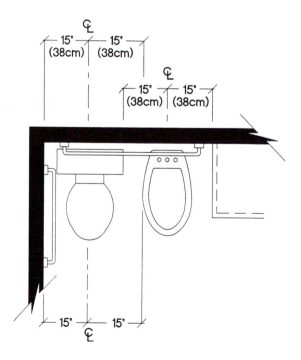

Figure 197 - **Guideline 23b - Clarification** - While a designer should always try to meet this goal, physical constraints of a job site may require deviation from the guideline. If a 16" (41cm) centerline clearance to an obstruction is unavailable, this centerline clearance may be reduced to 15" (38cm). Be aware that this compromise may not allow for full use by all people.

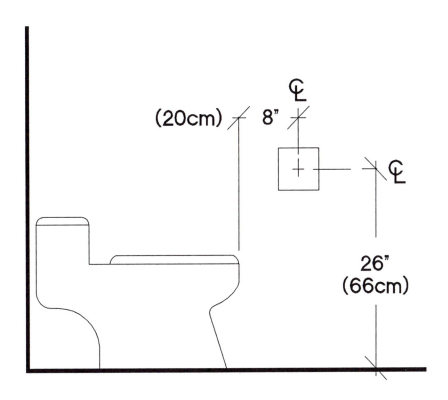

RECOMMENDED TOILET PAPER
HOLDER LOCATION

Figure 198 - **Guideline 24** - The toilet paper holder should be installed within reach of a person seated on the toilet. Ideal location is slightly in front of the edge of the toilet bowl, centered at 26" (66cm) above the floor.

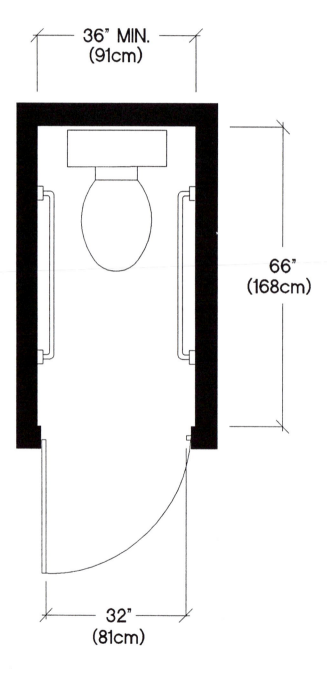

Figure 199 -   **Guideline 25** - Compartmental toilet areas should be a minimum 36" (91cm) x 66" (168cm) with a swing-out door or a pocket door.

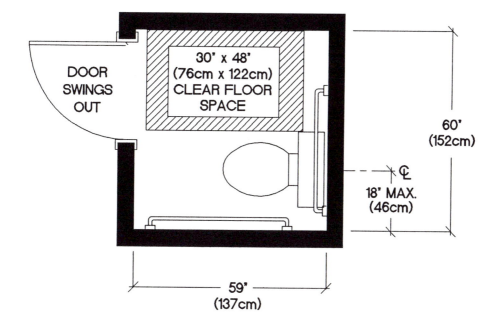

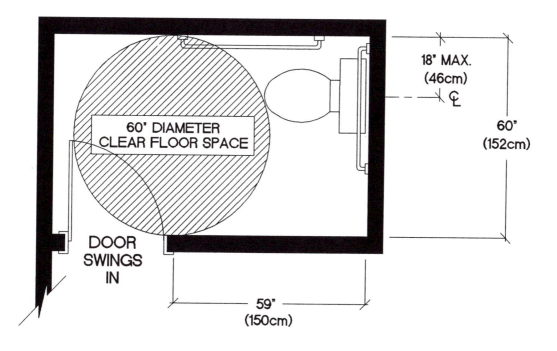

Figure 200 - **Guideline 25 - Clarification** - The amount of space needed for a private toilet area will be affected by the mobility of the person using it.

SECTION V: Grab bars, Storage and Flooring
Guideline 26 to Guideline 30

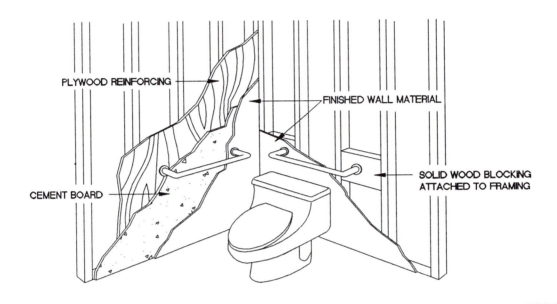

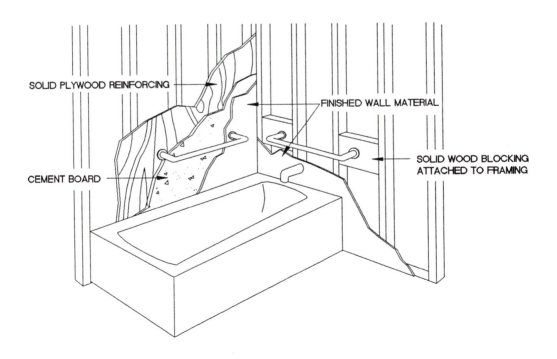

Figure 201 - **Guideline 26** - Walls should be prepared (reinforced) at the time of construction to allow for installation of grab bars. Grab bars should also be installed in the bathtub, shower and toilet areas at the time of construction.

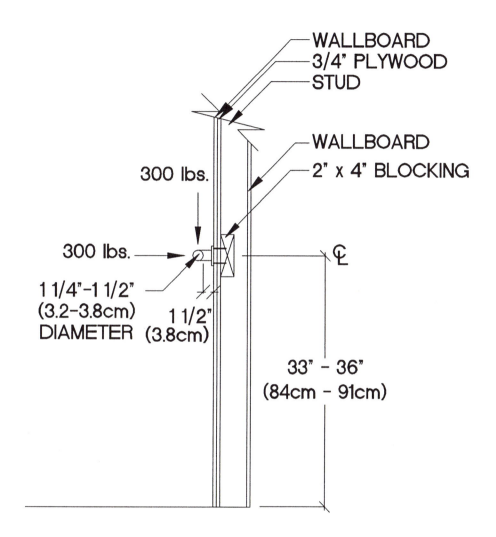

WALLBOARD
3/4" PLYWOOD
STUD

WALLBOARD
2" x 4" BLOCKING

300 lbs.

300 lbs.

1 1/4"-1 1/2"
(3.2-3.8cm)
DIAMETER

1 1/2"
(3.8cm)

₵

33" - 36"
(84cm - 91cm)

GRAB BAR SPECIFICATIONS

Figure 202 - **Guideline 26 - Clarification 1** - Reinforced areas must bear a static load of 300 lbs. (136kg). The use of cement board does not negate the need for blocking or plywood reinforcing.

Guideline 26 - Clarification 2 - Grab bars should be installed 33" - 36" (84cm - 91cm) above the floor, should be 1 1/4"-1 1/2" (3.2cm-3.8cm) diameter, extend 1 1/2 (3.8cm) from the wall, support a 300 lbs. (136 kg) load, and they should have a slip-resistant surface. When shapes other than round are used for grab bars, the width of the largest point should not exceed 2" (5.1cm). Towel bars must not be substituted as grab bars.

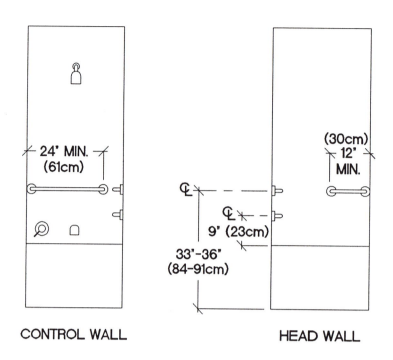

CONTROL WALL   HEAD WALL

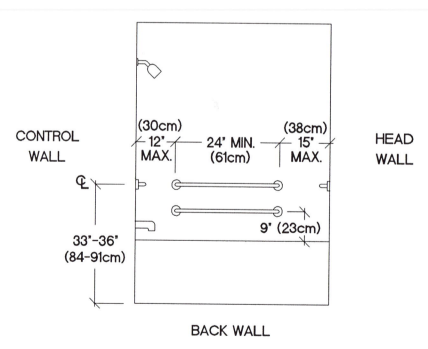

BACK WALL

Figure 203 - **Guideline 26 - Clarification 3** - Grab bars in bathtub/shower areas should be at least 24" (61cm) wide on the control wall, at least 12" (30cm) wide on the head wall and at least 24" (61cm) wide on the back wall, beginning no more than 12" (30cm) from the control wall and no more than 15" (38cm) from the head wall. If a second grab bar is desired on the back wall, it should be located 9" (23cm) above the bathtub deck, the same width as the grab bar above it.

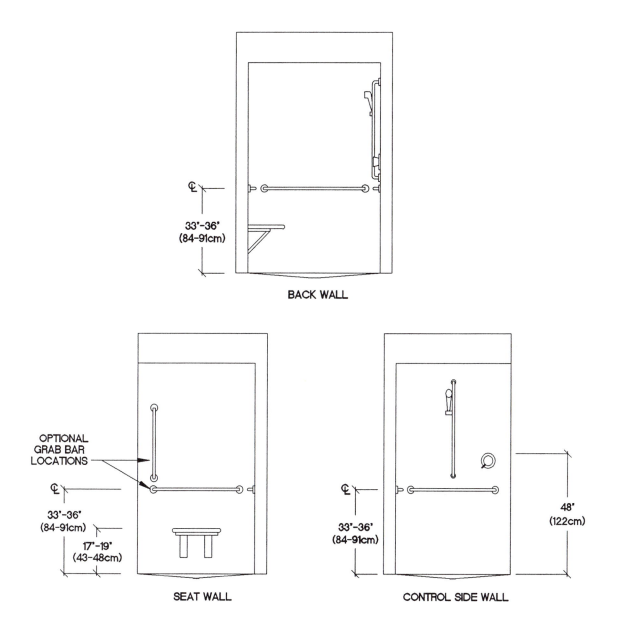

BACK WALL

OPTIONAL
GRAB BAR
LOCATIONS

33"-36"
(84-91cm)

17"-19"
(43-48cm)

SEAT WALL

33"-36"
(84-91cm)

48"
(122cm)

CONTROL SIDE WALL

Figure 204 -   **Guideline 26 - Clarification 4** - Grab bars in shower stalls should be included on each surrounding wall (optional on wall where bench is located) and should be no more than 9" (23cm) shorter than the width of the wall to which they are attached.

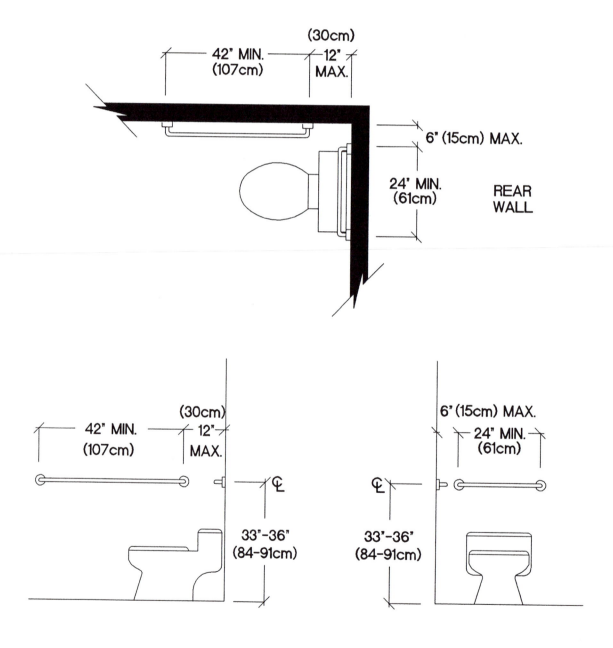

Figure 205 - **Guideline 26 - Clarification 5a** - The first grab bar in the toilet area should be located on the side wall closest to the toilet, a maximum 12" (30cm) from the rear wall. It should be at least 42" (107cm) wide. An optional secondary grab bar in the toilet area may be located on the rear wall, a maximum 6" (15cm) from the side wall. It should be at least 24" (61cm) wide.

**SIDE GRAB BARS ATTACHED
BELOW TOILET SEAT**

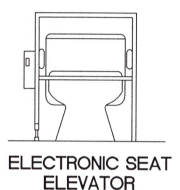

**ELECTRONIC SEAT
ELEVATOR**

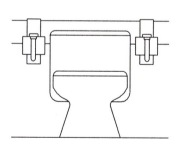

**RAIL SYSTEM WITH
SUPPORT ARMS**

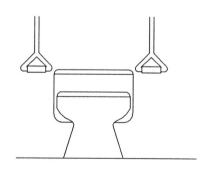

**HAND RAILS SUSPENDED
FROM CEILING**

Figure 206 - **Guideline 26 - Clarification 5b** - Alternatives for grab bars in the toilet area include, but are not limited to, side grab bars attached below the toilet seat, a rail system mounted to the back wall with perpendicular support arms at sides of the toilet seat, an electronic seat elevator or hand rails suspended from the ceiling.

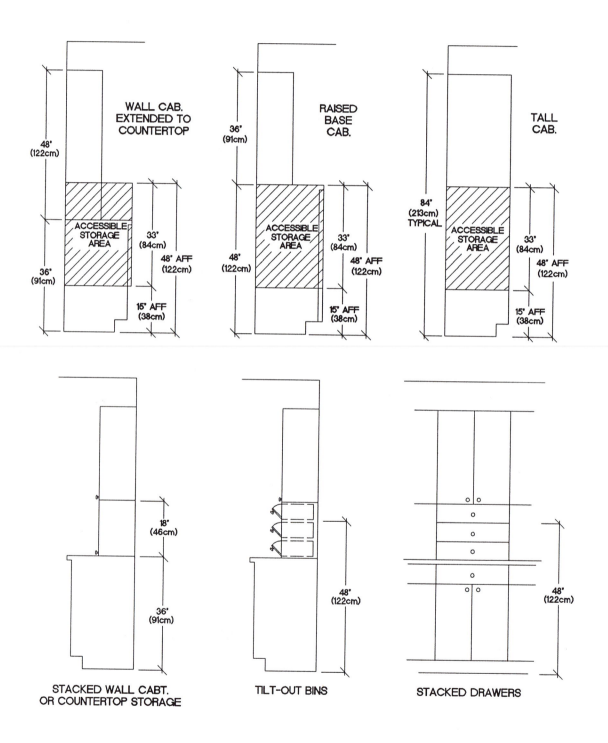

Figure 207 - **Guideline 27** - Storage for toiletries, linens, grooming and general bathroom supplies should be provided within 15"-48" (38cm-122cm) above the floor.

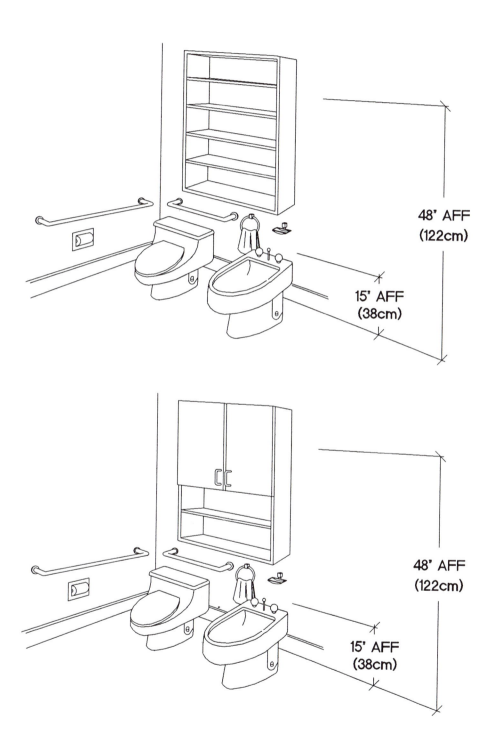

Figure 208 -   **Guideline 28** - Storage for soap, towels and other personal hygiene items should be installed within reach of a person seated on the bidet or toilet and within 15" - 48" (38cm - 122cm) above the floor. Storage areas should not interfere with the use of the fixture.

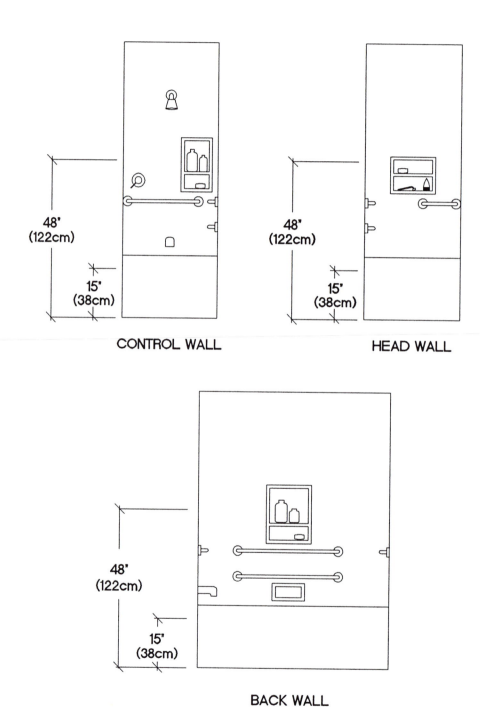

CONTROL WALL   **HEAD WALL**

BACK WALL

Figure 209 -   **Guideline 29** - In the bathtub/shower area, storage for soap, and other personal hygiene items should be provided within the 15" - 48" (38cm - 122cm) above the floor within the universal reach range.

Figure 210 - **Guideline 30** - All flooring should be slip resistant.

SECTION VI: Controls and Mechanical Systems
Guideline 31 to Guideline 41

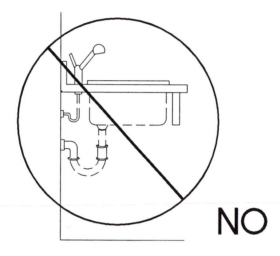

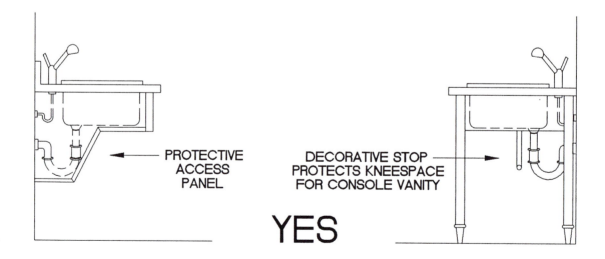

Figure 211 - **Guideline 31** - Exposed pipes and mechanicals should be covered by a protective panel or shroud. When using a console table, care must be given to keep plumbing attractive and out of contact with a seated user.

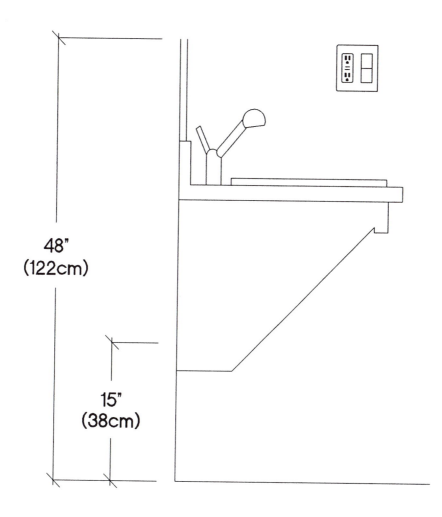

Figure 212 -   **Guideline 32** - Controls, dispensers, outlets and operating mechanisms should be 15"-48" (38cm-122cm) above the floor and should be operable with a closed fist.

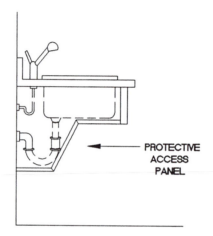

PROTECTIVE
ACCESS
PANEL

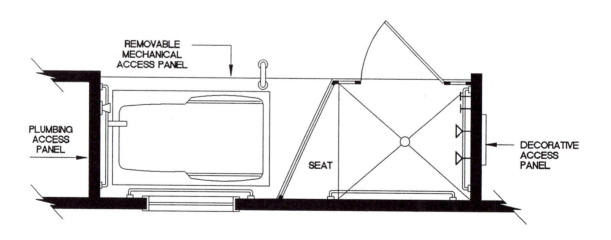

REMOVABLE
MECHANICAL
ACCESS PANEL

PLUMBING
ACCESS
PANEL

SEAT

DECORATIVE
ACCESS
PANEL

Figure 213 - **Guideline 33** - All mechanical, electrical and plumbing systems should have access panels.

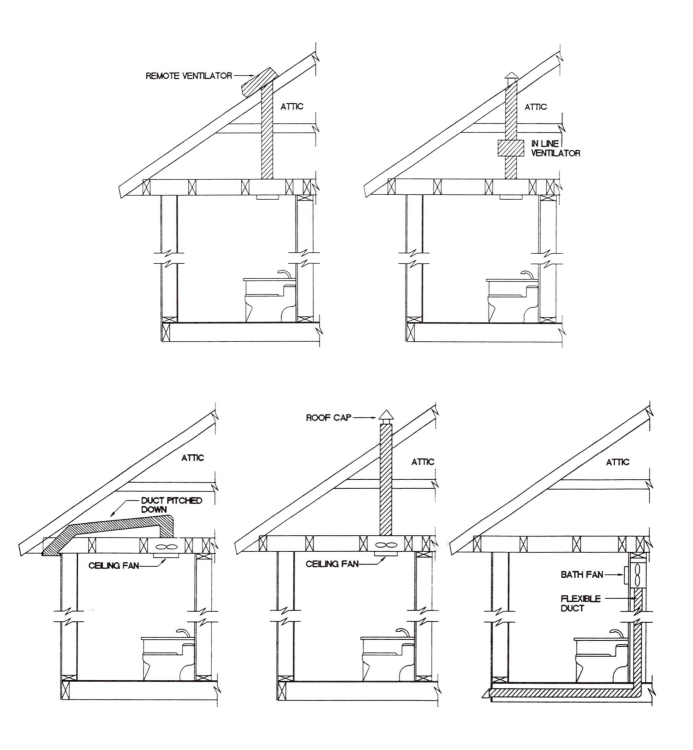

Figure 214 - **Guideline 34** - Mechanical ventilation systems to the outside should be included in the plan to vent the entire room. The minimum size of the system can be calculated as follows:

$$\frac{\text{Cubic Space (LxWxH)} \times 8 \text{ (changes of air per hour)}}{60 \text{ minutes}} = \text{minimum cubic feet per minute (CFM)}$$

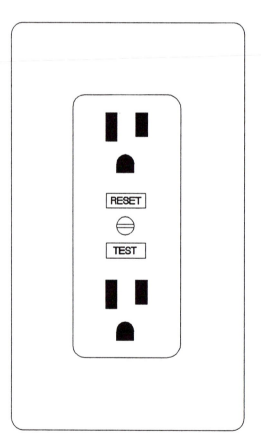

Figure 215 - **Guideline 35** - Ground fault circuit interrupters must be specified on all receptacles, lights and switches in the bathroom. All light fixtures above the bathtub/shower units must be moisture-proof special-purpose fixtures.

HEAT LAMP

HEAT/FAN/LIGHT

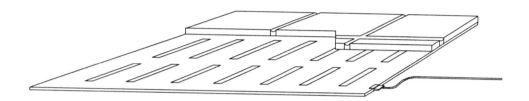

RADIANT FLOOR SYSTEM

WALL HEATER

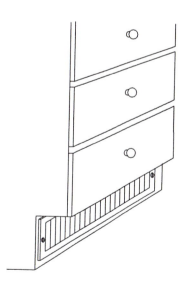

TOEKICK HEATER

Figure 216 - **Guideline 36** - In addition to a primary heat source, auxiliary heating may be planned in the bathroom.

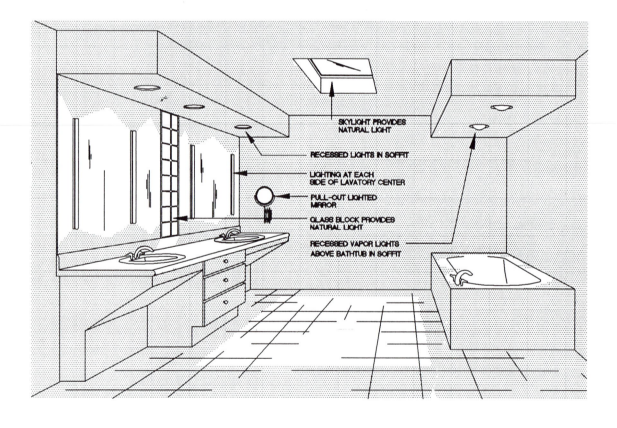

SKYLIGHT PROVIDES
NATURAL LIGHT

RECESSED LIGHTS IN SOFFIT

LIGHTING AT EACH
SIDE OF LAVATORY CENTER

PULL-OUT LIGHTED
MIRROR

GLASS BLOCK PROVIDES
NATURAL LIGHT

RECESSED VAPOR LIGHTS
ABOVE BATHTUB IN SOFFIT

Figure 217 - **Guideline 37** - Every functional area in the bathroom should be well illuminated by appropriate task lighting, night lights and/or general lighting. No lighting fixture, including hanging fixtures, should be within reach of a person seated or standing in the bathtub/shower area.

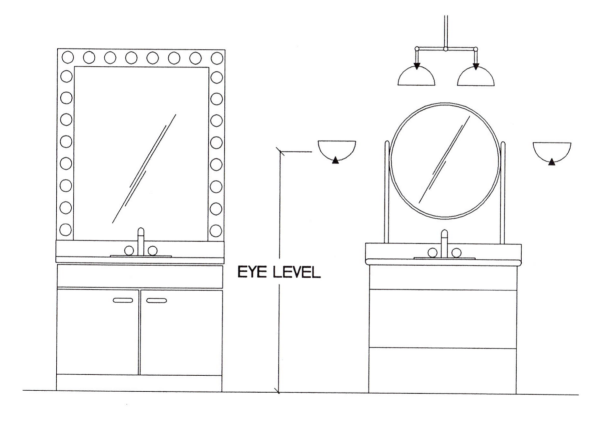

EYE LEVEL

Figure 218 - **Guideline 37 - Clarification** - The vanity area should include both overhead and side lighting locations. Side lighting may be planned at eye level which will be approximately 3" (8cm) below a users overall height.

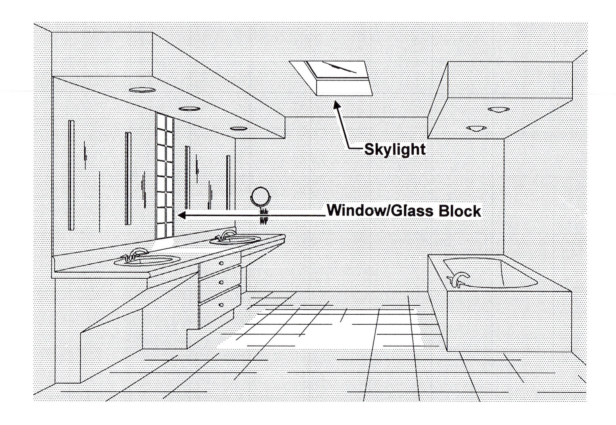

Figure 219 -   **Guideline 38** - When possible, bathroom lighting should include a window/sky-light area equal to a minimum of 10% of the square footage of the bathroom.

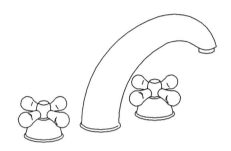

**EASY GRIP
TWO HANDLE
TUB FILLER/CONTROLS**

**SINGLE LEVER
SHOWER CONTROL**

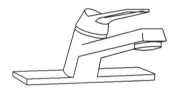

**SINGLE LEVER
LAVATORY FAUCET**

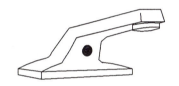

**INFRARED/MOTION SENSOR
LAVATORY FAUCET**

**TOUCH
SENSITIVE**

TOGGLE

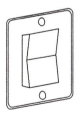

ROCKER

DEEP PULL

Figure 220 - **Guideline 39** - Controls, handles and door/drawer pulls should be operable with one hand, require only a minimal amount of strength for operation, and should not require tight grasping, pinching or twisting of the wrist. (Includes handles knobs/pulls on entry and exit doors, cabinets, drawers and plumbing fixtures, as well as light and thermostat controls/switches, intercoms, and other room controls.)

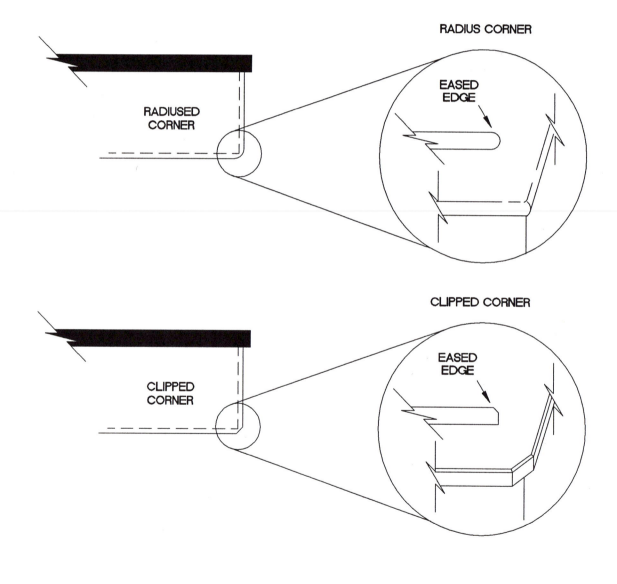

Figure 221 -   **Guideline 40** - Use clipped or radius corners for open countertops; countertop edges should be eased to eliminate sharp edges.

Figure 222 - **Guideline 41** - Any glass used as a bathtub/shower enclosure, partition, or other glass application within 18" (46cm) of the floor should be one of three kinds of safety glazing; laminated glass with a plastic interlayer, tempered glass or approved plastics such as those found in the model safety glazing code.

chapter 8

The Lavatory Area

The first of the three main functional areas of the bathroom, the lavatory area, requires careful consideration in terms of universal design. The space allowances, the style and installation, and to a lesser degree the material of the lavatory will have tremendous impact on safe and universal access to the area. This chapter will examine the lavatory and the spaces surrounding it, in terms of universal design.

SPACE CONSIDERATIONS FOR THE LAVATORY AREA

Universal space planning in the lavatory area involves several key considerations, all of which impact one another. They are:

- counter height
- sink depth
- plumbing location
- knee space height and width
- clear floor space for approach and use
- the impact on adjacent clear floor space
- storage.

Counter Height, Sink Depth, Plumbing Location, Knee Space Height

The maximum height lavatory for a seated user should be 34" (86cm), with 30" (72cm) being a more comfortable choice. Sink depth, and needed knee space height (based on height of wheelchair armrest) will impact this. NKBA suggests that a sink be no deeper than 6 1/2" (17cm). To function properly, 4" (10cm) is adequate. Given that the recommended knee space clearance is 27" (69cm) high minimum, and 29" (74cm) preferred to the bottom of the front edge or apron, the designer must work within these constraints to arrive at an optimum solution.

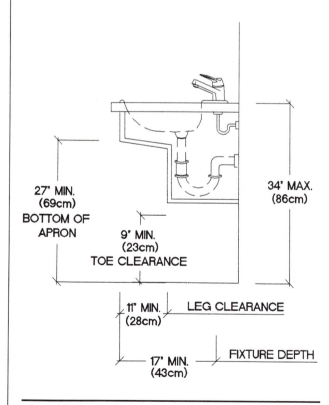

Figure 223 -   Kneespace at lavatory.

A comfortable height for a lavatory for a standing user is typically 36" - 38" (91cm - 97cm). Both the standing and seated user can be accommodated if there is room for two sinks or if an adjustable height sink can be used.

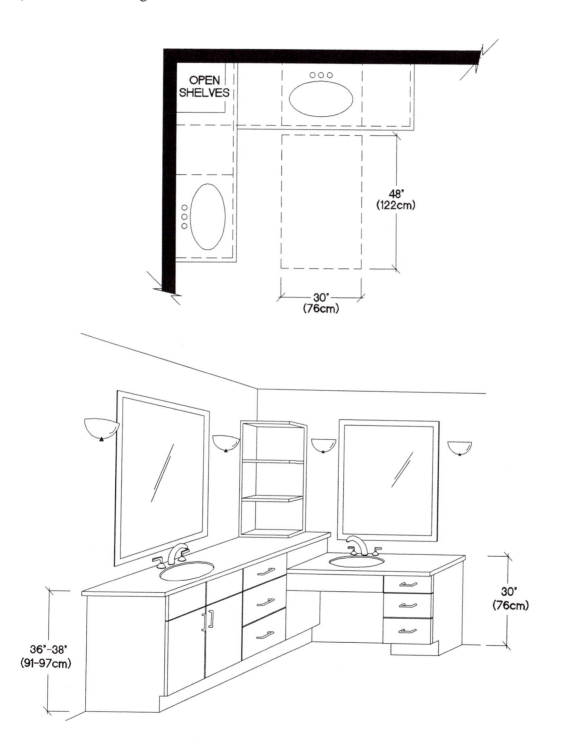

Figure 224 - Example of two lavatories at different heights.

Knee Space Width, Clear Floor Space and Storage

The minimum width for a knee space is 30" (72cm) with 36" (91cm) preferred. Remember that 36" (91cm) width will allow for a T-turn and 48" - 54" (122cm - 137cm) width will allow for enough clear space to include up to 19" (48cm) under the knee space to be used in a 60" (152cm) turning radius. When appropriate, planning the open knee space of the lavatory adjacent to the clear space at another fixture will be beneficial for maneuvering.

Storage in the lavatory area for towels, equipment, and supplies must be within the universal reach range of 15" - 48" (38cm - 122cm) and should be within reach of a person using the lavatory. Drawers adjacent to a knee space, open shelves on adjacent counter areas, or rolling storage help to achieve this convenience.

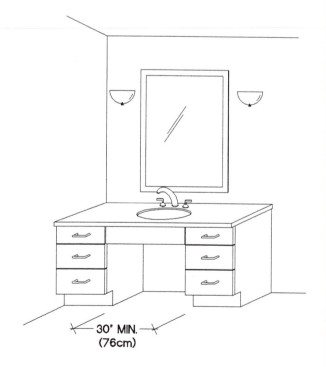

Figure 225 -   Minimum width kneespace.

Figure 226 -   36" (91cm) knee space allows for use in T-turn.

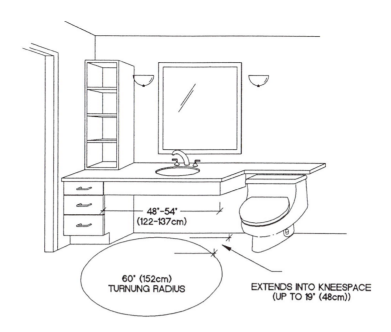

48"-54"
(122-137cm)

60" (152cm)
TURNUNG RADIUS

EXTENDS INTO KNEESPACE
(UP TO 19" (48cm))

Figure 227 -   48" - 54" (122cm - 137cm) wide kneespace, using up to 19" (48cm) to complete 60" (152cm) turning space.

THE FIXTURE

The lavatory or sink must be chosen carefully to provide functional counter and storage space while allowing for needed clear floor space. The main types of lavatories to be considered are Wall Hung, Pedestal, Drop-In, Undermount, Integral, and Console.

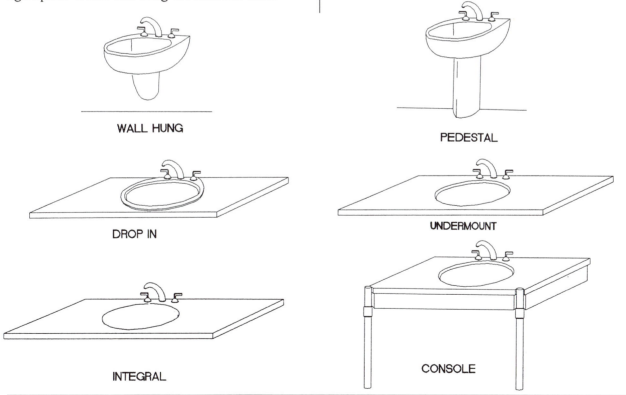

WALL HUNG

PEDESTAL

DROP IN

UNDERMOUNT

INTEGRAL

CONSOLE

Figure 228 -   Main types of lavatories.

Lavatory Designs

Certain characteristics will improve the universal design application for any of these lavatories. The maximum depth recommended for an accessible sink is 6 1/2" (17cm) . A sink depth of 4" (10cm) is sufficient, and a design that is shallower in the front, leading back to the deepest part of the bowl with a drain at the rear, is the preferred configuration.

If the space under the lavatory is to be open, it must include some type of protective covering for the drain and supply pipes. This covering should extend to the bottom side of the sink if needed to protect against heat, insulated for sound, and to cover any rough surfaces. A variety of options exist to do this attractively.

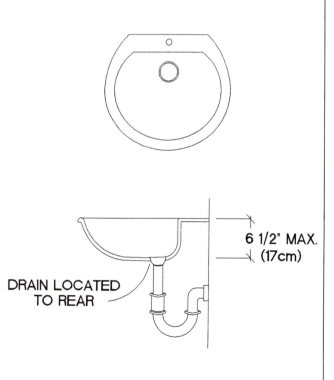

Figure 229 -   Ideal lavatory configuration.

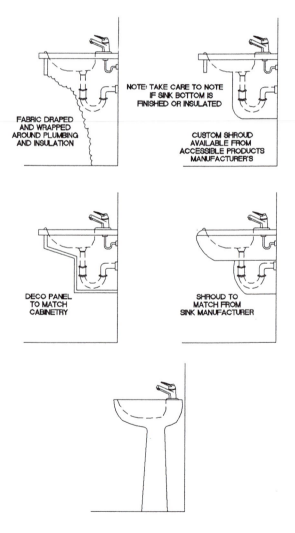

Figure 230 -   Options for covering pipes and sink underside.

Accessing the Knee Space

Several adaptable solutions would allow for the space under the sink to be used in a variety of ways. The face frame and doors of the cabinet might be made removable with the plumbing protected inside. This would allow the undersink area to be used for storage and when desired, removal of the face frame and doors would create a knee space for seated use. Another option would be to use retractable doors, taking care to allow for a 30" (72cm) minimum width interior space when the doors are in the retracted position. A third option would be to create bi-fold doors that fold 180° to lie flat on the adjacent cabinets. A hinge is available to facilitate this.

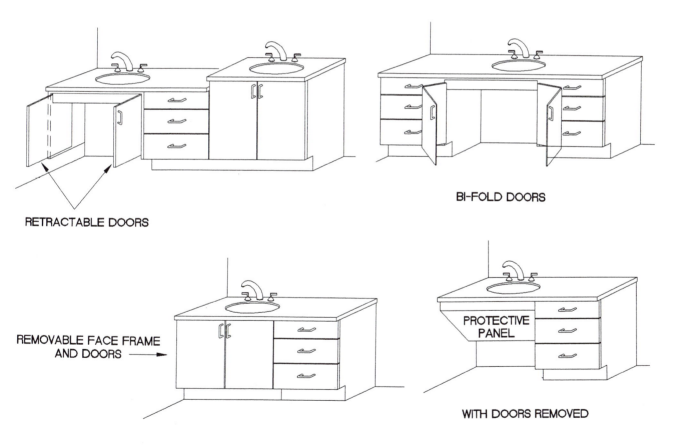

RETRACTABLE DOORS

BI-FOLD DOORS

REMOVABLE FACE FRAME AND DOORS ⟶

PROTECTIVE PANEL

WITH DOORS REMOVED

Figure 231 -   Adaptable lavatory options.

Wall Hung Lavatories

The wall hung lavatory provides great flexibility in the height of the area, with full clear floor space. However, it does not provide storage or counter options. Several solutions involve wall hung cabinets and the possible use of a counter or shelf above the sink, with care being taken to keep the counter surface within reach of users of various stature.

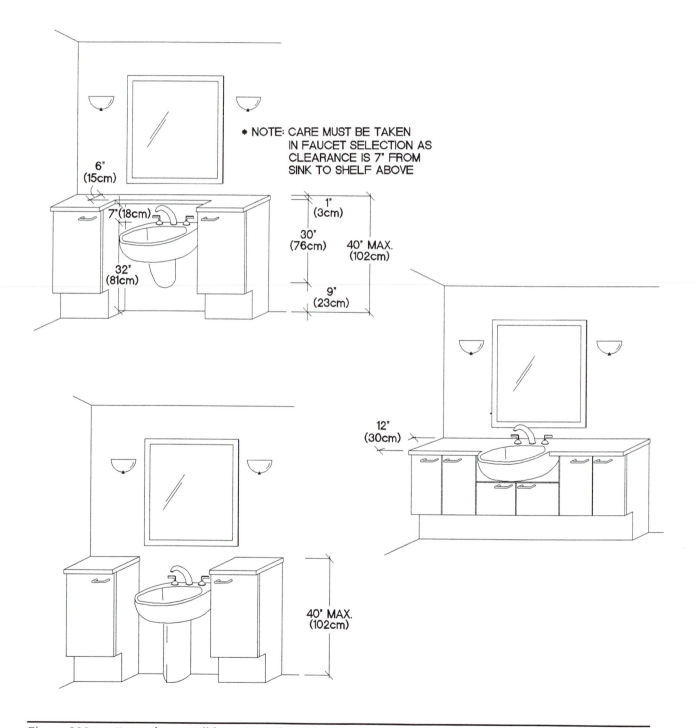

Figure 232 - Examples - Wall hung or pedestal lavatory areas.

Pedestal Lavatories

These same options apply to pedestal sinks.

The pedestal sink allows for clear floor space, with some interruption from the pedestal. Styles are available with the sink itself having an integral work surface.

In other designs, adjacent work surfaces can be created as illustrated for the wall-hung lavatory. The typical height of a pedestal sink is 30" (72cm), which will usually be too low to allow for a knee space, depending on the sink depth. The sink can be elevated by building a base for the pedestal.

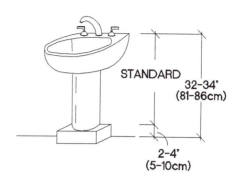

Figure 234 -   Pedestal Sink with Built-up base.

While the pedestal sink does provide some clear floor space, it may be desirable to opt for the same sink bowl with a matching wall shroud to make the knee space totally clear. Many pedestal sinks are available either way.

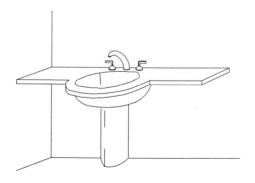

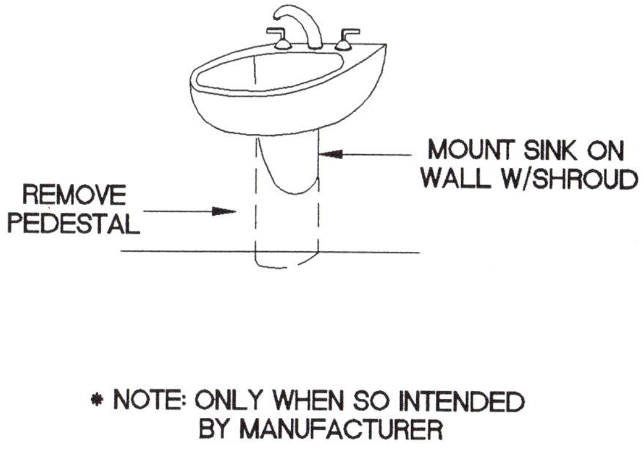

Figure 233 -   Pedestal sink with integral work surface.

Figure 235 -   Pedestal sink converted to wall hung sink with shroud

Drop-In and Undermount Lavatories

When using either a drop-in or an under-mount sink, the lavatory area can be univer-sally designed if the depth of the sink does not exceed 6 1/2" (17cm) and the drain is lo-cated to the rear. This would be done follow-ing the steps for creating a knee space. Unfortunately, the depth limitation makes most current sinks too deep when under-mounted, but there are a few models avail-able that will allow for this. The undermount sink eliminates any lip or rise in the surface around the sink rim, so it is desirable for a person with limited grip to access its interior.

Integral Lavatories

The integral sink fitted without apparent seams into the counter offers unique univer-sal design solutions, particularly when formed from solid surface materials that can be formed and shaped. The sink depth can sometimes be adjusted by trimming the bowl before it is bonded to the counter surface. The area immediately surrounding the sink can be trimmed and shaped to suit user and space needs. The front edge of the counter can be extended to create an apron to con-ceal support for the sink. Handholds and towel bars can be cut into the counter sur-face.

Console Lavatories

The console sink is an attractive way to provide a sink with a kneespace, provided there are sufficient clearances and maneuver-ing spaces. Carefully check the height of the console, the height of the kneespace below, and the adjacent clear floor space. The con-sole sink will also require special attention to protecting the user from exposed pipes and potentially sharp edges.

COUNTER CUT BACK
TO IMPROVE ACCESS
TO SINK

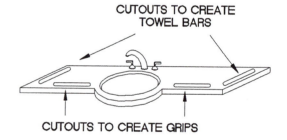

CUTOUTS TO CREATE
TOWEL BARS

CUTOUTS TO CREATE GRIPS

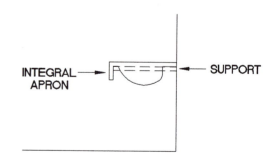

INTEGRAL APRON
TO CONCEAL SUPPORT

Figure 236 -   Options with solid surface/integral lavatories.

Adjustable Height Sinks

Several products exist that allow for height adjustment of the lavatory and/or adjacent counter area on a moment-to-moment basis. To use a motorized system, flexible plumbing lines must be installed which will require approval from local plumbing inspectors. While this is non-traditional, a careful examination of the system and its goals will usually result in approval. The system works via a motor installed against the wall that will raise and lower the counter, sink included.

The result is a totally flexible, easy-to-operate system that truly works for everyone.

Another product available includes the lavatory, flexible plumbing lines and a wall bracketing system that allows a person to adjust the position of the lav to the right or left or up and down by pressing a release lever.

These types of adjustability may be costly, but the total flexibility they provide will be worth the added benefits. A more moderately priced option would be a hand crank lift mechanism.

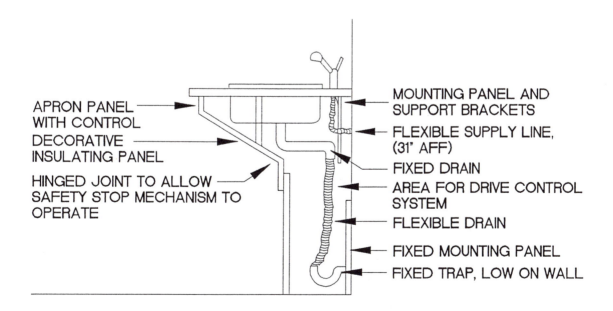

APRON PANEL WITH CONTROL

DECORATIVE INSULATING PANEL

HINGED JOINT TO ALLOW SAFETY STOP MECHANISM TO OPERATE

MOUNTING PANEL AND SUPPORT BRACKETS

FLEXIBLE SUPPLY LINE, (31" AFF)

FIXED DRAIN

AREA FOR DRIVE CONTROL SYSTEM

FLEXIBLE DRAIN

FIXED MOUNTING PANEL

FIXED TRAP, LOW ON WALL

Figure 237 - Flexible plumbing lines.

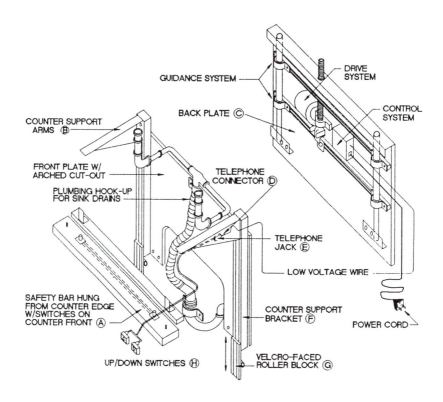

GUIDANCE SYSTEM

DRIVE SYSTEM

BACK PLATE Ⓒ

CONTROL SYSTEM

COUNTER SUPPORT ARMS Ⓑ

FRONT PLATE W/ ARCHED CUT-OUT

TELEPHONE CONNECTOR Ⓓ

PLUMBING HOOK-UP FOR SINK DRAINS

TELEPHONE JACK Ⓔ

LOW VOLTAGE WIRE

SAFETY BAR HUNG FROM COUNTER EDGE W/SWITCHES ON COUNTER FRONT Ⓐ

COUNTER SUPPORT BRACKET Ⓕ

POWER CORD

UP/DOWN SWITCHES Ⓗ

VELCRO-FACED ROLLER BLOCK Ⓖ

Figure 238 -   Drive assembly for motorized sink and counter support.

Figure 239 -   Adjustable lavatory. (Pressalit by American Standard)

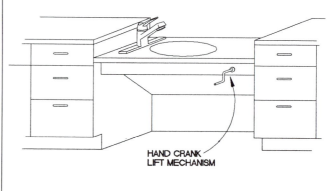

HAND CRANK LIFT MECHANISM

Figure 240 -   Hand crank lift mechanism.

Yet another option is to create adaptable-height lavatory and vanity areas. This will again require the use of flexible plumbing lines which must be approved. The counter, including the sink, is hung on support brackets. The brackets may be mounted at several heights without needing major construction changes. This type of adjustability is not meant for day-to-day changes, but for changes when users' needs change.

LAVATORY MATERIALS

Finally, the materials used to fabricate lavatories have some impact on universal design. Materials chosen should be slow to transfer heat and/or sound. The underside of the lavatory should be smooth and insulated to protect the legs of a seated user.

Stainless steel and other decorative metals are usually easy to maintain and several manufacturers are now insulating them against sound and heat transfer. There are

several stainless steel sinks that can be ordered with the depth and drain location called out by the designer.

Sinks of solid surface material are more costly, but they transfer less heat and sound. Also, they offer tremendous flexibility in fabrication. Cast polymer or cultured marble are less flexible in terms of fabrication, but manufacturers of these products have paid particular attention to universal design considerations, so there is a wide variety of standard shapes to choose from.

Vitreous china or cast iron lavatories are often deeper than the maximum 6 1/2" (17cm). There are growing numbers of china lavatories designed specifically to meet this need, so the selection is expanding.

For a more extensive discussion of materials, refer to the **NKBA® Bathroom Industry Technical Manuals**.

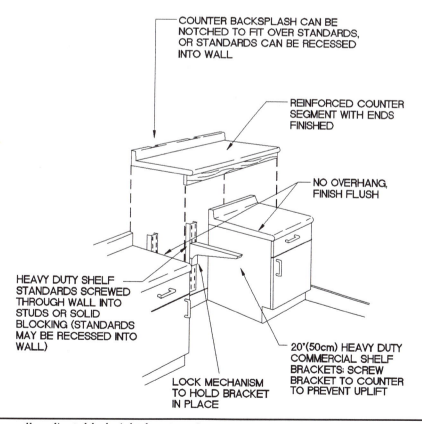

Figure 241 - Manually adjustable height lavatory/counters.

chapter 9

The Bathtub/ Shower Area

U niversal considerations for the bathtub or shower area include space planning, style and universal installation, material selection and controls. The main focus for the bathtub or shower area is on safe transfer into and out of the fixture and on ease of use.

SPACE CONSIDERATIONS FOR THE BATHTUB/SHOWER AREA

In planning the space for the bathtub and/or shower area, how the user will approach and transfer, into and out of the fixture will influence the use of space. A truly universal space would allow for a variety of approaches. In addition, the type of fixture and its intended use will affect the space plan. The three main fixtures are; a bathtub, a roll-in shower (large enough for a person using a wheelchair to roll into), and a transfer shower (a shower that a person using a wheelchair would transfer into).

The Bathtub

The bathtub space can be handled several ways. The first is to provide a seat or transfer surface in the bathtub space. One advantage to this option is that it requires the minimum amount of space, fitting within the bathtub. This is often a portable item, requiring no structural changes for its use. The disadvantages are that the seat will take up space wihin the bathtub, eliminating the option of soaking in the bathtub. Storage space must be provided when it is to be removed, and care must be given to ensure its stability. To create a better transfer surface, the bathtub seat should extend slightly beyond the edge of the bathtub.

Clear Floor Space at Bathtub

The clear floor space required at this type of bathtub is the length of the bathtub x 30" (72cm) with a preferred width of 36" (91cm).

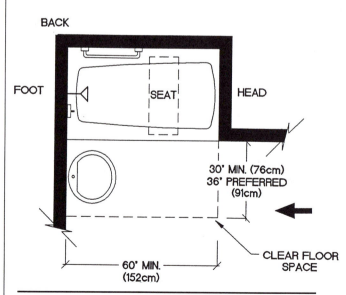

Figure 242 - Clear floor space - parallel approach.

For a perpendicular approach, the clear floor space required increases to a 48" (122cm) depth.

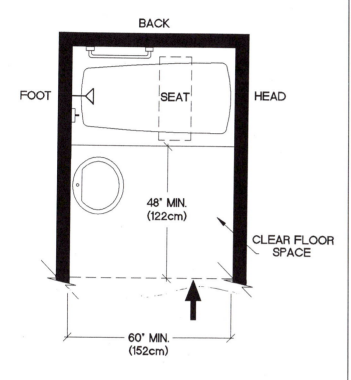

Figure 243 - Clear floor space - forward or perpendicular approach.

The preferred clear floor space would include 12" - 18" (30cm - 46cm) at both ends of the bathtub to allow for better access to controls and better maneuvering for a parallel transfer for a person using a mobility aid.

The added clearance at the foot of the bathtub allows for an added wheelchair footrest to extend beyond the control wall. The added clear floor space at the head of the bathtub allows for better positioning of the back portion of a wheelchair.

Another option for the bathtub area is to create a built-in transfer surface at the head of the bathtub. The depth of this built-in surface must be a minimum of 15" (38cm), with 20" - 24" (51cm - 61cm) preferred.

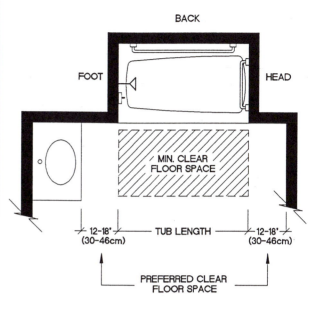

Figure 244 - Preferred clear floor space.

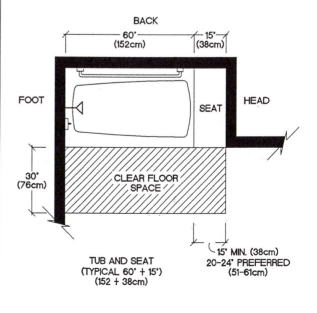

Figure 245 - Built-in seat at head of bathtub.

Remember, the minimum clear floor space required is 30" (72cm) x the length of the bathtub plus the seat. Better access to controls and better positioning of a wheelchair again call for an additional 12" - 18" (30cm - 46cm) clear floor space at the foot and the head of the bathtub.

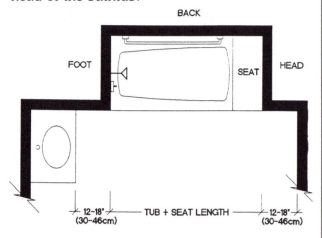

Figure 246 - Preferred clear floor space - bathtub with built-in seat.

Both the built-in or the removable bathtub seat must withstand a minimum of 300 pounds (136kg) of pressure. To construct a built-in seat, framing that will withstand this weight must be provided. In addition, the area must have a waterproof liner and should be sloped slightly toward the bathtub (1/4" per 12") (.64cm per 30cm) to avoid excess water standing on the seat.

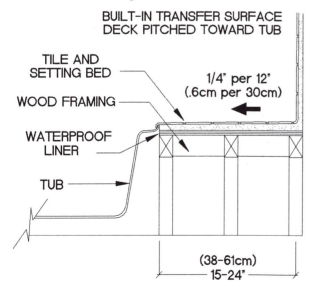

Figure 247 - Construction details - built-in transfer surface.

BATHTUB CONTROLS, ACCESSORIES AND GRAB BARS

Controls

Controls should be located at the foot of the bathtub below the grab bar and offset toward the outside of the bathtub. Sometimes, a second control and a handheld spray will be located on the back wall for ease of use by someone in the bathtub.

Showerhead

A fixed showerhead, if used, should be mounted at the standard 78" (198cm) above the floor. A hand-held showerhead should be mounted not higher than 48" (122cm) and in a position not to obstruct the use of grab bars. If the hand-held shower head is mounted on a slide-bar, the bar must allow for positioning the shower head with its lowest position not higher than 48" (122cm).

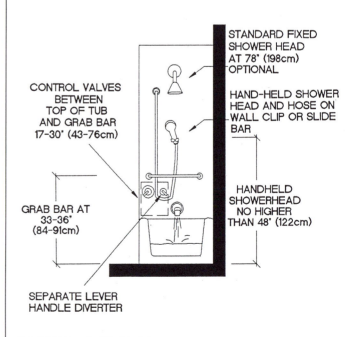

Figure 248 - Bathtub control wall.

Grab Bars

Grab bars improve safety and stability. While they are integral in certain bathtubs, they are optional with others, and the most universal choice is to build support into the entire bathtub surround so that grab bars may be added when and where needed.

Standards will dictate several locations for grab bars, yet it may not be a current need or desire of a client as you plan. Keep in mind that the point of entry where a person shifts from sitting to standing or from transfer surface down into the bathtub are the areas most likely to need grab bars.

The location of grab bars in the bathtub area will be affected by how a person intends to transfer into and out of the bathtub. A universal approach is to install blocking throughout the bathtub area, as previously mentioned, so that grab bars can be positioned when and where they will be most effective.

At the foot of the bathtub the grab bar should be a minimum of 24" (61cm) long beginning at the front edge of the bathtub. On the back wall, the grab bar should be a minimum 24" (61cm), although a longer bar is preferred. This bar may not be more than 24" (61cm) from the foot-end wall and not more than 12" (30cm) from the head-end wall.

A second grab bar, 9" (23cm) above the rim of the bathtub, the same length as the first should be included. The bar at the head of the bathtub is to be a minimum 12" (30cm) long, beginning at the front edge of the bathtub. If a built-in transfer seat is used, the bar at the head of the bathtub may be omitted and the grab bar(s) on the back wall becomes a 48" (122cm) minimum length, not more than 12" (30cm) from the foot of the bathtub and not more than 15" (38cm) from the head of the bathtub. For more information on how a person might transfer into the bathtub, *see Appendix 7, Bathroom Fixture Transfer Techniques.*

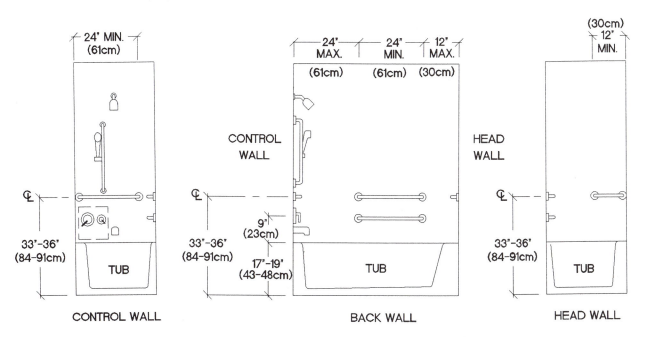

Figure 249 -   Grab bars at bathtub without built-in seat

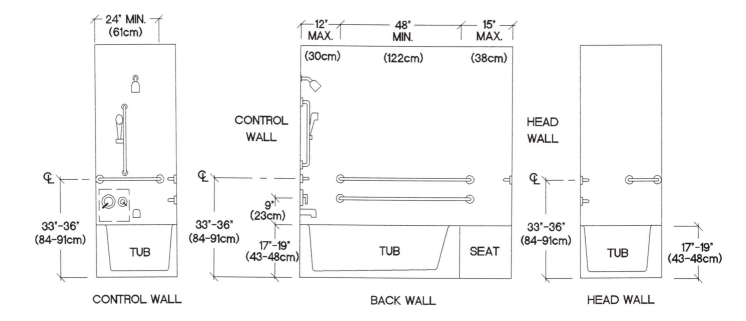

Figure 250 -   Grab bar locations for bathtub with built-in seat

THE FIXTURE

There are many varieties of bathtubs on the market today, with growing numbers of styles lending themselves to universal design. The traditional 30" w x 60" l x 14" - 21" d (72cm w x 152cm l x 36cm - 53cm d) bathtub can be challenging to even the most able-bodied user in terms of safe entry, exit and control.

- Any bathtub that does not include a seat in its design can be more safely installed by planning a transfer seat or surface into the decking around the bathtub.

- Changing from hazardous steps around a bathtub to an increased platform or deck will improve safe access for all, particularly if a handrail or grab bar is planned to further aid stability.

- A minimum depth of 15" (38cm) is recommended for a transfer surface, but if this is not possible, plan the deepest available space.

- Finally, a slip-resistant surface on the floor of the bathub will improve safe access.

Bathtub Styles

Although the style of the basic bathtub, which has never been user-friendly, has changed very little, there are a number of styles that provide assistance to the bather in entry and exit. Several bathtubs have doors.

In addition, molded bathtubs and surround systems are available with seats as an integral part of the bathtub.

Another option in the molded bathtub products may be fold-down seats or grab bars.

There are bathtubs with built-in lifts or seats that rotate out to allow a bather to transfer onto the seat, then back in and down to allow the bather to soak in the bathtub or whirlpool.

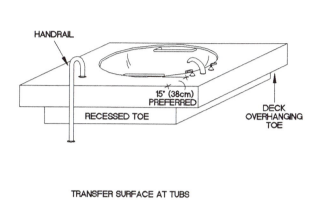

TRANSFER SURFACE AT TUBS

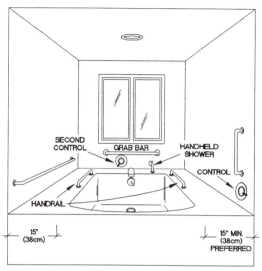

TRANSFER SURFACE AT TUBS

Figure 251 -   Transfer surface at bathtubs.

Several bathtubs are designed so that the floor of the bathtub is accessible by means of a door or rotating panel, and the bathtub floor is 18" - 20" (46cm - 51cm) high. This results in easy transfer directly onto the bathtub floor. It also means a person can sit while cleaning the bathtub or bathing a child, rather than kneeling on the floor.

Figure 252 -   Courtesy of Kohler - Bathtub with door.

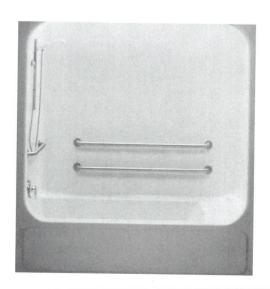

Figure 253 -   Bathtub with integral seat.

Figure 254 -   Bathtub with fold-down seat.

Figure 256 -   Bathtub with built-in lift.

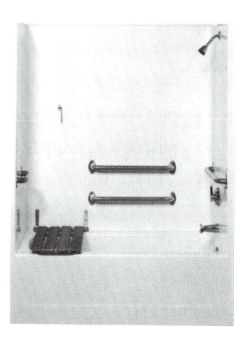

Figure 255 -   Bathtub with fold-down seat.

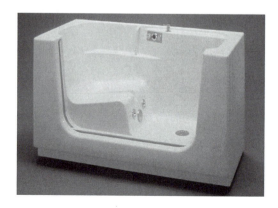

Figure 257 -   Bathtub with raised height floor and rotating front panel.

Bathtub Aesthetics

While the growing availability of accessible bathtubs are welcome, the institutional or medical appearance of many of them is unfortunate.

It requires continued effort from the manufacturers to improve the appearance of the bathubs and continued effort from the bathroom designer to create an area where function and aesthetics don't conflict.

Bathtub Materials

For the most part, materials used to fabricate bathtubs do not impact their universal application.

- Fiberglass, acrylic or molded materials typically retain heat better than cast iron, steel or china, but beyond that, there is little universal design advantage in using one over another.

- Custom bathtubs made of stone, tile, concrete, wood or other materials allow for custom shapes that can be universal, but care must be taken to make these surfaces slip-resistant.

- There is a soft bathtub on the market, created by using a fiberglass shell, lining it with foam and then sealing it with a non-porous elastomeric material. The result is a non-slip, soft surface that retains heat and decreases accidents and injuries from falls.

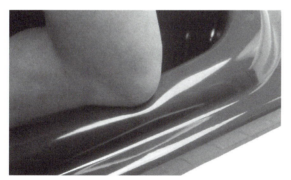 

Figure 258 - Soft bathtub.

Universal Design Critera for Bathtubs

Whether a bathtub is a whirlpool or not, standard size and shape or larger, intended for use by one or several, there are basic universal design criteria that should be applied in the selection process.

• First, entry and exit from the bathtub should be made safer by providing transfer surfaces and hand-holds.

• Second, non-slip surfaces should be chosen or added.

• Third, there should be easy access to the controls, whether the bather is inside or outside of the bathtub.

• Fourth, there should be a minimum amount of protruding objects in the bathtub area to avoid the risk of body parts bumping into anything.

Applying these criteria will improve safety and access for anyone using the bathtub.

THE SHOWER AREA

Space Considerations for the Roll-in Shower

A roll-in shower is a water-proofed area large enough for a person in a wheelchair to roll in and remain in the chair while showering. This type of shower lends itself to current trends toward the shower as a place of relaxation and retreat. It's size allows for one or more users and for the addition of multiple sprayheads, body sprays or rain bars. To be considered a roll-in shower, the area must be a minimum 60" (152cm) wide by 30" (72cm) deep, with no threshold greater than 1/4" (.64cm) high if square, or (1/2" (1.27cm) if beveled). Because this is a standard bathtub size, it allows for the conversion from bathtub to shower within an existing space. However, this size creates some problems in that 30" (72cm) is too shallow to retain water. A better size for the roll-in shower would be 60" x 48" (152cm x 122cm) or greater. Another option in designing the space is to waterproof the adjacent area and slope the floor slightly to the drain.

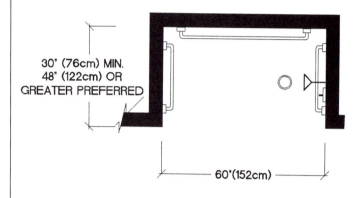

Figure 259 -   Roll-in Shower.

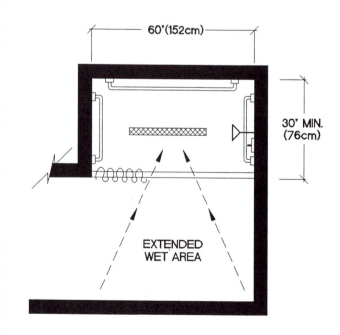

Figure 260 -   Minimum size roll-in Shower with extended wet area.

Clear Floor Space - Roll-In Shower

The clear floor space required adjacent to a roll-in shower is 60" x 36" (152cm x 91cm). An additional benefit to this dimension is that the combined space creates the clearance needed for a chair to turn 360°.

A preferred clear floor space would include 12" - 18" (30cm - 46cm) beyond the control wall to allow for better access to the controls.

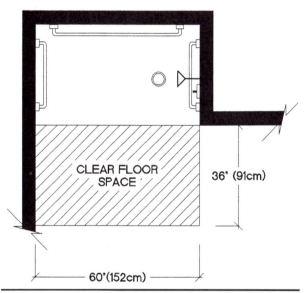

CLEAR FLOOR SPACE

36" (91cm)

60"(152cm)

Figure 261 - Clear floor space at roll-in shower.

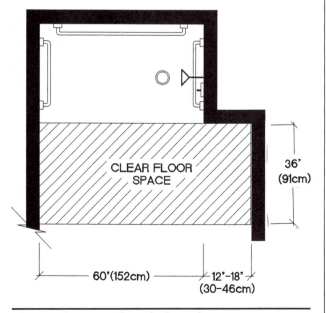

CLEAR FLOOR SPACE

36" (91cm)

60"(152cm)   12"-18" (30-46cm)

Figure 262 - Preferred Clear Floor Space at Roll-in Shower

Roll-In Shower Controls, Grab Bars and Accessories

Controls

Controls may be placed on any of the walls, in the area above the grab bars, no higher than 48" (122cm). Placement on either or both of the side walls improves access to controls for a person who is in the shower. This placement is safer and more convenient for adjusting water temperature and flow prior to entering the shower. A control on the back wall will be more accessible to a person seated in the area while showering.

Showerhead/Hand-Held Spray

If a fixed showerhead is used, 78" (198cm) is a good height for most people. A hand-held spray should be used, mounted no higher than 48" (122cm) in its lowest position. The use of an adjustable height hand spray may eliminate the need for a fixed shower head if the mounting bar allows for adjustment from 78" high to not more than 48" (122cm) above the floor.

Grab Bars

Horizontal grab bars should be placed on all three walls of a roll-in shower, 33" - 36" (84cm - 91cm) high. Vertical grab bars may be placed on the side walls to aid in balance and as a safety measure.

Transfer Shower

The transfer shower is designated at 36" x 36" (91cm x 91cm). Recent revisions to this standard acknowledge that a shower unit installed in a 36" x 36" (91cm x 91cm) space may result in an interior clear floor space slightly less, closer to 34" x 34" (86cm x 86cm) overall dimensions. Usually dimensions given are minimums, in this case the dimensions are the optimum. This type of shower is designed precisely to provide safe transfer for people with or without mobility impairments and it is one of the most universal of bathing options. It creates a space in which a person has both support and fixture controls within his reach at all times.

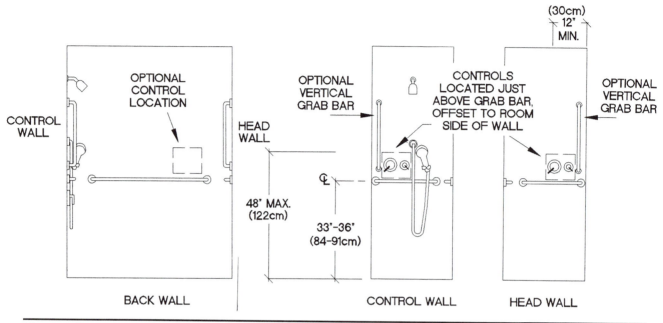

Figure 263 -   Control and Other Walls - Roll-in Shower.

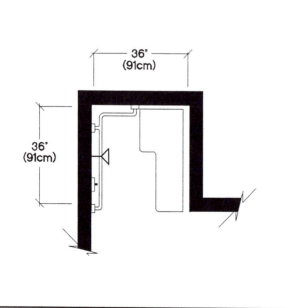

Figure 264 -   36" x 36" (91cm x 91cm) transfer shower.

The minimum clear floor space at a transfer shower is 36" x 48" (91cm x 122cm), measured from the control wall.

The preferred clear floor space would include an additional 12" - 18" (30cm - 46cm) beyond the control wall for better access to controls and to improve maneuvering space.

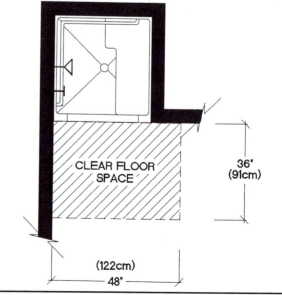

Figure 265 -   Minimum clear floor space at transfer shower.

Handedness or strength on one side or another will affect the location of the control wall and the seat.

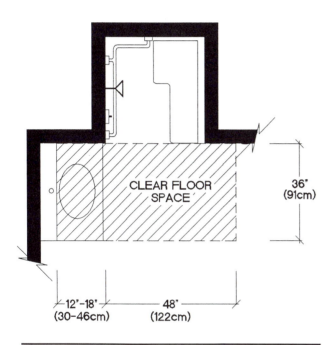

Figure 266 - Preferred clear floor space at transfer shower

Transfer Shower Controls, Grab Bars and Accessories

To create a true transfer shower, not only its size, but also the exact locations of the controls, the grab bar, and the seat are important.

Controls

The controls are to be located above the grab bar, not higher than 48" (122cm), offset to the room side on the control wall (opposite the seat).

Showerhead/Hand-Held Spray

The showerhead and the hand-held spray are to be centered on the control wall.

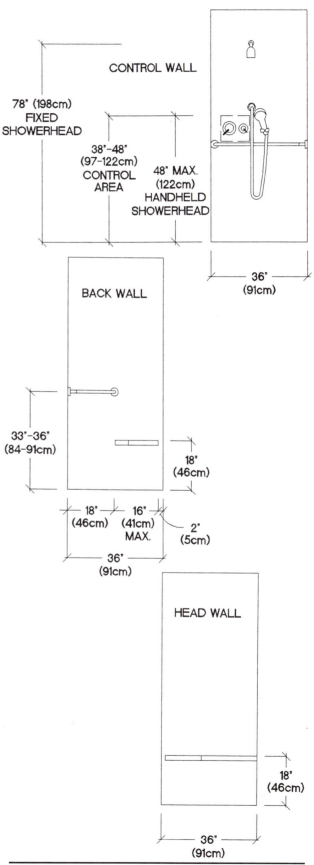

Figure 267 - Transfer shower - controls and other walls.

Grab Bars and Seats

The grab bar is to be L-shaped, the length of the control wall plus 18" (46cm) on the back wall. The seat may be L-shaped or straight. The dimensions of the seat, its location, and its shape are intended to provide maximum safety and support on two walls.

A fold-up seat is more universal in that it allows for use in a standing or seated position.

For more information and examples of how a person might transfer into this shower, see *Appendix 7, Bathroom Fixture Transfer Techniques*.

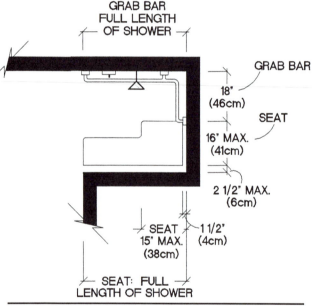

Figure 268 - Grab bar and seat configuration for transfer shower.

THE SHOWER FIXTURE

Transfer Showers

The transfer shower, created in a 36" x 36" (91cm x 91cm) space with an L-shaped grab bar, an L-shaped seat, and little or no threshold is the most versatile bathing fixture available. This shower allows a standing person support while showering and provides for transfer from a wheelchair with the greatest ease and privacy.

Keep in mind that this bathing system provides total independence for most people using mobility aids who can stand to transfer. While this shower can be a molded unit or one made with separate component parts, its dimensions and specifications are precise to create a space where anyone using the shower will have support and control within their reach at all times. Choosing a folding seat allows a person to stand or sit while showering.

USE OF THE 36" X 36"(91 x 91cm) TRANSFER SHOWER BY WHEELCHAIR USERS

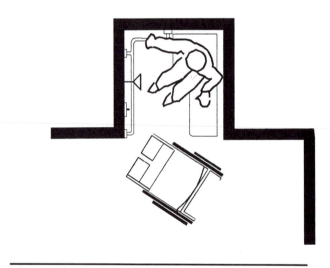

Figure 269 -   Transfer shower.

Although not essential for a transfer shower, little or no threshold, 1/2" (1.27cm) maximum is preferred as it makes transfer and entry easier and safer. Because the space is small, and water may escape the shower, care must be given to retain the water. The floor of the shower and adjacent floor space should be waterproofed and sloped towards the shower drain (suggested pitch is 1/4" per 12") (.64cm x 30cm). In some cases, a grate-type drain will ease in the containment of water, but it should not interfere with the floor surface.

Often times a shower curtain is preferred over a door because the curtain in no way interferes with maneuvering. A shower curtain of extra length will assist in retaining water. The exact dimensions of the space must be followed for a transfer shower to work properly. Transfer showers are available in molded units with fold-up or integral seats, and with grab bars and controls.

Figure 270 - Transfer shower module.

Figure 271 - Transfer shower module.

Roll-In Showers

The roll-in shower is simply a water-proofed area large enough for a person in a wheelchair to remain in the chair to shower. While this seems at first to be the easiest showering system, in fact usually the person in a wheelchair must transfer into a shower chair, so transfer is still a part of the process.

In addition, shower chairs often do not have front controls and must be pushed from behind, which translates to the need for an assistant to move a person into and out of the shower. For those who can transfer, the 36" x 36" (91cm x 91cm) transfer shower may offer greater independence.

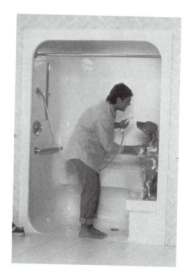

Figure 272 - Roll-in shower module.

That said, the roll-in shower does have tremendous flexibility and universal design appeal. The aesthetic appeal of a shower area or wet room is wonderful. The size of the space lends itself to a variety of uses - bathing pets, sitting or standing to shower, in or out of a wheelchair, and multiple users at one time. It's size also reduces concerns for water escaping the shower area, and provides useful clear floor space for ease in maneuvering.

The minimum size for a roll-in shower is 30" x 60" (72cm x 152cm), good for replacing a traditional bathtub, but small for water retention. As mentioned previously, planning adjacent wet areas will help to take care of the water concern. A size of 36" - 48" x 60" (91cm - 122cm x 152cm) is better, with a 60" x 60" (122cm x 122cm) roll-in shower having the added advantage of providing a full turning circle.

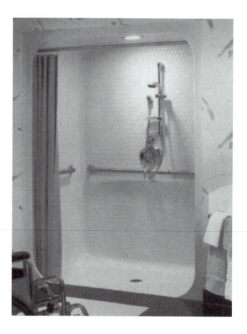

Figure 274 -   Roll-in shower module.

WET AREAS

The concept of a wet area eliminates many of the concerns in other bathing systems. A wet area is created by making the space adjoining the shower waterproof as well, sloping the entire floor towards the shower.

Creating a wet room means that fewer walls and divisions of space are needed. So a person can more easily maneuver using a wheelchair, walker or crutches and has a choice of whether to use a seat to shower. It is important to waterproof the entire area and to locate GFI electrical outlets out of the spray and splash of the water.

Figure 273 -   Roll-in shower module.

There are molded units with or without fold-up seats and grab bars in the 30" x 60" (72cm x 152cm) size. These units must be designed with low (maximum) or no thresholds for a true roll-in surface. In some cases, the base of the unit will have a curb and in such cases, the floor of the module must not be recessed greater than 1/4" (.64cm), (1/2" (1.27cm) beveled from the front edge.

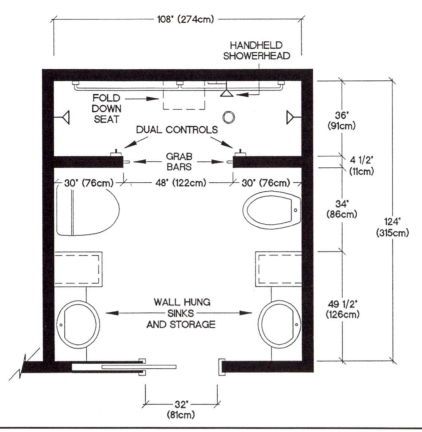

Figure 275 -   Wet room.

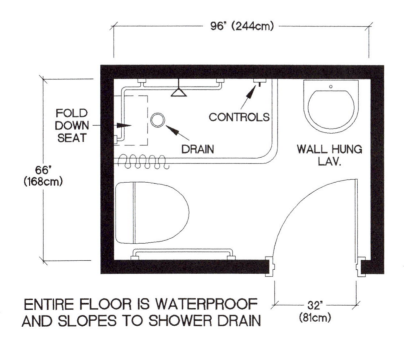

Figure 276 -   Wet room.

Materials and Aesthetics

Transfer showers are available in molded units with fold up or integral seats, and with grab bars and controls. They can also be fabricated from tile, solid surface, stone, or concrete, following the specifications. As with any bathing system, when planning for a shower area this size, blocking in the walls will provide for easy addition of the seat and grab bars.

One way to create a custom universal shower is to begin with a shower base designed to have a flush threshold. These are available with slight ramps which eliminate the need for a floor recess, and removable thresholds. Another option is a custom shaped shower base made of solid surface material with an integral curve to help retain water but allow easy access.

The base can also be formed from tile, small tiles being the better choice as they help with slip-resistance and they most easily incorporate the floor sloping to the drain. Once the base is created, wall treatments can be personal preference.

When planning the use of materials, consider contrast at entry, controls and grab bars, and seats for visual cuing. Keep in mind that the floor in and beyond the shower must be waterproof and that reinforcing should be in all the walls for installation of seats and grab bars.

Figure 278 -   Solid surface custom base without threshold.

Universal Design Criteria for Showers

Whatever the style or material used in a shower, the following universal design criteria will apply.

- The floor should be non-slip and the threshold should be low or flush.

- Hand-holds for support and flexible seating should be planned either for present or future installation.

- The clear floor space approaching and in the shower should allow for flexibility.

- Safety and ease of use benefit everyone.

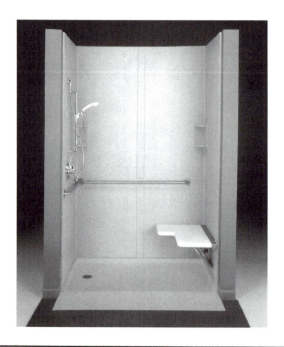

Figure 277 -   Shower base with flush threshold.

c h a p t e r 10

The Toilet and The Bidet

L̲ike the bathtub or shower, the toilet and the bidet require transfer. The same careful consideration must be given to space, materials, fixtures and supports, to ensure safe transfer and ease of use.

SPACE CONSIDERATION FOR THE TOILET/BIDET AREA

In planning the space for the toilet and bidet area, mobility, balance, handedness, and transfer will again be important. Planning appropriate storage space in this area is also important and should not be overlooked.

The addition of a bidet or an integral personal hygiene system in the toilet is particularly beneficial to a client who is unable to clean in traditional ways.

Codes and Standards

While the bidet is not mentioned in codes or standards, space considerations similar to those of toilets may be applied.

Most codes and standards detail toilet areas as part of non-residential spaces, but not as clearly for private residences. Both ANSI and the Fair Housing Guidelines provide some specification for toilets in residential baths.

The following is based on these two sources of information and draws from codes and standards. The configuration of the toilet area includes one side wall to return a minimum 54" (137cm), and a back wall width a minimum of 32" (81cm).

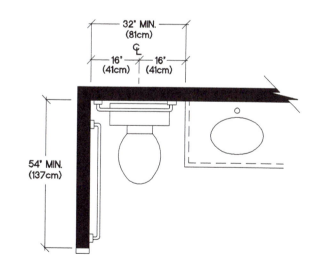

Figure 279 -   Toilet area.

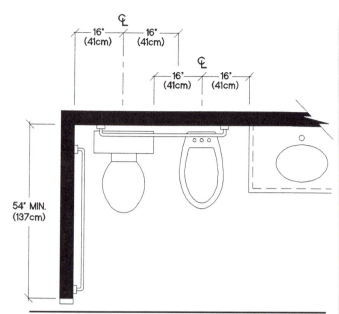

Figure 280 - Toilet and bidet area.

Clear Floor Space

The clear floor space suggested at a toilet is 48" (122cm) in front of the fixture by 48" (122cm) off the side wall.

This would allow a person to transfer from a perpendicular approach or a forward approach (*see Appendix 7 - Bathroom Fixture Transfer Techniques*), making it fairly flexible and universal.

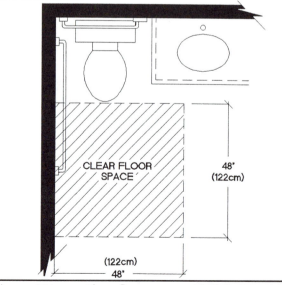

Figure 281 - Clear floor space at toilet.

Increasing the clear floor space off the side wall to 60" (152cm) with no lavatory directly adjacent to the toilet, increases the transfer options to allow for a parallel transfer. In this case recessing the back wall adjacent to the toilet further improves maneuvering space. Rolling storage of personal hygiene equipment can be a flexible way to use this space.

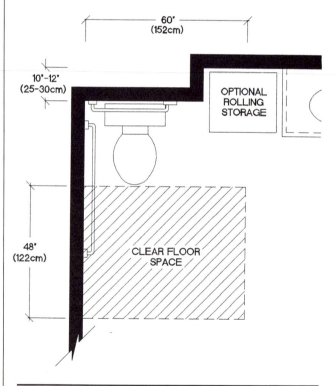

Figure 282 - Optional plan for clear floor space at toilet.

When a toilet and a bidet are located adjacent to each other, the clear floor spaces will overlap, with the clear floor space extending at least 16" (41cm) to either side of the center line of both fixtures.

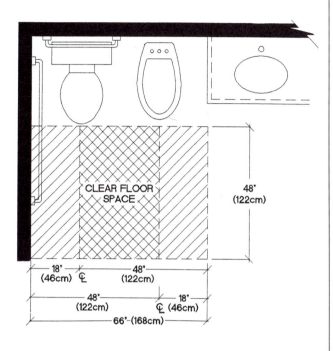

Figure 283 -   Overlapping clear floor space at toilet and bidet.

Location of Grab Bars, Controls and Accessories

If there are space constraints, some alternatives can be found by examining the following minimums for toilets.

The grab bars are to be located 33" - 36" (84cm - 91cm) off the floor, on both walls. One is to be on the side wall not more than 12" (30cm) off the back wall and a minimum 42" (107cm) long. The second one is to be a maximum 6" (15cm) off the side wall and a minimum 24" (61cm) long. This grab bar on the back wall must be a minimum 12" (30cm) on either side of the toilet center line.

Often the side wall does not in fact extend far enough to allow for a 42" (107cm) grab bar. While this would not meet code requirements, there are options that would improve the safety and function of the area.

First a grab bar that folds down off the back wall on the opposite side of the toilet may be used. This would be particularly useful if a bidet is adjacent.

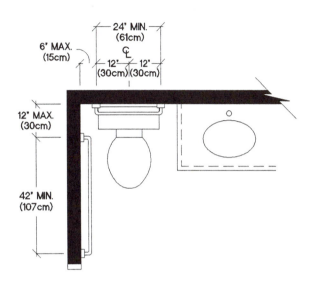

Figure 284 -   Grab bar locations at toilet.

Another option might be to install a seat with integral bars on the toilet.

When possible, extending the grab bar length on the back wall will improve safety and transfer options. In any case, providing support throughout the area at 33" - 36" (84cm - 91cm) off the floor will allow for the addition of desired grab bars.

The toilet tissue holder and the towel storage for the bidet should be placed within the universal reach range of 15" - 48" (38cm - 122cm). The preferred location for the toilet tissue holder is slightly in front of the seat, 8" (20cm) is ideal, and 26" (66cm) off the floor.

When locating a towel holder, care must be given not to obstruct the use of the grab bar. Placement a minimum of 1 1/2" (4cm) below the grab bar will avoid any interference.

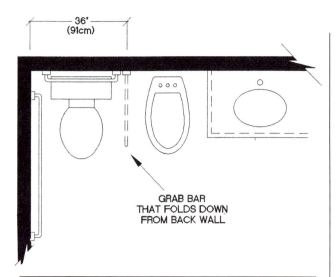

Figure 285 -   Optional grab bar location.

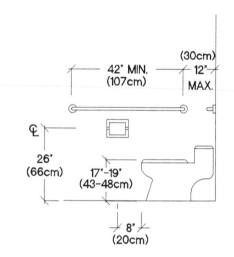

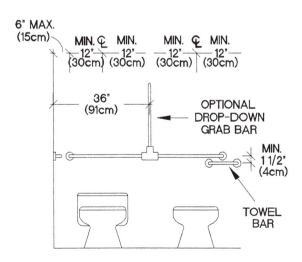

Figure 286 -   Accessories/grab bars at
toilet/bidet area.

THE FIXTURE

Style and installation of the toilet and bidet have much more impact on universal use than material which is typically vitreous china. This section will look first at the toilet and then the bidet in terms of universal design and its impact on style and installation. There are three main styles of toilets:

• floor-mounted
• wall-hung
• wall-hung with concealed tank

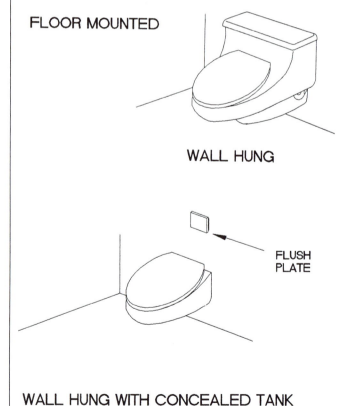

Figure 287 -   Styles of toilets.

Floor-Mounted Toilets

Floor-mounted toilets are by far the most common. They adhere to universal design principles if the toilet seat is at the right height and the clear floor space around them is sufficient.

Figure 288 -   Floor-mounted toilet.

Wall-Mounted Toilets

Wall-mounted toilets, while less common, have more advantages in terms of universal design. They can be mounted to create the appropriate seat height, and they provide greater clear floor space and easier maintenance.

Figure 289 -   Wall-mounted toilet.

Wall-Mounted Toilet with Concealed Tank

The wall-mount toilet with concealed tank is the most universal design choice. In this style, the tank is designed to be concealed in a 4 3/4" (12cm) space in the wall. The average toilet extends into the room 27" - 30" (69cm - 72cm) off the back wall. This type of unit extends only 22 1/2" (57cm), depending on the model, saving around 6" (15cm) of clear space. In addition, it may be installed at the appropriate height and it provides total clear floor space below it as it is off-the-floor, easing cleaning and maneuvering. Finally, this design creates a quieter flushing action which is particularly desirable as hearing abilities decrease.

There are not many models of this style to choose from and it is somewhat pricey, but the benefits may well outweigh the price.

Figure 290 - Wall-mounted toilet with conceled tank.

Toilet Seat Height

After clear floor space, the seat height on a toilet is the main universal design concern. No single height is right for all users.

- Low seats are not good for anyone, with the exception of small children, and there are portable seats to address their changing needs.

  Low seats are difficult for people with mobility impairments who have trouble standing from a low position. They are also difficult for people using wheelchairs, as they may transfer on easily, but have trouble transferring from the lower seat to their higher wheelchair seat.

  Finally, anyone with back strain (pregnant women for example), reduced strength or joint conditions (like arthritis) will have more difficulty standing from a low position.

- High seats are better for most people who can stand, with or without mobility aids. If they are too high, they will be difficult or impossible for people using wheelchairs to transfer to without assistance.

  In addition, too high a seat will be difficult and uncomfortable for shorter people because their feet won't touch the floor.

  The range of heights specified for toilet seats in residential spaces is 15" - 19" (38cm - 48cm). The compromise recommended by most experts is 18" (46cm), the same as many wheelchairs.

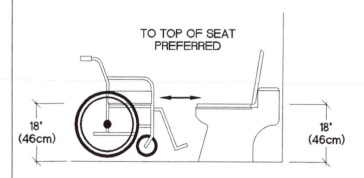

Figure 291 - Optimum toilet seat height for most users.

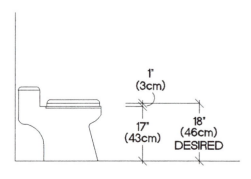

Figure 292 - Measure toilet height to top of seat.

Few toilets are designed with a seat height of 18" (46cm). The vast majority are the traditional 15" (38cm) height. There are a few "*designed for people with special needs*" that unfortunately end up at 19" - 20" (48cm - 51cm) high, which is too high.

In examining the product offerings from two major manufacturers, there were many toilets with a 15" (38cm) seat height, three toilets at 19" - 20" (48cm - 51cm) seat height, two wall hung fixtures that would allow for an 18 seat height, and two floor models with 18" (46cm) seat heights. Of 50 toilet models, four could provide the desired seat height without further alteration.

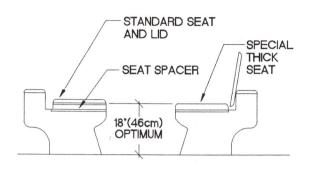

Figure 294 - Elevated seats on traditional height toilets.

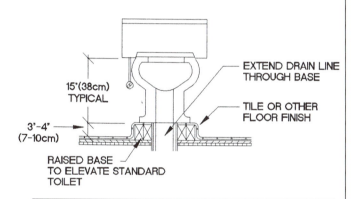

Figure 293 - Elevated base for toilets.

In defense of manufacturers, people want what they are accustomed to, and that is 15" (38cm) high toilet seats. The truth is that able-bodied adults can use these toilets because they have adapted to them. But a higher seat would be more appropriate, even for those able-bodied people. Perhaps this is an area for the bathroom designer to break with tradition and begin to incorporate the higher toilet seat as a matter of course.

Because there are so few products designed for the 18" (46cm) seat height, it is important to look at alternative ways to accomplish this. The first is to mount the standard height toilet on a raised base to bring the seat to the desired height.

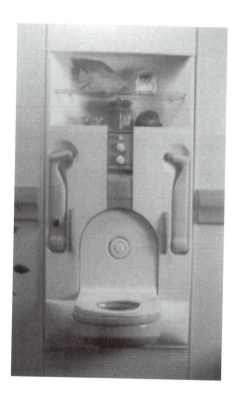

Figure 295 - Modular toilet system adjusts in height.

Second, special thick toilet seats or spacers that fit between the toilet seat and the rim of the toilet bowl will adjust the height up from the standard 15" (38cm). While these usually have a more institutional look, they have the advantage of flexibility in that they can be easily changed as needs change. Care must be given to selection and installation to be sure these seats are stable.

A toilet module has been designed that adjusts easily and instantly to accommodate the height of a standing or seated user. Hand rails fold down for use by those who desire them. The entire system folds up against the wall when not in use for easy cleaning and flexible maneuvering. This system is wonderfully flexible and truly universal. It is not yet on the market and will have to pass some plumbing and cost hurdles before we can easily use it.

Another product, readily available and easily installed is the electric powered toilet seat elevator. This mechanism actually tilts and raises or lowers the seat to assist a person in moving from a standing position to a seated position, and again to a standing position.

A more low-tech assistive device for standing and sitting are seat mounted grab bars which work well for many people who can stand but are a barrier for people in chairs who slide to transfer.

The bidet is a wonderful option for self-care, particularly for people whose physical disabilities make independent personal hygiene difficult. The standard bidet will be a challenge for those who have trouble sitting or standing, but problems will be reduced by adding support (grab bars) and storage within reach of the seated user. Building up the base or using wall-hung models will make height adjustment possible, but the lower position is more appropriate for personal cleaning.

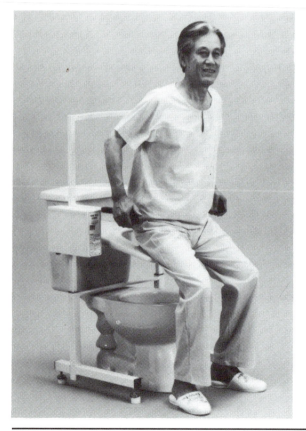

Figure 296 -   Powered toilet seat elevator.

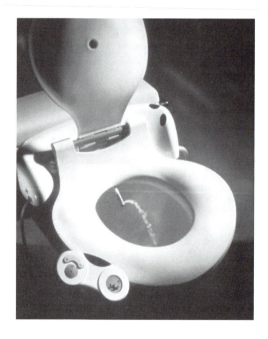

Figure 297 -   Personal hygiene system at toilet.

The real boon to personal hygiene for people with mobility impairments is the toilet mounted bidet. These systems attach behind and under the toilet seat or replace the toilet seat and supply a warm water cleaning spray and a warm air drying spray.

Traditionally, the bathroom has been a place where people adapted to existing fixtures and systems. Lately, though, the bath fixture industry has begun to put the needs of people first.

As universal bathroom designers, we must work carefully to stimulate and promote these changes, breaking our own patterns and habits along with those of our clients and the manufacturers.

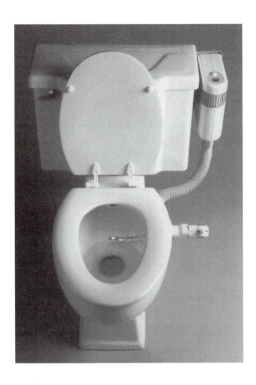

Figure 298 - Personal hygiene system at toilet.

Figure 299 - Bidet.

Figure 300 - Wall hung bidet.

chapter 11

Bathroom Fittings, Controls and Accessories

Universal design principals impact both the selection process and the design for installation of faucets and controls, support systems, and accessories in the bathroom. As manufacturers respond to consumer needs, new features are appearing to make accessories and the space safer and more accessible. In addition, the designer must think in terms of universal principles when creating the centers of the bathroom, including installations that sometimes break with tradition.

FAUCETS AND CONTROLS

The single lever faucet is the most universal in design. It allows temperature and flow adjustment with one control, easier for one-handed use or for use when both hands are occupied. A pull-out hand shower adds flexibility. Several models are available with a loop-type lever handle that make use easier for a person with grip or dexterity limitations.

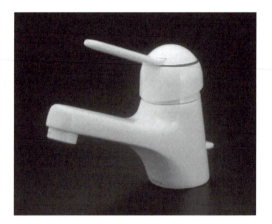

Figure 301 -   Single lever faucets.

Lever or wrist blade handles also allow for ease of use. Round or square handles that require grasping and twisting are the most difficult to use.

Figure 302 - Faucet with lever or wrist blade handles.

Touchless electronic faucets are available that automatically turn on when they sense motion. For the most part, temperature and flow rate are preset. Models are available now that include handles for manual override control and prototypes exist for a retrofit system that allows temperature adjustment through sensors in the front of the sink. These options require no hand dexterity and may be worth their expense in certain situations.

Figure 303 - Touchless electronic controls.

Touchpad controls are also available that allow for control of water temperature and flow from a remote location. These are relatively new on the market and are much higher in cost.

While there are many faucet styles that lend themselves to universal use, the drain control is often a problem, especially when it is a tiny round knob or button on the back of the faucet. A large or remote lever is more accessible. Another alternative is to install a separate drain plug that can be manually put in place.

The controls for the shower and/or bathtub, including the showerhead, the hand-held spray and the diverter (when required) should follow the same guidelines as faucets. First, controls, whether for flow and temperature, for diverting, or to release a sliding spray head, should be assymetrical and preferably a lever design. Push plates and electronic touch or voice-activated controls will also provide accessibility.

Mentioned previously, a hand-held spray unit on a sliding bar must have its lowest position no higher than 48" (122cm) off the floor. If it is to double as a showerhead, its highest position should be close to 78" (198cm). The hose on a hand-held spray should be a minimum 72" (183cm) long. Button or push-pull diverters should be avoided. Products are available with the hose of the hand spray attached at the fixed showerhead. This concept is acceptable as long as the diverter is not at the connection point on the arm of the shower head, but in a location within the universal reach range of 15" - 48" (38cm - 122cm). Likewise, the push-pull diverter often located on the top of the bathtub fill spout is very difficult for many people to grasp.

Sometimes a desirable option is to have more than one control, one for use from outside the bathtub or shower and one that controls the hand-held spray for use while in the bathtub/shower.

Antiscald temperature control and pressure-balance systems should be used. These features mix and regulate the water so that it cannot exceed a pre-set temperature. In addition, the pressure-balance system adjusts the flow of hot and cold water to ensure no dramatic temperature changes occur because of sudden changes in pressure in the system.

Visual cuing on controls is desirable, including high contrast, color-coding or raised characters to identify temperature adjustments.

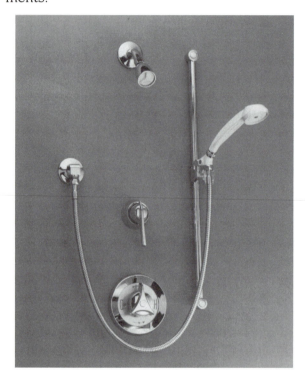

Figure 304 -   Controls and hand held sprays.

SUPPORT SYSTEMS

Grab Bars and Other Supports

Grab bars or railings placed in the bathroom must be capable of supporting 300 pounds (136kg) and must be 1 1/2" (4cm) from the wall. This clearance must be exact as it allows ample space for the user's hand and not enough for the user's arm to slip through.

Grab bars should be 1 1/4" - 1 1/2" (3cm - 4cm) in diameter (or less than 2" (5cm) at the largest point if their shape is other than

round) and should have a slip-resistant surface.

The recommended height for grab bars is usually 33" - 36" (84cm - 91cm) off the floor. A simple solution to the question of appropriate placement for a specific client is to plan and install plywood reinforcement throughout the bathroom. This allows the client to actually test the space and determine exact locations. It also allows for a minimum amount of rails or grab bars at the time of the project and easy installation of additional grab bars as needed or desired.

Horizontal grab bars are the basic and most useful choice. In addition, vertical grab bars can sometimes be helpful to a standing person for entry/exit from the bathtub/shower. Some experts discourage the use of vertical or diagonal grab bars because of a concern that a hand is more likely to slip along bars in this position.

NKBA guidelines require at least one bar in the bathtub/shower area and recommend additional grab bars at each workstation in the bathroom as well as reinforcement for future additions.

Grab bars come in all shapes, sizes, materials and colors. One interesting design option is to use a continuous bar around the entire room as a functional and decorative feature. Hanging towels (or anything else) should not interfere with use of grab bars. There is a risk that anything within reach may be grabbed by someone in need of support. Proper wall support and installation of grab bars as towel bars will eliminate the risk of a person mistaking a towel bar for a grab bar.

Along with the familiar grab bar, other support systems exist, also in many colors and materials. Grab bars that fold down off a back wall are useful where support is needed and there is no side wall.

Ladder or triangle supports can be ceiling installed, with proper reinforcement, for assistance where there are no adjacent walls or where greater flexibility is required.

Figure 305 -   Fold-down grab bar.

Figure 307 -   Triangle support.

Grab bars are available from adaptive equipment manufacturers that attach to the bathtub or toilet, requiring no alterations in construction. Although these are not usually specified by the bathroom designer, it is good to be familiar with them. These items are relatively inexpensive, easy to install or remove, and cumbersome to store. Unfortunately, they have not, as yet, been designed with a residential appearance. They are the answer in certain situations.

When selecting a grab bar that attaches to a fixture, it is important to examine the method of attachment for its strength and stability.

Bathtub and Shower Seats

Portable or removable bathtub and shower seats provide the options of sitting when desired or needed and standing or soaking upon their removal. The concept of sitting is relaxing and provides assistance to people with limited strength, endurance, or balance. The flexibility of a removable seat is often desirable, but requires storage space when not in use.

Figure 306 -   Ladder support.

SEAT TYPES

Several types of seats are available. The following examples from the Center for Inclusive Design and Environmental Access at SUNY Buffalo, will provide an awareness of them allowing the designer to guide each client to the best choice.

Bathstool

With no backrest, the bathstool is suitable for a person of slight to medium build. Compact in size and economical, it works well in narrow tubs and can be stored easily. It is available with a hard or padded seat, can be contoured, and may have hand grips on the sides of the seat. Careful attention must be given to its intended use as it is less stable than other options.

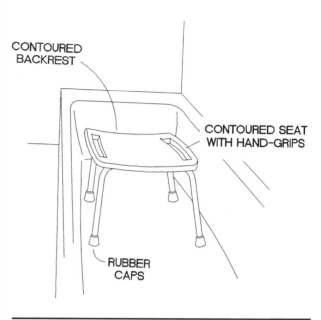

Figure 309 -   Bathstool hand grip.

Bathchair

The bathchair provides improved stability, greater support and more comfort. It is available with firm or padded contoured seat, hand grips, and is adjustable in height. The backrest improves bathing for a person with back conditions and the padding is easier on those with sensitive skin. The bathchair may not fit in narrow bathtubs, requires more storage space, and hinders easy access to a person's back and lower body.

The hand grip bathchair is ideal for leisurely bathers who need assistance in maintaining an upright position. The hand grips are useful to provide support while reaching various parts of the body. The contoured seat and backrest provide comfort to the bather.

With variable seat and backrest heights, the height adjustable chair accomodates persons of different stature and provides custom seating conditions. While there are various mechanisims for adjusting seat and backrest heights, the most common is the twist mechanism. Located on each of the legs,

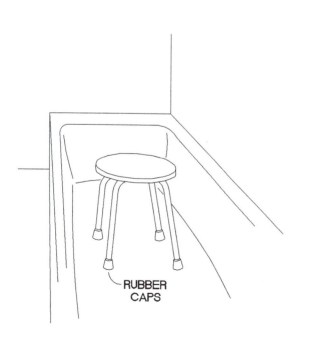

Figure 308 -   Bathstool.

these mechanisms are easily locked and un-locked by hand. Constant adjustment, how-ever, tends to loosen them, which can cause the chair to collapse unexpectedly.

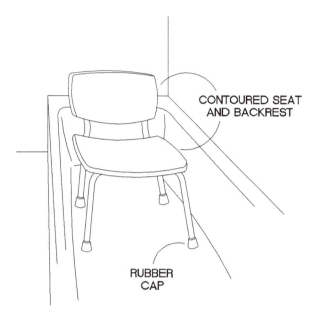

Figure 310 - Bathchair.

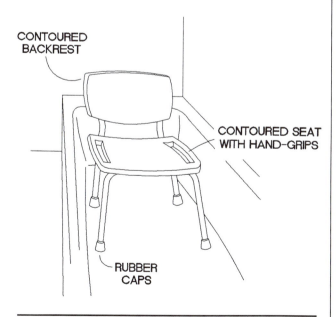

Figure 311 - Hand grip chair.

Figure 312 - Height adjustable bathchair.

Horseshoe Bathstool

The horseshoe bathstool or seat has a unique shape that is helpful to a person who has difficulty accessing and cleaning them-selves while sitting on the bathtub floor. One style is designed at a 6" (15cm) height which allows a person to soak in the bathtub. This style is not good for a person who has dif-ficultly sitting down and getting up.

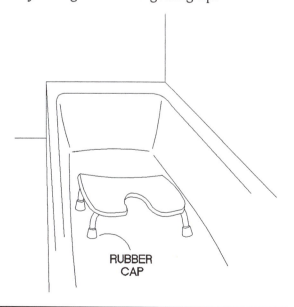

Figure 313 - Horseshoe bathseat.

Other styles are available with adjustable height, contouring, padding, and backrests to provide for a variety of support.

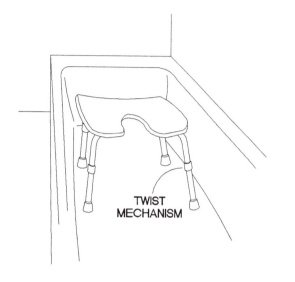

Figure 314 -   Horseshoe bathstool.

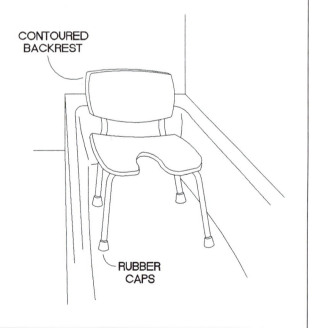

Figure 315 -   Horseshoe bathchair.

Bathtub Board

The bathtub board is suitable for people with strong backs who wish to sit to bathe. It is made from two pieces of vinyl-coated steel that slide into one another to fit a variety of bathtub sizes, and is padded on the underside to prevent scratching. Easily moved and stored, this option must be used with care as it can be unsteady.

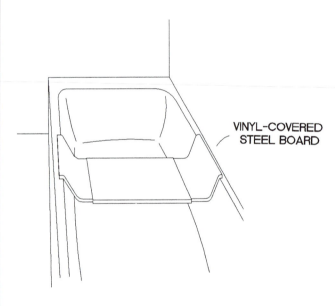

Figure 316 -   Bathtub board.

Transfer Bench

Using the handrest for support, the bather transfers into the bathtub by gradually sliding across the seat. The slatted seat allows water to drip into the bathtub and the slot at the bathtubs edge enables the person to draw the curtain for privacy. While the bench is portable, its size makes it difficult to store.

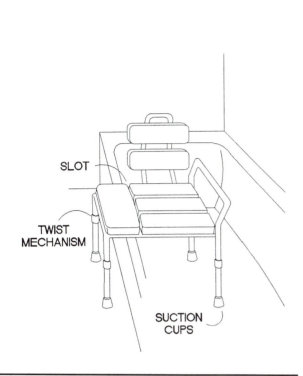

SLOT

TWIST
MECHANISM

SUCTION
CUPS

Figure 317 - Padded transfer bench.

Showerseats

Showerseats are available that are removable or that fold up when not in use, with or without armrests, in a variety of styles and materials. Models are available that are adjustable in height, padded, and with easy access to body parts for cleaning. The shower seat is desirable for those who wish to sit for part or all of a shower.

For further assistance in safe transfer into and out of the bathing fixture, chair designs and other equipment exist that allow a person other means of access into a shower or bathing fixture. These options should be explored through a medical health care professional.

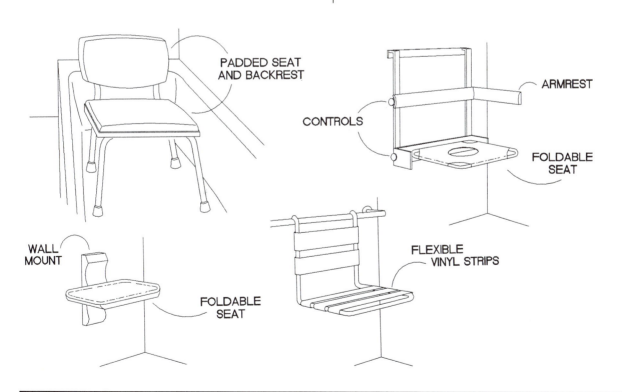

PADDED SEAT
AND BACKREST

ARMREST

CONTROLS

FOLDABLE
SEAT

WALL
MOUNT

FOLDABLE
SEAT

FLEXIBLE
VINYL STRIPS

Figure 318 - Showerseats - adjustable, portable, foldable.

Shower Wheelchair

The shower wheelchair transports non-ambulatory persons into the shower. It is lightweight and is constructed completely from rust-resistant hardware. The seats horseshoe shape enables easy cleaning of ones underside. The swing-back arms simplify transfers in and out of the wheelchair, and swing away footrests adjust to various positions. The chair is usable only in shower stalls accessible to wheelchairs.

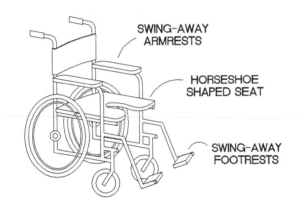

Figure 319 -   Shower wheelchair.

BATHTUB LIFTS

Although not typically thought of as standard usage equipment of the bathroom designer, lifts may be specified through a doctor or occupational therapist. A basic understanding of the types and their function will help a bathroom designer in planning the overall space and in discussing options with the client and therapist.

Inside Bathtub Lifts

Bathtub lifts typically function with a special hose and hardware that connect the lift to the bathtub faucet. These lifts are portable, but their size and weight make them difficult to store. Usually these lifts will transfer people up to 200 pounds (91kg), but water pressure must be adequate and consistent.

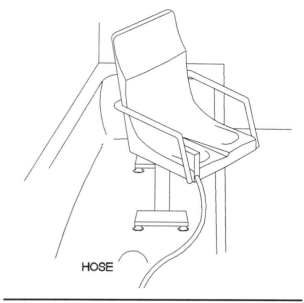

Figure 320 -   Inside bathtub lifts.

Outside Bathtub Lifts

Outside bathtub lifts may be permanently installed, with hose and hardware that connect to the water supply. Typically they will allow a person to move lower into the bathtub, desirable for soaking. Consistent and adequate water pressure is also imperative.

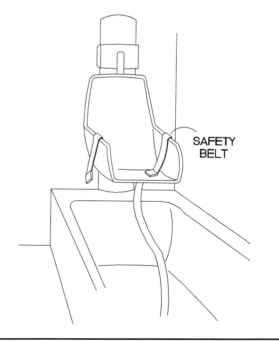

Figure 321 -   Outside bathtub lifts.

Hydro-Cushion

The hydro-cushion attaches via a hose to the bathtub filler. The bag or cushion is filled with water to elevate. A person sits on the cushion and empties it to be lowered into the bathtub.

To exit, the cushion is refilled, again raising the seat. This product usually will support 300 pounds (136kg) and again relies on constant water pressure.

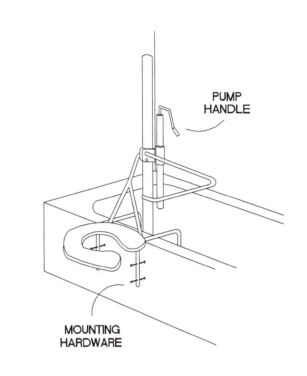

Figure 323 -   Bathchair lift - bathtub mounted.

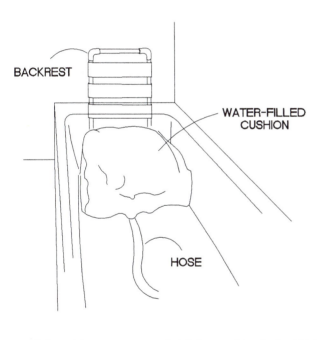

Figure 322 -   Hydro-cushion.

Bathchair Lift

The bathtub or floor mounted bathchair lift usually requires assistance from a care provider. The user sits on the seat and is rotated up and over the bathtub rim. The floor-mounted version takes considerable space in the bathroom, and the bathtub-mounted version takes less.

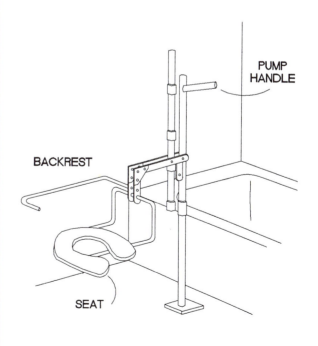

Figure 324 -   Bathchair lift - floor mounted.

Hoyer Lift

Floor Mounted, the Hoyer Lift is a portable lift that assists people who need a caregiver to help in transfer. The person is transferred into a suspended cloth sling. A hydraulic or mechanical system lifts and supports the person, rotating to allow for easy bathtub entry and exit. This type of lift is heavy and requires large clear floor spaces and storage areas. However, it carries up to 400 pounds (182kg) and provides for transport as a person can be lifted from a bed, transported to the bathtub and lowered in. It is a great assistive device for trained caregivers.

Figure 325 -   Hoyer lift.

Electrically Powered Lift

The electrically powered lift can provide independence for people with mobility impairments. The person sits in a harness that is moved along a track with motion controlled by a low-voltage remote control. This lift can be used by a caregiver or in some cases, by the person needing assistance.

All lifts require planning, installation, and operation by skilled professionals.

Figure 326 -   - Electrically powered lift.

ACCESSORIES

Many simple adaptive devices or adaptive designs of existing accessories are available to make the bathroom safe and accessible. The selection and installation of accessories should be based on their ease of reach and operation as well as their aesthetic value. Any accessory that frees one's hands is good.

- Shampoo and soap dispenser, installed in the bathtub/shower within the reach of the intended user, is good.

- Wall-mounted hair dryers that require one or no hands are also available.

- Mirrors are available that tilt so that they can be positioned for people of any height.

- Lighted magnifying mirrors are available that can be pulled into position for use by people of varying heights to improve function for people with visual, height or mobility differences.
- Reachers, graspers and aids for dressing oneself are examples of the types of products available through assistive products catalogs.

Items such as toothbrushes, hand-sprays, or comb and brushes with handles that are a comfortable size (use recommended grab bar size of 1 1/4"-1 1/2" (3cm - 4cm) as a guide) will be easier for those who have less gripping ability.

While some of these things will be specified by others, a familiarity with them will help the bathroom designer to overcome traditional barriers in the bathroom.

As accessories are chosen, attention should be given to cuing for people with visual, hearing and cognitive differences.

- A white grab bar on a white wall might be difficult to see. It will be more effective if it is accented with a bright color.
- An assistive device that sounds or flashes a light when the curling iron is left on will improve its safe use.
- A faucet and counter edge in high contrast to the counter and lavatory will reinforce safe and easy usage.

Manufacturers are beginning to respond to these criteria, and bath designers must take the time to find the right accessories for each space.

c h a p t e r 12

Bathroom Storage

Reach range parameters, varying height counters, and knee spaces make adequate amounts of storage a key issue in the universal bathroom. Because of the nature of activity in the bathroom, storage must be planned to house needed supplies and equipment in close proximity to each of the centers. Often, the space is small, which makes careful consideration of needs and options imperative.

GOALS/CONSIDERATIONS TO KEEP IN MIND

• One main goal is to plan the maximum amount of storage within the 15" - 48" (38cm - 122cm) universal reach range and to make it as safe and easy to access as possible.

• Another goal is to make stored items easy to see. As always, storing items near their point of first use is a good guide, or in several locations if they are used in several places. Because overall storage in the bathroom is limited, these goals should be applied first to items used frequently, such as toothbrushes or hair dryers, with items used less frequently, such as back-up bathroom tissue, stored in the remaining spaces.

• If a client has particular storage needs for assistive equipment or personal hygiene supplies, these must be measured and planned for in convenient locations.

• Drawers on full extension slides and open shelves eliminate the need to maneuver around a drawer to access the stored items.

• An open shelf also allows for easy view of stored items, helpful when memory fails or vision is impaired.

• Lighting the interiors of storage areas will also improve visibility.

• Tall storage takes advantage of the full universal reach range - 15" - 48" (38cm - 122cm).

• Because many items used in the bathroom will fit in a small space, wall cabinets or storage systems 12" (30cm) deep or less will meet many needs.

• In some cases, recesses created between studs will allow for storage that does not use clear floor space or create a protrusion.

• Rolling storage has several advantages in the universal bathroom because of its flexibility. It can be moved out of an area to give more clear floor space and it allows for stored items to be moved into place easily when in use.

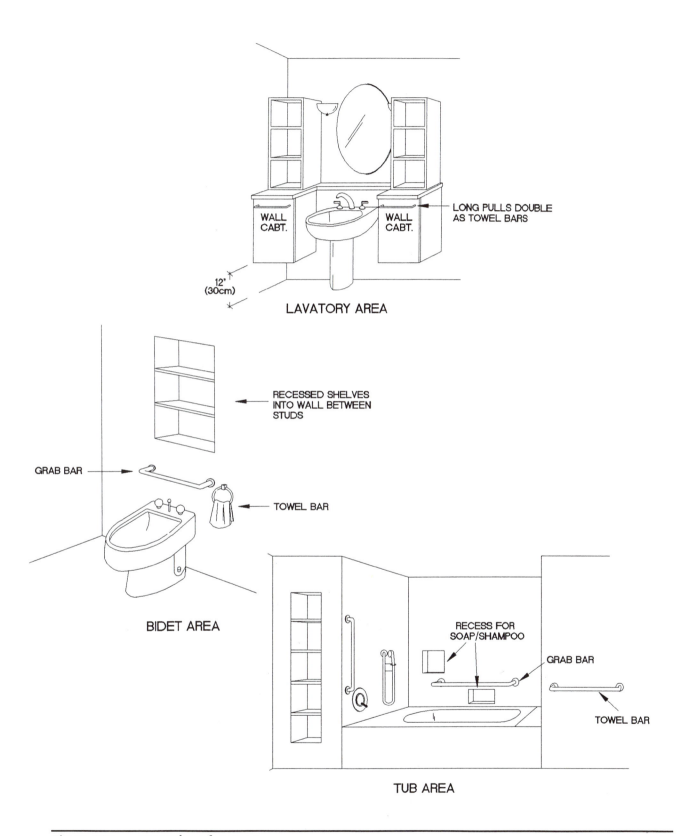

Figure 327 - Examples of storage.

Figure 328 -   Examples of storage.

CABINETRY CONSTRUCTION AND HARDWARE

Several options in cabinetry or storage and hardware selection have impact on universal design.

Frameless Cabinetry

A benefit of frameless construction is total accessibility to the interior of the cabinet, and the same is true with much of today's framed construction.

Raising toekicks to 9" - 12" (23cm - 30cm) high provides clearance for wheelchair footrests and other walking aids. This option is available on most custom lines and some stock lines as well.

Door Options

A variety of options are available for moving doors out of the way.

- Hinges that allows doors to swing completely open to 180° are helpful.

- In addition, a hinge is now available that folds the doors back against themselves and flat against adjacent cabinets, making the doors less obstructive.

- Doors can also be hinged to be retractable, but this option takes up as much as 6" (15cm) on each side, which translates to needing 42" (107cm) for a 30" (72cm) knee space.

- Doors mounted on removable face frames can be used for adapting to knee space by removal of the door and frames.

- Tambour doors or doors that slide or open upward on wall cabinets also eliminate the concern for moving safely around them.

Hardware Considerations

Decorative hardware should be easy to use and should not require strength or dexterity to operate.

- Pulls should be chosen in place of knobs. Pulls that are integral and are easy to grasp are ideal because they do not protrude.

- Touch latches eliminate the need for any grasp or strength.

Material Selection

Finally, material selection should consider durability in terms of finish.

- Particularly at 12" (30cm) above the finished floor and below, cabinetry may be exposed to tremendous wear from repeated impact from mobility aids.

- High-gloss or finishes that create glare should be avoided.

Beyond this, selection of cabinetry is not impacted by universal design.

c h a p t e r 13

Finishing the Space

To finish the universal kitchen and bathroom, several key factors must be considered: lighting and electrical, including ventilation, heating, flooring and wall surfaces.

LIGHTING

Lighting is crucial to the universal environment, particularly for those with visual impairments. As we age, our vision changes. The quality of light in a space is determined not only by the light source, but also by the colors, amounts of contrast and reflective quality of surfaces in the room.

Light Adjustability

It is important to provide adjustability and increased available ambient and task lighting without glare or harsh shadows. People with visual impairments and aging eyes typically benefit from increased light, but this is not always the case. Consultation with qualified professionals (medical, lighting designer) is recommended.

LIGHT SOURCES

Natural Light

Natural light sources are best and should be generous in the plan. Avoid glare from natural light sources with shades or blinds or glass surface treatments that deflect glare but allow light to come through.

Incandescent/Fluorescent Light

To supplement natural light, lamp fixtures should be chosen that produce a high-accuracy color rendering. A color rendering accuracy rating of 85 or higher for either incandescent or fluorescent is desirable. Though it is true that the eye yellows with age, changing how we see color, lighting experts suggest that as long as there is good color rendering, either type of lamp may be used.

Halogen Light

Halogen is another option, although the amount and intensity of heat produced by a halogen lamp may be less than ideal in terms of safety. The fixture should be designed to conceal the light source and diffuse light in an effort to reduce glare. Glare creates hazards as it can be blinding, and research shows that it contributes to confusion associated with aging.

Lighting Plan

The lighting plan in the universal space should include generous ambient and task lighting and offer flexible controls. One eye condition might need greater general lighting, but another might benefit from reduced ambient lighting and increased task lighting.

Flexibility in controls allows for a variety of users to function in the bathroom. In addition, the plan should take into account reflectant qualities in the room surfaces and eliminate harsh shadows.

For example, side lights added to down lights in a vanity area will eliminate shadows. Another example would be to direct a light into the cabinet space from outside or above and use transparent shelves to cut down on harsh shadows in the storage area.

Surfaces

- In choosing surfaces in the room, avoid glossy and harsh white surfaces that will reflect light and can create glare.

- Consider the size of the space and the color and reflectant quality of surfaces when planning the amount of light needed.

- A room with dark cabinetry will require more light than one with light surfaces.

Along with reflection, consider color and contrast. They have a major impact on how practical a room is for a person with vision impairments.

- Because of the yellowing and thickening of the eye's lenses that occurs with age, it becomes difficult to differentiate colors that do not contrast.

- Navy, black and brown might look similar, or pastel colors might blend together. For this reason, contrast judiciously and with safety in mind.

- Placing light objects against darker ones, or vice versa, makes them stand out.

- Contrast can be used effectively in counter edges, flooring, control locations, on/off indicators, etc. **This same benefit can become a hazard if overused.** A black and white checked floor becomes a hazard as it affects depth perception.

Lighting design requires intense review of the parameters of each project.

FLOORING

Goals/Considerations

There are several goals in choosing flooring for the universal space.

- The floor should be low-maintenance and durable.

- It should be resilient to allow for minimum injury or breakage from drops or falls, and it should be a fairly smooth or regular surface for ease of use by persons with mobility or balance impairments.

- It should be matte finish, as highly polished surfaces can create glare and are usually slippery.

- The most important goal in selecting flooring is to choose flooring that can be as slip-resistant as possible.

While no flooring choice is ideal in every respect, most flooring materials can be used effectively if these goals are considered in the selection process.

Slip-Resistant Flooring

Slip-resistance in kitchen and bathroom flooring, always a key concern, becomes even more important when universal design concepts are applied.

The floor that is somewhat slippery and less safe for an able-bodied person is even more of a hazard when the person is a toddler or has difficulty with balance or uses crutches.

Flooring manufacturers use a slip-resistance rating called the **coefficient of function**, with higher numbers indicating greater slip resistance. When using a **COF rating** to evaluate a floor surface, it is important to determine the rating when wet for bathroom use.

Research at **Pennsylvania State University** estimated that 88% of the population would be protected by a COF of .6 (.8 for ramps). There are a number of ceramic and vinyl surfaces available with ratings at least this high.

In addition, slip-resistant strips or coatings are available to reduce the risk of falls in particular areas, but heavy use, water, and continual cleaning can reduce the practicality of their usefulness.

Ceramic Tile

The appropriate ceramic tile can be a good choice.

• First, check manufacturers recommendations for use, durability, and slip resistance. A slip-resistant glazing can be of help.

• Choose tiles that are smooth or even-surfaced with a minimum of grout to create a level floor.

• Choose tile and grout that is stain and moisture resistant.

• Mosaic tiles provide added insurance against slipping.

Although tile is not resilient, the value of tile in a universal bathroom is its durability in wet situations, its easy maintenance and the opportunities for patterns to create the desirable contrast.

Stone Flooring

When considering a stone floor, pay attention to the surface and the porosity. Often stone is highly polished, making it a slippery surface, or tumbled, making it an irregular surface. For the universal space, a matte finish level surface and a denser stone that will be more resistant to stains is the better choice.

Vinyl Flooring

Vinyl flooring products, including sheet goods, solid tiles and composition tiles, are another good option.

They are durable, low-maintenance and somewhat resilient, and they are available in a variety of patterns and colors. With certain products, the designer can create a pattern that allows for effective contrast to help with *way-finding*. A surface with less sheen will reduce glare and may be more slip-resistant.

If choosing either type of vinyl tiles, pay attention to the amount and depth of grout lines. A fairly smooth and minimal grout line is best, chosen with attention to levelness.

• Vinyl composition tiles perform much like vinyl sheet goods and allow the designer to create patterns and color schemes.

• Solid vinyl tiles usually have more of a matte finish, which can help in slip resistance.

With any vinyl flooring, consider the finish and the maintenance requirements.

Wood Flooring

Wood floors have good resilience and require varying degrees of care. Given the characteristics of wood in regard to moisture, a strong or penetrating sealer should be used. Wood floors should also be designed to be slip-resistant.

Carpet

Although carpet is frequently avoided in the bathroom because of concerns for maintenance, it has some merit in the universal bathroom.

A firmer, more industrial carpet with minimal or no padding is generally more stain resistant. This carpet provides warmth, resilience and a smooth surface for ease of travel. In addition, patterns can be created with carpet for contrast for *way-finding*.

Cork

Cork tile flooring is an interesting option for the universal space. Made by sandwiching ground cork and a layer of wood or cork veneer between vinyl layers, it provides cushioning and insulation created by air pockets in the cork. With a surface similar to vinyl goods, it offers easy care and durability. It also provides a low glare, level finish with the added benefit of cutting down on ambient room noise, especially helpful to people with hearing impairments. Care must be given to seal the tile seams against stains or moisture, especially when there is concern about spills left standing.

Contrast/Way-Finding Considerations

When choosing floor patterns and finishes, consider contrast as a *way-finding* detail. A light tile floor with contrasting tiles around the perimeter of the bathroom and its major components will help to indicate area and edges. On the other hand, an all-over pattern can create problems in terms of depth perception. A matte surface on the floor will most likely be more slip-resistant and will reduce glare.

Thresholds should be flush and level, and again, there should be no irregularities in the floor.

FLOORING MATERIALS/UNIVERSAL CONSIDERATIONS

Material	Maintenance /Stain Resistance	Slip Resistance	Resilience	Level	Low-Glare
Ceramic Tile	choose non-porous, careful on grout, very easy care	mosaics, slip-resistant glaze, slight texture, can be slippery when wet, but above will help, check rating	hard surface	choose only level tiles	honed color, matte finish
Stone	choose denser stone, non-porous, can be easy care	no polished stone texture	hard surface	choose only level tiles, minimum grout no tumbled stone if surface is irregular	no polished stone
Vinyl Sheetgoods	no wax, very easy care	matte or low gloss, slight texture	consider underlayment, very resilient	very level	no high gloss finish
Vinyl Composition Tiles	review manufacturers care and installation guide on seams, otherwise, easy care	matte or low gloss, slight texture, minimum grout helps	fairly resilient	very level	no high gloss finish
Solid Vinyl Tiles	easy care, check manufacturers for stain resistance	matte finish and grout, good for slip resistance	very resilient	minimum grout, very level	matte finish
Wood Flooring	easy daily care, more long term maintenance	slippery when wet	resilient and warm	very level, no grooves in seams	low-gloss finish
Carpeting	choose tight industrial type/stain resistant	firm, resistant to slip, no padding	very resilient and warm	very level	no glare
Cork Flooring	easy maintenance, caution with seams	similar to vinyl sheetgoods	resilient, warm, sound insulator	very level	non-glare

WALL FINISHES

The selection of wall surfaces in the universal space requires only that established parameters be reviewed and emphasized.

- Ambient sound can become more of a problem for a person with hearing impairments.

- Wall and window treatments that absorb some of this room's noise include cork, carpet and fabrics.

- Surfaces that reduce glare enhance the space for everyone, particularly those with vision impairments.

- The natural sunlight that creates warm ambient light can also create glare, and there are glass and window treatments to eliminate the glare while allowing the light and the view.

- Wall colors and patterns should be chosen with consideration of the total room in terms of contrast and light.

- Consider the possible rigorous wear on the lowest 12" (30cm) of wall surface from mobility aids. One solution is to continue the flooring right up the wall 12" (30cm) and trim it at the top.

ACCESSORIES

It is not always the role of the kitchen and bathroom designer to accessorize these spaces, but a good designer should be familiar with the options, particularly those that make a kitchen and bathroom safer and more accessible.

Cabinet accessories go a long way toward making the space usable for more people. In reviewing accessories, choose those that are flexible and stable.

- A footstool that allows safe access to storage otherwise out of reach is only practical if it can be easily retrieved and set up. Designs are available for footstools that hang on the inside of base cabinet doors and set up and fold up with a simple lever movement.

- A recycling bin will be easier to use if it slides in and out of storage and does not require lifting above its physical height to be emptied.

Careful review and testing of accessories will allow the designer to make the best choices from the many options available.

Selecting and locating small appliances in the kitchen should include a review of their operation and safety features. Apply the standards for controls - no round or smooth knobs, but rather lever or touch pad controls, dual cuing and automatic shut-offs, one function per control.

Because these features are not always available, there are a number of assistive devices available to cut down on the barriers to universal use. These assistive devices are available thru mail-order distributors or home health care equipment stores. An occupational therapist or rehabilitation engineer will be familiar with them. A few of them are presented here to raise your awareness.

Assistive Devices

- Reach and grasp aids assist in reaching things more than an arms length away.

- A lighted magnifying glass allows easier reading of appliance controls.

- Large non-slip grips on utensils allow for ease of use when hand strength is limited.

- Electric and manual can and jar openers allow opening with one hand.

- Gripping mats that rest on counters help to hold things in place and allow food preparation with one hand.

- Cutting boards with prongs hold an item in place while it is cut and raised curbs prevent spilling.

- Right-angle knives make cutting from a sitting position easier and safer when strength is limited.

- A pan holder mounted on a cooktop holds the handle of a cooking pan in place.

- A slicer holds food and knife in place for safe and easier one-handed slicing.

- A cutting board that is black on one side and white on the other, provides a work surface of contrast for foods of any color.

- There are large-print timers that produce sound and a flashing light when time is up.

- There are wrist timers that sound and/or vibrate when time is up.

- *Dual-cuing* smoke alarms produce both a sound and a flashing light when set off.

- There are alerting devices that sound and flash light when an appliance is in use.

CONTROLS, ELECTRICAL AND VENTILATION SYSTEMS

Controls for ventilation, lighting, and any electrical systems in the bathroom should be mounted within the universal reach range of 15" - 48" (38cm - 122cm).

In addition, **controls must follow codes and safety guidelines.**

The possible addition of a security system, a safety alarm system, or a telephone will allow a person in need of help in the bathroom to call for assistance. The type and location of the system should be discussed with each client to ensure effectiveness.

c h a p t e r *14*

Kitchen and Bathroom Safety

Safety, created by ease of use, is a main principle of universal design. That same improved accessibility may be seen as a hazard in some situations. *"Keep medications out of reach of children"* is a well-known rule of home safety.

Universal design guidelines would provide a safe access to a high space via a stepstool or a system that lowers that high storage into the universal reach range, where everyone can access it. Improved accessibility minimizes bending, reaching, stretching and using undue force, making safer and more independent use possible. Yet designers and clients must recognize the relative risks in a space to be used by many people.

Careful consideration must be given to those who will be operating in the kitchen and bathroom. **Barriers must be eliminated and safety checks must be created as a part of the design process.**

In most cases, safety concerns relating to increased access have to do with improper use by children or those who are confused or forgetful. Some of the solutions covered in the appliance chapter included; programmed lockout or wiring to an outlet or circuit that can be shut off, a microwave oven that has both a flashing light and sound signal to indicate a completed cooking cycle.

SAFETY AIDS

Aids include redundant cuing such as sound and flashing light to indicate when an appliance is left on or when water is running. Automatic shutoff is another safety check and is commonly available on curling irons and hair dryers. In addition, locking away those items that are unsafe for a particular user will help.

HOME CONTROL SYSTEMS

There are home control systems that allow a person to check on the status of the household via a control panel or even by calling in on the telephone. From these remote locations, a user can adjust room temperature or shut off appliances. Or with a preselected program, a user can execute the usual morning operations, such as turning up heat, starting coffee and lighting the path to the bathroom.

These devices respond to commands by visual and auditory cuing. When the right button is pushed or the time arrives, a voice says *"Good Evening"* and the heat and lights are turned down, appliances are checked and shut off and the doors are locked.

While this is definitely high tech, it goes a long way as a safety check.

WAY-FINDING

Way-finding is a simple concept normally achieved by using high tactile or visual contrast borders such as a dissimilar colored countertop edge or a border tile pattern which follows a path of egress.

Way-finding techniques are an excellent way to assist those who may be forgetful or who have a visual disability.

FIRE SAFETY

Safety relating to fire may include extinguishers that are easy to reach and use. Work aisles and pathways should include a clear means of leaving the space should a fire occur.

SECURITY CONCERNS

The addition of a security system can add to the safety of the bathroom in that it provides an easy method of calling for help should a problem arise.

Security systems can be activated by the typical means with the control in the universal reach range and supplemented by controls throughout the baseboard to allow a person who falls to call for help. Another control option is one that the user wears, which is within reach all the time.

OTHER SAFETY CONSIDERATIONS

What can be easily seen and understood is more apt to be used safely.

- Lighting that eliminates glare and harsh shadows and components that are self-evident in their use reduce the risk of misuse by anyone.
- Safety related to reducing the risk of falling has several components. The use of slip-resistant flooring, as discussed in the section on flooring, is first.
- In addition, hand-holds or grab bars can be used wherever there is a concern about slipping.
- Items stored within reach will eliminate unnecessary leaning, stretching or climbing.
- Spatial design that requires the least maneuvering and that provides for easy draining of excess water on the floor will also help.

Whenever possible, discuss each decision with the intended user to make the safest choices.

Safety concerns should guide, not limit the design of universal kitchens and bathrooms.

c h a p t e r 15

Kitchens That Work

The kitchens featured in this chapter attempt to tie together many of the design and planning techniques discussed in this book.

Here, you will visually see how kitchens can be planned utilizing creative common sense applications of universal thinking.

Several of the ideas you'll discover are totally new, others expand on commonly thought of concepts and some... are not new at all, just good design. As you explore the photos and drawings featured on these pages, attempt to mentally identify the use of the individual and overall work center spaces which you will see include usage for people of varying sizes and abilities.

KITCHEN PROJECT #1

General Electric Kitchen "Real Life Design"

Sponsored by General Electric Appliances and designed by National Kitchen & Bath As-sociation professional teaching instructor, Mary Jo Peterson, The *"Real Life Design Kitchen"* features design concepts that adapt to people, rather than people adapting to design. It acknowledges a wide range of physical and mental abilities in todays families. The result is a kitchen that makes sense in any home.

Client Profile

This kitchen was designed to accommodate the needs of a family in today's *"sandwich generation"*. Family members include two parents in their 40's, a 17 year old son, a seven year old daughter and a grandmother who is 72. Since both parents work, the grandmother and the children look after each other during the day, and all family members participate in kitchen activities.

Ensuring that the kitchen is safe and functional for the varying sizes and abilities of the family members was a special concern.

- Both parents and the teenage son have full mobility, strength, dexterity and cognitive skills.

- The grandmother has arthritis and the potential for a change in vision, hearing and memory as she ages. She sometimes uses a walker and is most comfortable functioning in a familiar space with safety checks to remind her of the use of the kitchen.

- At seven years old, the daughter has sharp senses and a short attention span. Safety checks, functional storage and work areas within her reach are a help to her.

Design Solution

To allow for this variety in sizes and abilities, the design solution is spacious and flexible.

- Walkways and work aisles are generous.

- Work surfaces and storage areas are planned at varied heights.

- Cabinetry is accessorized to bring maximum storage into everyone's reach as much as possible.

- In the main work triangle, pullout work surfaces at lower heights, a built-in step stool and wall cabinet storage that can be lowered make the space more flexible, as does the sink that can be adjusted in height to suit the user.

- A secondary work triangle is designed with work surfaces at a lowered height to allow for use by the shorter or seated cooks.

- Heat resistant counter surfaces near cooking appliances allow for minimum lifting and transfer, particularly of hot items.

- Two rolling carts and a rolling table further limit the need to carry items and increase the flexibility of the space.

The overall look of the kitchen is somewhat informal with soft creme and contrasting cobalt blue. The selection of materials creates a light and comfortable space, while responding to safety and visual needs.

- The light counters are without glare and have contrasting raised edges to aid in maneuvering in the kitchen.

- Contrasting borders in the flooring add beauty and help all users to navigate around the space. Generous windows and adjustable lighting meet the needs of various cooks and functions.

- Tile patterns in the counter and backsplash create interest and provide dark surfaces for working with light foods, as well as light surfaces for working with dark foods.

- Glass doors, open shelves and plate racks add to the visual setting and eliminate the need to remember where items are stored.

- Appliances with large graphics, high-contrast indicators and easy-to-use touch-pad controls are incorporated.

Careful selection of the components help make this kitchen remarkable for its aesthetics and for its function.

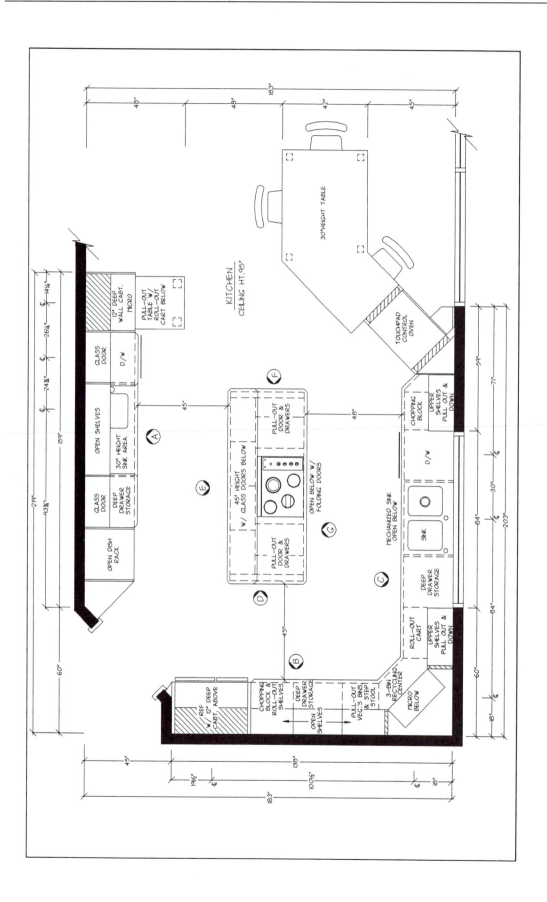

General Electric Appliance Kitchen "Real Life Design" - Floor Plan

General Electric Appliance Kitchen "Real Life Design" - Photo

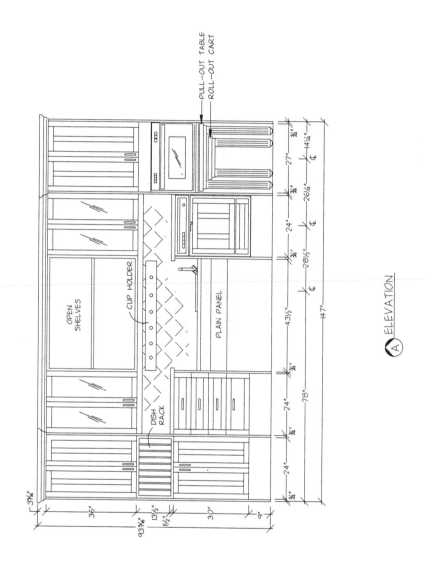

A ELEVATION

General Electric Appliance Kitchen "Real Life Design" - Elevation A - • This area is intended as a secondary work or snack area. • The raised toekicks allow a greater clear floor space for mobility devices such as a walker or wheelchair. • The 24" wide (61cm) tall cabinet includes roll-outs for pantry storage and a plate rack within the universal reach range. • The plate rack provides convenient usable storage, as does the cup rack over the sink. • The four drawer base cabinet features full extension slides. • A pull-out work surface is located in the second drawer, placing it approximately 30" (76cm) above the finished floor, a good height for anyone seated and working in this area. • The sink section features an open knee space, lowered counter height and an instant hot water dispenser for quick snacks and meal preparation. • The raised dishwasher allows for easy access and was positioned opposite shallow dish and glass storage located at the back of the island as seen in Elevation E. • The right side of the elevation includes a microwave/convection oven with a drop down door at table height, allowing items to be removed from the oven by sliding them onto the door and then onto the heat resistant table. • The pull out table located below the micro/convection oven may be extended for use as a work surface. • A roll out cart located below the pull-out table is used to transport items to other areas of the kitchen. • The center wall cabinet section has been aesthetically developed with glass doors and open shelves for easy identification.

General Electric Appliance Kitchen "Real Life Design" - Photo Elevation A - • Storage within universal reach range. • Raised toekick for clearance of mobility aides. • Telephone and switches at appropriate height as you enter room. • Pantry storage at varied heights. • Plate rack in reach range. • Counter surfaces throughout the kitchen are a light color with a dark 1/2" (1cm) raised curb on the top surface which provides a tactile path. • Snack area at 30" (76cm) for seated user. • Open shelf storage. • Rolling cart and table. • Lever faucet and instant hot at sink. • Base cabinetry with roll out storage. • The work surfaces at varied heights. • Microwave/Convection oven features a door that drops down to provide resting area, touchpad controls, sensor cooking in microwave, micro and convection options, sure grip handles.

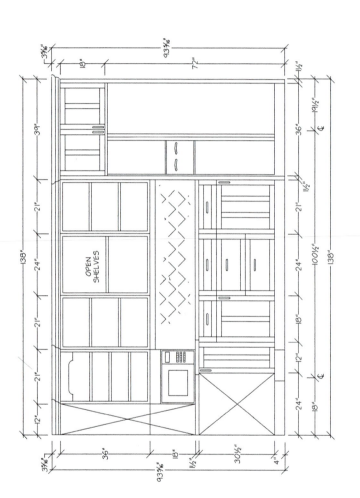

B ELEVATION

General Electric Appliance Kitchen "Real Life Design" - Elevation B - • Refrigerator on the right is a side-by-side model which provides food storage at varied heights. This unit features ice and water in the door and easy-grip handles that allow a hand to pass through. • Over the refrigerator, tray dividers make good use of a difficult space. • The wall cabinet center section has open shelves to allow for visible storage. • While the counter below is at 36" (91cm), a pull-out work surface in the 18" (46cm) base cabinet provides lower flexibility. • Deep drawer storage on full-extension slides and vegetable bins that pull-out provide additional accessible storage. • A step-stool also installed on the door of the 18" (46cm) base cabinet allows more access to the wall cabinets. • The corner base cabinet is a recycling center that allows removal of the bins without much lifting. • The microwave on the counter in the corner allows one to slide items from the refrigerator to the microwave eliminating the need to lift food items.

General Electric Appliance Kitchen "Real Life Design" - Photo Elevation B - • Side by side refrigerator - ice and water in door, storage at varied heights for all users, roll-out, non-spill shelves, easy grip handles, clear view of stored items, slide out freezer baskets, 150° door swing. • Pull-out work surface at 30" (76cm) height. • Step stool. • Pull-out vegetable bins. • Microwave - touch controls, timer, sensor cooking, cooking complete reminder, word prompting, side swing door allows items to be slid onto counter at microwave and from there to work surface without lifting. • Waste receptacles.

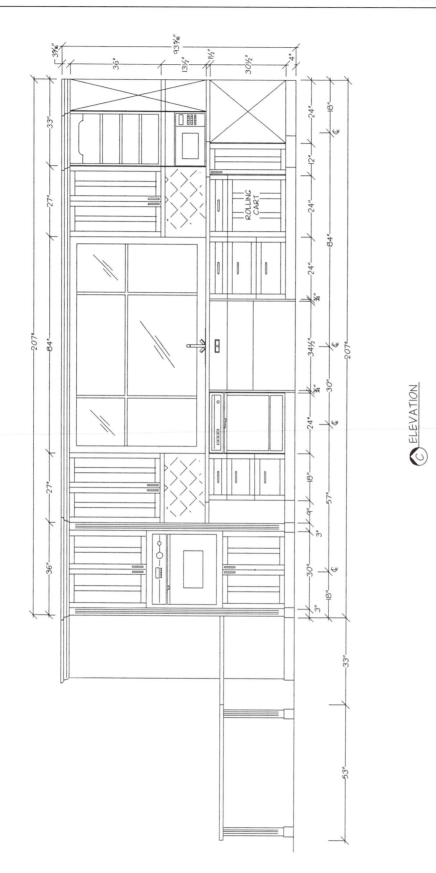

ELEVATION

C

General Electric Appliance Kitchen "Real Life Design" - Elevation C - • Wall cabinets in this elevation have interiors that pull out and down, bringing storage into the universal reach range. • A rolling cart with a tile top to allow items to be moved around the kitchen. • A motorized sink assembly permits its height to be adjusted between 32" (81cm) and 42" (107cm), allowing for comfortable use by any member of the family. • A pull-out work surface to the left of the dishwasher provides further countertop height flexibility. • The oven has large number characters with touch controls, a lock-out feature and improved lighting with the light at the front of the interior oven cavity. It has been installed at a lower height, placing the controls within reach and allowing the oven door to open at the table height. • The adjacent table features a heat resistant surface, creates a knee space and cuts down on lifting and carrying items from the oven.

General Electric Appliance Kitchen "Real Life Design" - Photo Elevation C - • The oven is positioned with the interior shelf at height of adjacent table, control lockout, self-clean, touchpad controls, graphic display time and temperature, audible preheat, 4 rack positions, sure grip handle. • Eating area - adjacent to oven for ease of transfer - heat resistant surface, open knee space adjacent to oven, open shelving for cookbooks, message center. • Rolling cart - heat resistant surface for transfer from oven with curbs on 3 sides, allows transport of items around the kitchen (i.e., pots from sink to cooktop and back or dishes from dishwasher to table). • Sink with knee space, motorized adjustable, rear drain, shallow sink, lever handle faucet. • Dishwasher with control lock-out, touchpad controls, feature flexibility in loading (fold down tines, smart baskets), graphic display, quiet, indicator for rinse aid. • Adjustable height wall cabinet storage.

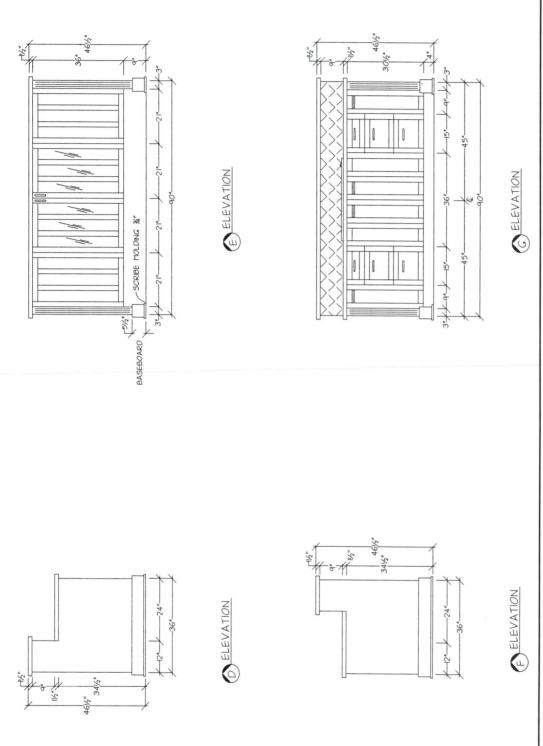

General Electric Appliance Kitchen "Real Life Design" - Island Elevations D, E, F & G - • The island has a heat resistant surface and a smooth-top cooktop, allowing for ease of transfer from the counter to the cooktop burners and back again. • Deep drawers on either side of the cooktop provide pot and pan, condiment and spice storage. • The doors below the cooktop fold back on hinges that fold them back and out of the way, revealing a knee space for cooks who wish to sit. • The back side of the island faces the snack area (Elevation A) and features an increased toekick height. • Heat resistant surfaces are ceramic tile with areas of color contrast for ease in visual acuity. • Areas of color contrast, along with the raised counter curb, assist people with visual difficulties, to locate the counter edge.

General Electric Appliance Kitchen "Real Life Design" - Photo Elevation D, E, F and G - • Glass smooth top cooktop with high contrast controls, safety indicator stays on until unit cools down. • Open knee space below with pull-out stool behind foldback doors. • Heat resistant surface for sliding pots off cooktop. • Downdraft venting system with control within reach range. Pot and condiment storage on either side of cooktop. • Contrasting floor "border". • Raised edge counter shaped to be spill-proof with contrasting edge. • Increased day lighting via window above cabinetry. • Cove lighting for non-glare indirect general illumination. • Increased task lighting and general illumination. • Adjustability in lighting via switches.

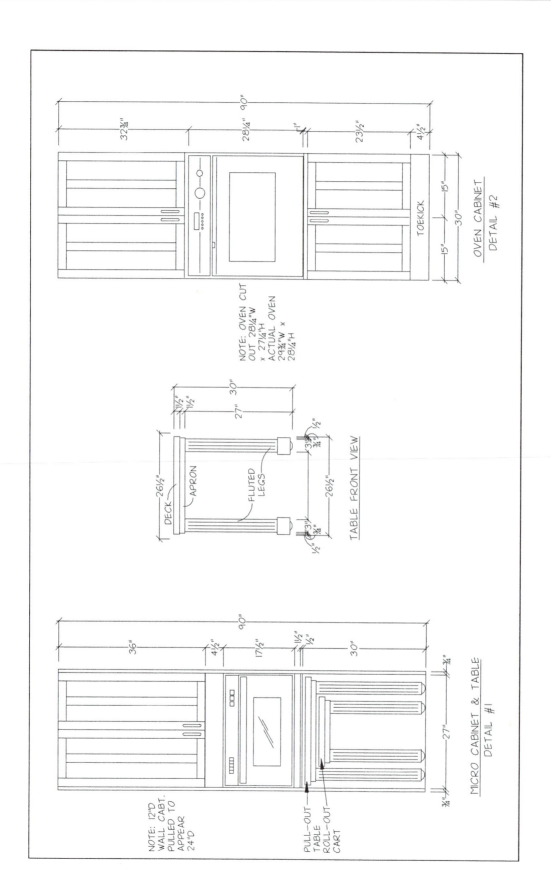

General Electric Appliance Kitchen "Real Life Design" - Detail drawings.

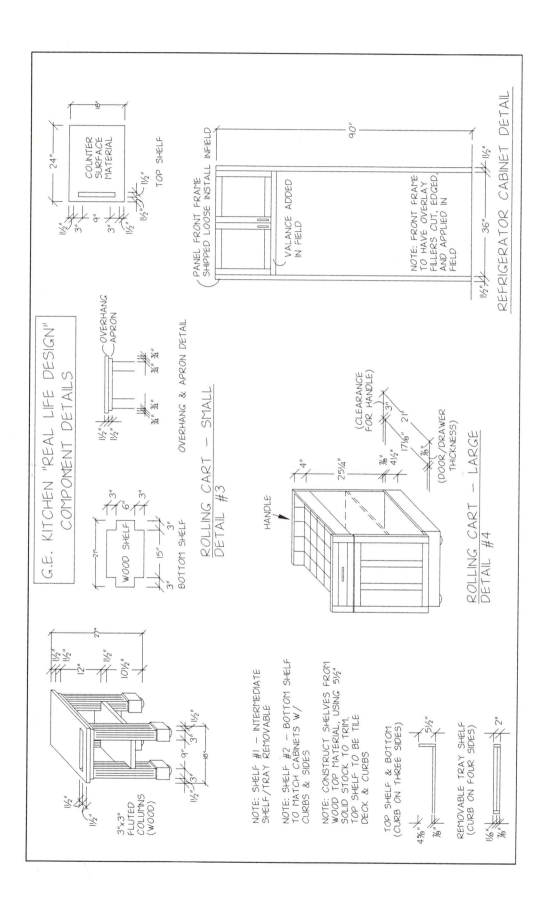

General Electric Appliance Kitchen "Real Life Design" - Detail drawings.

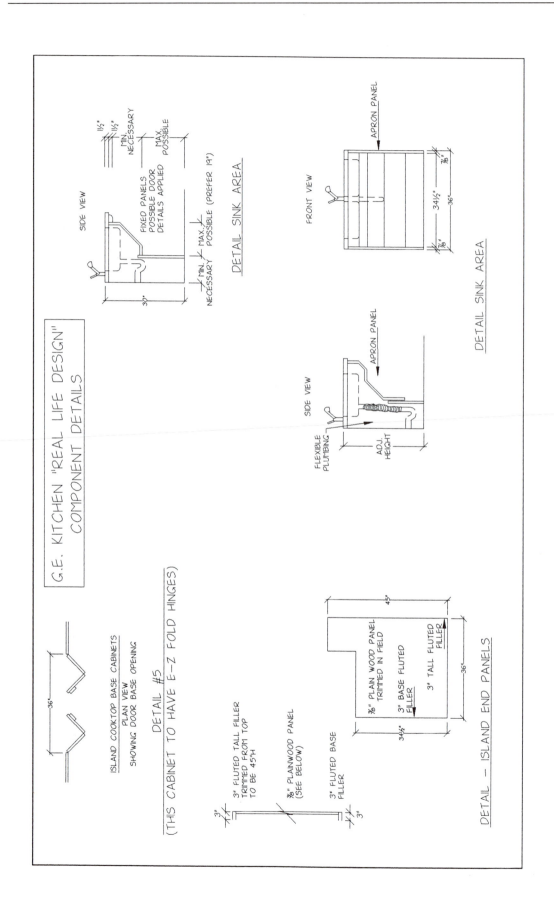

General Electric Appliance Kitchen "Real Life Design" - Detail drawings.

KITCHEN PROJECT #2

Maytag Kitchen
"The Accommodating Kitchen"

Sponsored by Maytag Company and designed by National Kitchen & Bath Association professional teaching instructor, Jim Krengel, CKD, CBD, *"The Accommodating Kitchen ... Accessibility with Substance ... and Style"*, encourages consumers to ask themselves very pointed questions before they build or remodel their dream kitchen. With the idea in mind to accommodate physical needs throughout peoples lives, Jim also shows us how we can employ the design concepts featured in this book to the benefit of every consumer.

A Kitchen for all Seasons was reproduced from Better Homes and Gardens Special Interest Publications.

Better Homes and Gardens® Special Interest Publications - Kitchen and Bath Ideas Fall 1994 - ©Copyright Meredith Corporation 1994 - All rights reserved.

A KITCHEN FOR

ALL SEASONS

By Marsha A. Raisch

Retractable undercabinet doors, varied counter heights and lowered cabinets and storage units allow this multifunction kitchen to adapt to the changing needs of any cook. From newlyweds to a houseful of children to the retirement years, this is a once-for-a-lifetime kitchen!

"*The beauty of this kitchen is that it's very good-looking without any of the obvious trappings of a kitchen designed specifically for someone with limited reach or mobility," says designer Jim Krengel. The doors below the sink are retractable - allowing anyone unable to stand for an extended period to pull up a chair to the sink area. If this is not a need, the space below the sink becomes a handy storage area.*

A KITCHEN FOR

ALL SEASONS

I f you're planning to remodel or build a new kitchen, take some time before the sawdust flies to examine what the future may hold for you and your family. Making this initial time investment will help ensure that your new kitchen can comfortably accommodate a lifetime of changes. For instance, do you now - or do you plan someday - to have children who will help out in the kitchen? Do you have a parent who may someday come to live with you? Do you plan to retire in this home? Thoughtfully considering the future phases of your life before remodeling or building will likely net you a kitchen like this one - designed to meet the lifetime needs of any cook.

Sponsored by Maytag, and designed by Jim Krengel, design director of the Maytag Kitchen Idea Center, this kitchen showcases a number of design features to fit the needs of a host of cooks. "We created this kitchen to illustrate how thoughtful planning and design can allow a space to serve people of all ages and limitations," says Krengel. "This type of kitchen is well suited for any home."

The 20x13-foot kitchen is L-shape, with a tri-level island taking center stage. The L-shape floor plan is the most functional design in any home because it allows you to enter the kitchen on one side and leave on the other with no retracing of steps," explains Krengel. Three solid-surface counter levels at the island (30, 36 and 42 inches) make it a three-sizes-fits-all work area. At 30 inches - 6 inches below the standard 36-inch countertop - the island's lowest level is the perfect height for stirring or mixing ingredients, rolling out dough, and for accommodating pint-size kitchen helpers or a cook of shorter stature. Thirty inches puts the working surface at a comfortable level for someone seated and also gives enough clearance for a wheelchair.

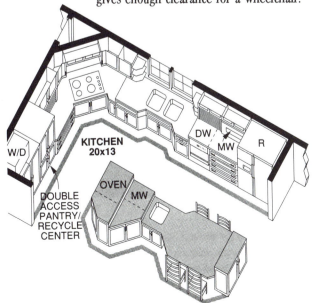

A tri-level center island offers a work surface tailored to fit a cook of any size. The 42-inch counter at one end of the island - which accommodates a tall cook better than a standard 36-inch counter - tops a dish storage unit, making table-setting an easier task for helpful little tykes. The contrasting-color edges on the countertops keep anyone who has lost vision acuity and depth perception from missing the edge of the counter. To save unnecessary bending - particularly for those with lower back pain - the dishwasher is elevated 6 inches.

ALL SEASONS

Convenient Comforts

Not only must a kitchen be functional, it should also be convenient for anyone who will be using it. To ensure its usability by all, kitchen designer Jim Krengel recommends considering these criteria when remodeling or building a kitchen.

- *Concentrate the work triangle to limit needless step.*

- *Use nonglare finishes and lighter colors, especially for older eyes.*

- *Install glare-free lighting to make the space comfortable for all eyes.*

- *Lower light switches or install voice-activated or remote-control light switches.*

- *Lower wall cabinets for elderly persons and children*

- *Remove cabinet doors or use touch-latch doors, eliminating the need to grasp knobs or pulls.*

- *Install vertical pullouts, roll-outs, and lazy Susans for maximum accessibility.*

- *Lower windows in the eating and sink areas to allow the wheelchair-bound to see outside.*

- *Design spans of continuous counter for dragging or sliding items instead of carrying them from one work center to another.*

- *Build a step stool into the toekick for help reaching wall cabinets or a microwave oven.*

- *Store dishes in a 42-inch-high wall cabinet on the floor, making access convenient for everyone.*

- *Raise the dishwasher 6 to 16 inches to curb stooping.*

- *Install faucets and soap dispensers with easy-grasp lever handles on the side of the sink for easier reach.*

- *Install faucets with retractable spray heads to aid those with limited reach.*

- *Install the microwave oven below the counter for children and anyone in a wheelchair. be sure to provide a pullout cutting board or landing counter nearby for safety and convenience.*

- *Leave the area under the cooktop and sink open so a wheelchair or chair can fit beneath.*

Both ends of the island feature 42-inch-high counters sure to please any tall cook who resignedly has become accustomed to stooping when slicing vegetables on a standard-height countertop. At one end of the island, the 42-inch-high counter tops a dish storage unit that allows easy access at mealtime. Now when Mom or Dad asks the kids to set the table, the youngsters can be self-sufficient helpers and get the dishes all by themselves!

Dish storage and varying work-surface heights are not all this multifunction island affords. Housed within the island are two of the kitchen's appliances: a built-in oven and an undercabinet microwave oven. Unlike in a typical kitchen - where the oven is usually located under a standard-height counter - the oven in this kitchen is built into one of the island's 42-inch counters, raising it an additional 6 inches to reduce back wrenching. The undercabinet microwave oven is also lowered for easier access by younger cooks; steaming hot baking dishes are less likely to be tipped when the cook looks down rather than up at the container as it is removed from the oven.

With a side-mounted faucet, the island's auxiliary sink - complete with a built-in dispenser - is within easy reach of little helpers when it's time to wash up. The sink is also convenient for rinsing produce or for scraping the dinner dishes. A hot-water dispenser makes it easy to fix a quick cup of instant coffee or a relaxing cup of tea.

Besides offering abundant food storage, the side-by-side refrigerator gives all users easier access than a model with the freezer on the top or bottom. Chilled water and crushed or cubed ice are available through the door - within anyone's reach. Placement of the refrigerator was also calculated; it's next to a second microwave oven for a casserole's quick commute from freezer to oven. And because a refrigerator is called into action just as often in setting and clearing the table, it's also in close proximity to the dining area.

Placing often-used items or heavier small appliances within close reach is a good idea in any kitchen - and particularly in a kitchen where accessibility is top of mind. In this kitchen, two tambour-door appliance garages stand ready to store anything from a heavy-duty mixer to items used every day - like the toaster and coffeepot. "Recent statistics show that a 65-year-old woman will likely have difficulty lifting something that weighs more than 10 pounds," says Krengel. "Including lowered cabinets and appliance garages in a kitchen you're designing today

An angled mirror above this 30-inch-high smooth-surface cooktop reflects the contents of a simmering or boiling pot permitting a young cook or a cook unable to stand for lengthy periods to keep tabs on what's cooking. The retractable doors can accommodate any kind of chair. for anyone who suffers from a height disadvantage, this two-step stool is always handy to help give a leg up. When not in use, the stool tucks out of the way into the toekick under the base cabinet.

ALL SEASONS

Built into the island, this microwave oven is at a safe height for younger cooks who are less apt to tip a hot baking dish when they don't have to reach up to remove it from the oven. The feature stripe in the vinyl floor has a twofold purpose: It adds a decorative element to the room, and provides a visual clue of the cabinet's proximity for those with vision problems. In the case of a blind person, the strip could be textured, allowing a foot to feel its way around the kitchen.

may be for convenience, but as the years go by, these conveniences in the same home may become necessities. In both cases, they not only make it easier for the cook but also facilitate meal preparation."

The electric, smooth-surface cooktop - placed at a 30-inch height - makes cooking easier for a young cook or a cook unable to stand for long periods of time. The doors under the cooktop are retractable, allowing a seated cook adequate access, too. Above the cooktop, an angled mirror reflects the contents of a simmering or boiling pot to any cook not tall enough to keep a watchful eye on its contents.

One of the kitchen's most innovative features - a double-access pantry - will appeal to anyone who has struggled unloading groceries from the back of the car and lugging them into the house, only to unload them again into kitchen cupboards. Opening on the back side in an attached garage, this pantry is handy for unloading canned foods and packaged goods directly from the trunk into the kitchen. Dual recycling bins in the lower portion of the pantry - one for plastics and the other for aluminum - are also accessible from the kitchen side for storage, and from the garage side when it's time to clean out for a visit to the recycling center.

In todays busy household, stationing a clothes-washing facility in the kitchen is a resourceful way to get two jobs done at the same time - combining kitchen and laundry duties. The space-saving stacked washer/dryer unit in this kitchen hides behind a retractable door when not in use. And, while it can save building costs because the unit shares the same plumbing and electrical sources as the other kitchen appliances, in a homeowner's later years it can also eliminate the need for navigating steep basement stairs.

Safety Solutions

Of all the rooms in a home, the kitchen is one of the most likely to invite accidents. Jim Krengel suggests following these safety precautions to lessen the likelihood that anyone will be injured in your kitchen.

- *Use contrasting edges to help discern counters more easily, particularly in a monochromatic setting.*
- *Pull out and lower work counters so both children and those seated can work more safely.*
- *Use nonskid floors, which offer better traction - especially for those using a walker or on crutches.*
- *Use tambour units to put heavy small appliances at countertop height.*
- *Install late-night timers to ensure that any appliances left on will be automatically shut off.*
- *Provide a hot-water limiter to avoid scaldings.*
- *Lower the cooktop for a more comfortable and safer reach.*
- *Install an angled mirror above the cooktop to help seated users see contents of cooking vessels.*
- *Use cooktops with staggered burners to avoid the need to reach over a hot element.*
- *Avoid exposing a sleeve to an open flame by specifying an electric range.*
- *Specify cooktops with front-mounted controls and knobs that are a least 11/2 inches in diameter for easy grasping.*

"Building a kitchen that meets the needs of a family today - as well as how those needs will progressively change - makes good sense," says Krengel, who believes that adaptable design is on its way to becoming a building industry standard. "Besides the obvious benefit of an adaptable-designed kitchen that provides a safe environment tailored to fit the needs of every family member, there is a second advantage as well. If properly designed at the outset, an adaptable kitchen can be built for the same dollar value as one that is not; but should you decide to sell your home, the resale value may actually be enhanced because your kitchen will also serve the needs of any buyer." □

Photographer: Hopkins Associates
Kitchen designer: Jim Krengel, CKD, CBD
Photo stylist: Nancy Wall Hopkins

Opening on the back side to an attached garage, this food pantry will make trips home from the supermarket a breeze. Packaged goods and canned foods transport from the trunk to pantry with minimal effort and with an added bonus: The fresh-from-the-store items remain in the back of the pantry while older items are pushed forward flagging earlier usage. Pullout recycling bins can also be loaded from the kitchen side and unloaded from the garage side. (In some areas, building codes require a security lock on any access into the home.)

KITCHEN PROJECT #3

Whirlpool Corporation
"The Less Challenging Home"

Every person has some type of physical or mental limitation that makes certain tasks more difficult to accomplish than others. But often people forget to take these limitations into consideration when designing a kitchen or laundry area. The result can be choices that turn simple day-to-day tasks into difficult chores.

Sponsored by Whirlpool Appliances, this space was designed to help expand the approach to planning a kitchen. Simple and inexpensive design elements have been combined to create a kitchen that works for nearly everyone, regardless of age or physical condition.

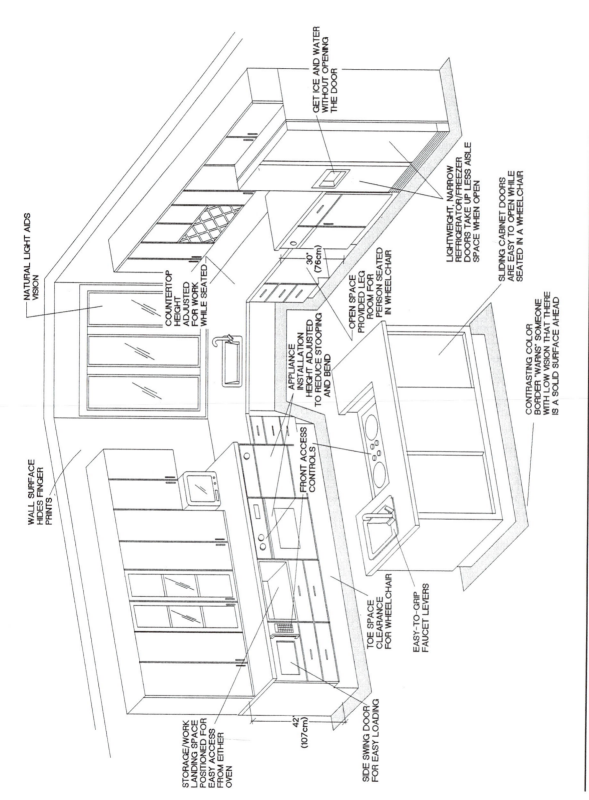

NATURAL LIGHT AIDS VISION

COUNTERTOP HEIGHT ADJUSTED FOR WORK WHILE SEATED

WALL SURFACE HIDES FINGER PRINTS

STORAGE/WORK LANDING SPACE POSITIONED FOR EASY ACCESS FROM EITHER OVEN

SIDE SWING DOOR FOR EASY LOADING

42' (107cm)

APPLIANCE INSTALLATION HEIGHT ADJUSTED TO REDUCE STOOPING AND BEND

FRONT ACCESS CONTROLS

TOE SPACE CLEARANCE FOR WHEELCHAIR

EASY-TO-GRIP FAUCET LEVERS

OPEN SPACE PROVIDED LEG ROOM FOR PERSON SEATED IN WHEELCHAIR

30' (76cm)

GET ICE AND WATER WITHOUT OPENING THE DOOR

LIGHTWEIGHT, NARROW REFRIGERATOR/FREEZER DOORS TAKE UP LESS AISLE SPACE WHEN OPEN

SLIDING CABINET DOORS ARE EASY TO OPEN WHILE SEATED IN A WHEELCHAIR

CONTRASTING COLOR BORDER "WARNS" SOMEONE WITH LOW VISION THAT THERE IS A SOLID SURFACE AHEAD

Whirlpool Corporation "The Less Challenging Home" - Modified to accommodate a person using a wheelchair, this design eliminates many of the common barriers in kitchens. Pointed out in the drawing are examples of concepts that create a more accessible space.

Whirpool Corporation "The Less Challenging Home"

Whirpool Corporation "The Less Challenging Home" - Dropped wall cabinets increase accessible storage.

Whirpool Corporation "The Less Challenging Home" - Raised toekick provides clear floor space.

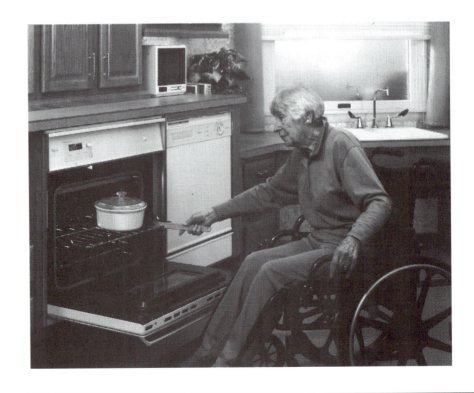

Whirpool Corporation "The Less Challenging Home" - Placing appliances at a more comfortable height for everyone.

c h a p t e r *16*

Bathrooms That Work

The bathrooms featured in this chapter attempt to tie together many of the design and planning techniques discussed in this book. Here, you will see how bathrooms can be planned utilizing creative common sense applications of universal thinking. Several of the ideas you'll discover are totally non-traditional, others expand on commonly thought of concepts and some are not new at all, just good design.

As you explore the photos and drawings featured on these pages, attempt to mentally identify the use of the individual and overall work center spaces which you will see accommodate people of varying sizes and abilities.

RACHEL'S BATHROOM

This remodeling project includes a kitchen and a bathroom, designed by **Mary Jo Peterson** for the Burgess-Goldberg family. This story and the space that evolved, provide designers with not only the "*how-to*", but equally important the "*why bother*" of universal bath design.

The Burgess-Goldberg family includes a working widowed mother, a teenage son, and Rachel, a 13 year old girl who uses a wheelchair and has multiple physical disabilities. As we approach the project, their house has a number of barriers for Rachel.

In the kitchen for example, only one cabinet is within her reach and the space is so cramped that most movement in her wheelchair results in banging or bruising a wall or cabinet surface.

In the bathroom Rachel's mother has to lift her into and out of the bathtub, a task that is becoming difficult and dangerous as Rachel grows. The rest of the space is limiting for Rachel and difficult for other family members as Rachel's assistive devices occupy more of the already limited space. In the family room is a small second bathroom that Rachel cannot access at all.

Project Goals

The main goal of the project is to create kitchen and bathroom spaces without unnecessary barriers, allowing Rachel optimum safe levels of activity. As Rachel reaches adulthood, one way to provide her with maximum independence would be for her mother to move out of the house, allowing Rachel to live with a care-giver and thus be truly independent.

With this in mind, the team that made this goal a reality was formed. Members of the team include Rachel, Rachel's mother and sister (a physical therapist), Rachel's own occupational therapist, Mary Jo as designer, and an outstanding contracting team led by **Dale Zimmerman**.

The New Plan -
Meeting the Requirements

The new plan involves relocating both the kitchen and bathroom. The kitchen is now moved into what had been the family room and second bathroom. A new bathroom is now where the old kitchen had been.

Existing conditions predetermined that the new kitchen and the new bathroom would be elevated 6" (15cm) from the existing grade to accommodate the transition.

- The new space plan is more open, with the existing living room flowing into the kitchen, incorporating what was a small dining room into this more flexible space.

- Vaulted ceilings, sky lights, and window expand the space.

- The change from smaller separate spaces to one larger and more open space also translates to ease of movement for Rachel and reduces wear and tear on walls and doors exposed to the exuberant movements of a young girl in a wheelchair.

The Plan Implementation

The new bathroom is a space that is not only safer and more accessible to Rachel and those assisting her, but also a space that reflects the high levels of energy, activity, and pleasure that are the personality of this household.

- To begin, the bathroom is entered through an oversized pocket door. The door is actually the maximum size opening that allows for its pocket and the pre-existing location of the utility space.

- Grab bars continue through the room, functioning as support and as a decorative detail.

- A countertop extending over the lavatory area knee space and the adjacent toilet, allow for resting space for frequently used items.

- The sink itself is relatively shallow with a rear drain to allow for optimum knee space, and the single lever faucet is easy to use and is familiar.

- The actual 32" (81cm) height of the knee space is based on Rachel's wheelchair arm height, so that she can roll up close for grooming.

- In the toilet area, Rachel and her mother opted for a standard height toilet with an elevated seat and integral grab bars. Past experience has taught them that this setup is most conducive to Rachel making best use of her strengths and abilities for transfer and stability.

- In addition the ceiling is re-enforced for hanging assistive triangle supports installed at the lavatory and toilet area.

- Adjacent to the toilet, the roll-in shower increases access to the toilet for transfer and provides for Rachel and a care giver for grooming and hygiene.

- Grab bars surround the area and an added adjustable support drops down from the ceiling.

- Controls include the hand-held spray with an extended hose for ease of use by everyone.

- The walls of the shower are kept to a minimum, extending only, as far as necessary to retain water, so that Rachel's entry, movement, and exit can occur without interference.

- Continuing around the room, there is a ramp and a second exit. The ramp is necessary due to the change in floor levels. The door exists because typical traffic patterns would allow her mother to assist Rachel from the shower to her bedroom in the evenings. This route would be the most direct. Exiting through the secondary door provides a direct route out the front door in case of emergency.

- To combine safety and aesthetics, the floor tile was patterned in this area to emphasize the ramp, with a contrasting arrow at both ends of the slope.

- The fourth wall of the bathroom includes some storage space that is fixed and some that is movable. Closed area storage is provided for typical bath products as well as personal hygiene supplies.

- The rolling storage basket allows access to the utilities through a pre-existing panel. Rachel can roll her stored grooming items to where she needs them and again, out of the way, as needs for the clear floor space change.

Aesthetics and Finishes

Aesthetics of this bathroom, chosen with Rachel's guidance, definitely reflect the personality of the family.

- Gray and white wall tiles with a mottled gray floor tile were her mothers choice for their ability to look clean under any circumstances.

- Red accents in the grab bars, window treatment and accessories call out safety features and brighten the space.

- Bright yellow in the hanging support system ties into the overall theme as Rachel's choice, Mickey Mouse ties together the colors of red, yellow, black and white.

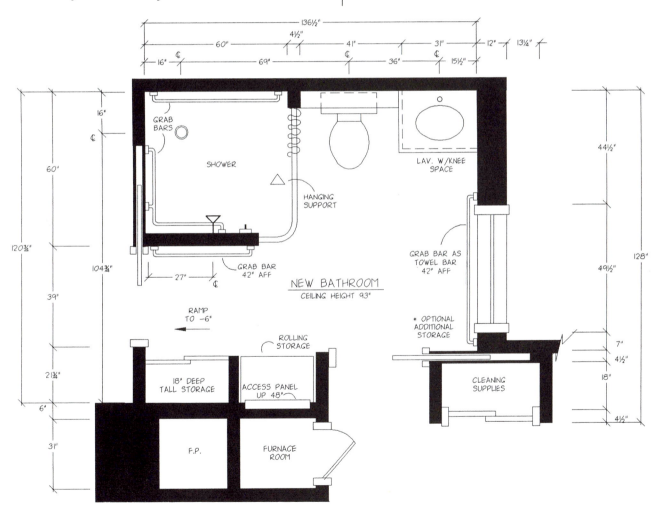

Figure 329 -   Burgess-Goldberg Bathroom.

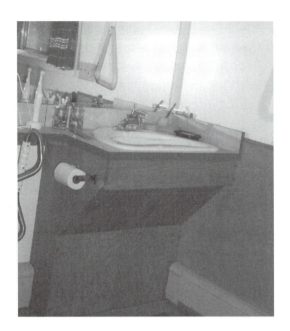

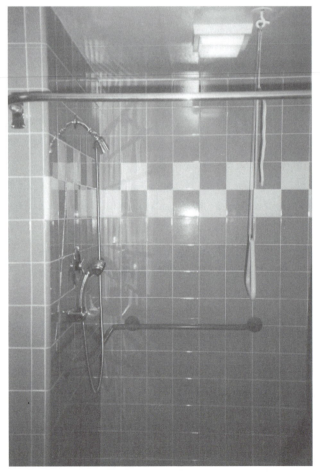

Figure 330 - Burgess-Goldberg Bathroom.

THE DOBKIN BATH

This master suite was and is a labor of love, created by designer Irma Dobkin, ASID, for herself and her husband. The plans, along with Irma's descriptions will inform and inspire bathroom designers to incorporate universal design concepts as an integral part of the beauty and function of every bathroom space.

Irma, a design student in her early forties, now faced with the reality of the aging process, gained considerable insight from her own mother's aging. The aging process creates inevitable changes in physical as well as mental abilities. Accommodations for these changes are reflected in the design she has created.

Floor Plan of Original Suite

The Dobkins sat down and evaluated the strengths and weaknesses of the existing bedroom and compiled a wish list of how a remodeled room would work and look. The list included concerns for accessibility should a wheelchair ever be needed. Independence was of paramount consideration as an acceptable solution.

The Users and Their Needs

An empty-nest, professional working couple, they are art collectors who entertain frequently. Their desire was to create a dramatic and romantic bedroom, bathroom and dressing area using the following criteria.

- A self-contained living environment, eliminating the need to travel through the house and negotiate steps to the kitchen and the laundry room.
- The space would be universally designed and wheelchair accessible (to some degree).
- A shower without a curb and threshold in case a wheelchair, crutches or other walking aids would be needed.

- A separate area for the toilet and bidet close to the sleeping area would be convenient for middle of the night visits.
- An organized, dramatic and compartmentalized suite.
- Separate grooming areas would provide convenience when both users were in the space.
- A bed facing the entry door and angled fireplace wall provided a fabulous view.
- Sensitivity toward cost dictated the reuse of the existing toilet and bidet. However since each stood 14 1/4 inches (37cm) AFF to the seat, they would be built-up.
- Acoustics were a concern (difficulty discerning foreground from background sound). So the architectural finish materials selected had to be evaluated in light of their acoustical properties.

The Design

The new master suite restores romance, integrating safety, accessibility, and beauty. The space anticipates the physiological changes of aging.

- Special assistive devices are woven into the tapestry of the compartmentalized space.
- Judicious selection of materials assures safety and operational ease.
- Automated draperies, mechanical beds, and lighting now require little strength or dexterity.
- A soaring architecture elevates the spirit, neutrals and niches provide surrounds for art and sculpture.

The Details

- A curbless shower, using large-scaled floor tile, led to the design of a trough for water management.
- Grab bars, used as a rail detail, are integrated throughout.

- *Way-finding* is logical. Multiple routes avoid congestion, as do the wide passages and doorways.

- Frequently used, the toilet is the space's hub.

- The bumper designed for the pocket door permits effortless operation regardless of dexterity or strength.

- The physical separation of sink areas permits individualized solutions; one being fully wheelchair accessible.

- The custom nightstands puts light and bed controls along the bedside for safety and convenience

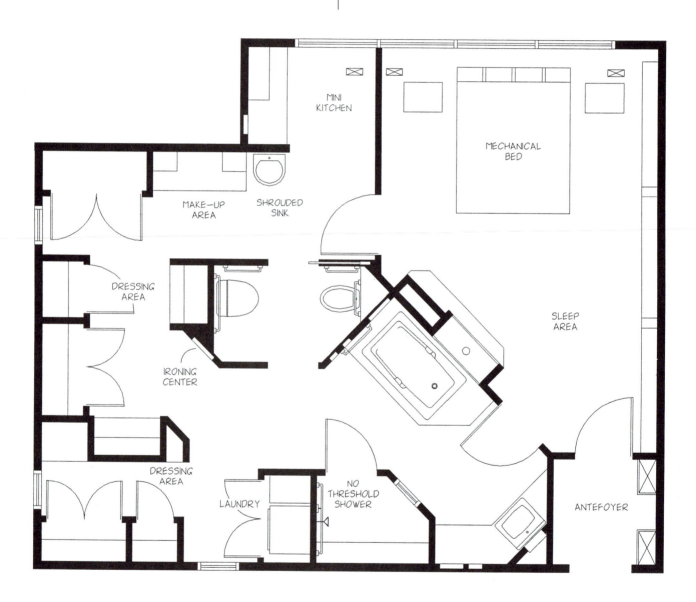

Figure 331 - Dobkin Bathroom.

Figure 332 -   Dobkin Bathroom.

THE KLINE BATH

The client profile for this universal bathroom project, designed by Annette DePaepe, CKD, CBD, ASID, is not unlike the profile for many custom bathroom projects.

The Klines are a couple in their late forties looking to create a master bathroom that will be both functional and beautiful, an environment that will feel like a sophisticated spa retreat and flow naturally with their bedroom's contemporary Japanese influence. John Kline is 5' 7" (170cm) and Harriet is 5' 3" (160cm) and they want a space that suits their physical characteristics.

Recent attention to *"the aging boomer"* has helped them to appreciate design details that while subtle, will allow them to enjoy their space for as long as they wish.

Design Requirements

The space to be utilized is an addition on the east end of the bedroom. Parameters include:

- Access to the bedroom and to an exterior patio to be built on the north wall.

- An open roll-in shower with large seat, stool or bench area adjacent to the shower, toilet with space for side transfer, lavatory with kneespace, storage closet and a 60" (152cm) wheelchair turning space.

The New Plan - Meeting the Requirements

The new plan responds to the client's desires and offers more.

- With doors on east and north walls, a clear floor space of 60" (152cm) is maintained, creating the flow the Klines had requested while providing the clearance needed for a wheelchair to turn 360°.

- A custom 31 1/2" (80cm) high pedestal sink accommodates both standing and sitting use and provides kneespace.

- The shower is designated by four columns that frame the 36" (91cm) wide seat and window areas.

- Controls are placed at the entrance, with a hand-held showerhead on the seat deck for easy access.

- All glass used is tempered for safety.

- The 1/2" (4cm) high beveled curb is easy to roll-over with a wheelchair and adds to the open flow of the space.

- The floorspace at the shower entrance provides the 90° turning space required for a wheelchair.

- The vertical towel warmer allows towels to be hung at a wide range of heights above the floor.

- A solid surface bench opposite the shower provides for towel drying and aids in transfer.

- The remaining floor space accommodates the toilet and side transfer space.

- All corners are eased to eliminate any sharp edges and surfaces are of tile and solid surface for easy maintenance.

- In order to provide the spa retreat feeling requested, a special reflecting pool for floating candles and potpourri lies between the shower and lavatory and drains into the shower.

- The semi-circular protrusion of the lavatory front is mirrored in the back splash and mirror top.

- The square motif, picked-up from a shoji screen in the bedroom, is used throughout the bathroom to create a unified theme.

- Squares are found in the molding, cabinet door style, lighting, floor and bench/lavatory supports.

- The neutral with black accent colors help to create a feeling of understated sophistication.

The finished space is remarkable for its beauty and more subtly for its foresight and flexibility, providing for a longer lifespan.

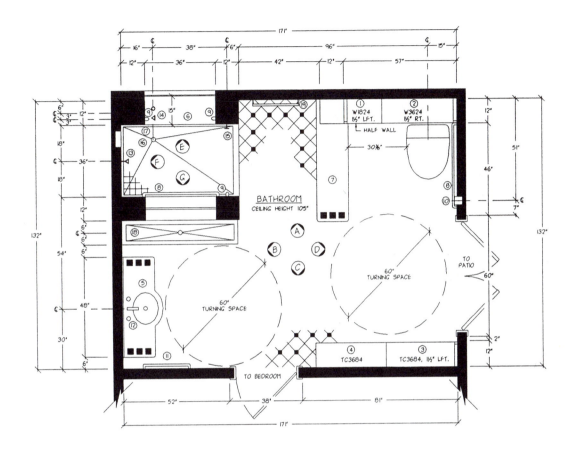

FLOOR PLAN

SPECIFICATIONS

① W1824, 1½" EXT. LEFT, UNDER CABINET LIGHT, DOOR 1½" LONGER THAN CASE TO CONCEAL LTS.

② W3624, 1½" EXT. RIGHT, UNDER CABINET LIGHTS, DOORS 1½" LONGER THAN CASE TO CONCEAL LTS.

③ TC3684, 1½" @ LEFT, 6 ADJ. SHELVES AND TOUCH LATCH DOORS

④ TC3684, 6 ADJ. SHELVES & TOUCH LATCH DOORS

⑤ CUSTOM LAVATORY SOLID SURFACE BRAND ABC, COLOR 123, UNIVERSAL DESIGN SINK MODEL #U911

⑥ CUSTOM SOLID SURFACE SEAT BRAND ABC, COLOR # 123, 36" WIDE x 12" DEEP

⑦ CUSTOM SOLID SURFACE BENCH BRAND ABC, COLOR # 123, 62" LONG x 12" DEEP, SUPPORTS COLOR # 134

⑧ 2-42" HORIZONTAL GRAB BARS, ONE AT TOILET ONE IN SHOWER, BRAND XYZ, #42-CKS, @ 33" AFF

⑨ 3-30" VERTICAL GRAB BARS IN SHOWER, BRAND XYZ #30-CKS, @ 33" AFF

⑩ RECESSED TOILET PAPER HOLDER, BRAND XYZ, MODEL #765

⑪ 24" TOWEL BAR, BRAND ABC, #759, 39" @ AFF

⑫ FAUCET BRAND XYZ, MODEL #123, 8" SPREAD

⑬ PRESSURE BALANCED SHOWERHEAD BRAND XYZ, MODEL# 123, 78" @ AFF

⑭ HAND-HELD SHOWERHEAD WITH DIVERTER BRAND XYZ, MODEL #123 ON TOP OF BENCH

⑮ SHOWER CONTROL BRAND XYZ, MODEL 123, 42" @ AFF

⑯ CUSTOM BUILT SHOWER PAN 36" x 60" WITH BRAND ABC TILE, 4" x 4", BLACK (NON-SKID) MATTE FINISH & ½" BEVELED THRESHOLD IN SOLID SURFACE #123

⑰ SHOWER WALLS TO BE SOLID SURFACE BRAND ABC, COLOR 123.

⑱ REFLECTION POOL WITH DRAIN SURFACED IN SOLID SURFACE BRAND ABC, COLOR 123.

⑲ TOWEL WARMER 24" W. x 48" H. BRAND XXX, MODEL #1234, 21" @ AFF

⑳ BRAND ABC TILE FLOOR 8" x 8" COLOR #123 ON DIAGONAL W/ 1" x 1" COLOR # 456 DOT BORDER, ALL TILE W/ MATTE NON-SKID FINISH

Figure 333 - Kline Bathroom.

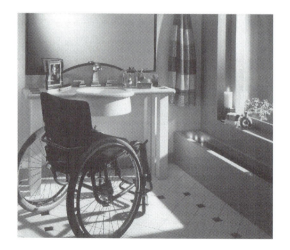

Figure 334 -   Kline Bathroom.

THE HEATHER BATHROOM

Lorraine and George Heather are in their fifties and wish to update and change their home to accommodate their changing lifestyles. George is 6' 2" (188cm) tall, a large man and Lorraine is 5' 4" (163cm), operating from a power wheelchair as an injury from a car accident has resulted in the loss of the use of her legs.

Design Requirements

Having retired from teaching, Lorraine still has an interest in helping young people and has decided to offer her home and herself as a source of rehabilitation for young people who are recovering from injuries similar to hers.

In addition, because George is involved in town politics and their home is often a place where varieties of people congregate, they have decided to make one bathroom on the main floor a flexible and accessible space where people of varying size and ability can function.

To accommodate the Heathers' desire for flexibility in their guest bathroom, the new space allows for adjustment in the major work areas and in the storage areas.

The New Plan -
Meeting the Requirements

- As you enter the bathroom, storage and mirrors are located on either side of the door.

- In both corners fixed storage is 18" (46cm) deep and just 66" (168cm) high, placing most of the storage within the universal reach range. Between the units and the door are full length mirrors to allow for full view for a person who is seated or standing.

- In front of each mirror is a rolling storage unit with a hinged top and drawers.

These units allow a person to move stored items easily and the surface doubles as a counter when needed.

- Moving into the shower area, a sloped floor to the drain and a 60" x 48" (152cm x 122cm) curtained area help to retain water.

- The seat can be adjusted, both horizontally and vertically, or folded out of the way for varied preferences in showering.

- The control wall includes a hand-held spray which can be adjusted in height or used in-hand.

- Water temperature can be preset or adjusted with the pressure balanced valve eliminating the risk of scalding. A separate on/off lever allows for volume control.

- The lavatory area is flexible as well, with a sink that can be adjusted vertically or horizontally by pushing a lever up, and using one hand, easily positioning the fixture, then pushing the lever down to lock into place. This adjustability lends itself to people of varying size, age and ability. The ability to move the sink left or right changes the clear floor space as desired for showering and toileting.

- In the toilet area, flexibility in surrounding grab bars and the adjacent lavatory provide clear floor space for a variety of approaches and transfers. Grab bars can be raised, lowered, or folded out of the way to suit the abilities and preferences of the user.

- The gray and white theme in the bathroom is accented by bright red. The room has generous task and ambient lighting, including natural light. Adjustability in switches allows for differences in visual needs. The overall effect is light and spacious.

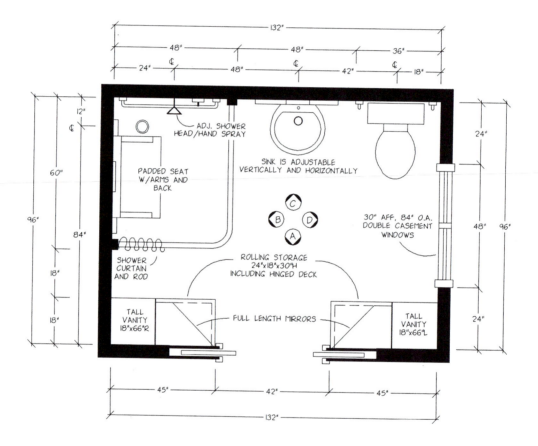

Figure 335 -   Heather Bathroom.

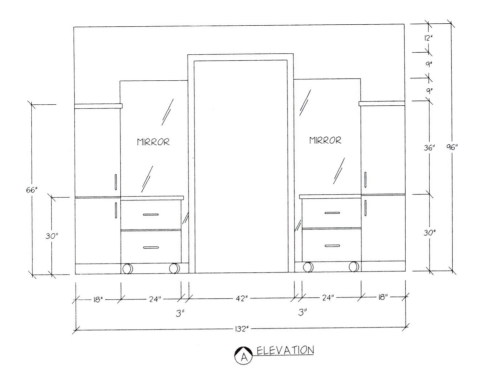

MIRROR   MIRROR

12"
9"
9"
36"   96"
66"
30"   30"

18"   24"   42"   24"   18"
3"   3"
132"

A ELEVATION

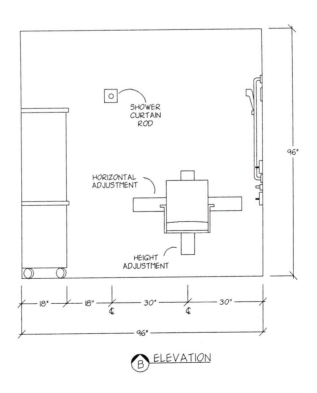

SHOWER
CURTAIN
ROD

HORIZONTAL
ADJUSTMENT

96"

HEIGHT
ADJUSTMENT

18"   18"   30"   30"
96"

B ELEVATION

Figure 336 -   Heather Bathroom.

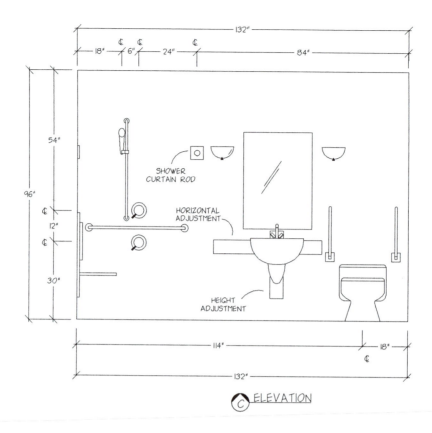

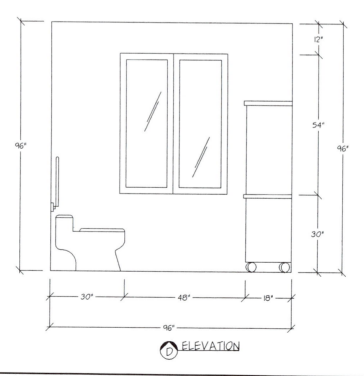

Figure 337 - Heather Bathroom.

Figure 338 -   Heather Bathroom.

c h a p t e r *17*

Understanding

Disabilities

and

Functional

Considerations

FUNCTIONAL ASSESSMENT OF KITCHEN AND BATHROOM SKILLS

When planning kitchen or bathroom modifications for an individual with an injury or disability it is imperative to start with a full assessment of the person's functional capabilities. In other words, it is important to consider the total person and the environment, not just his or her component parts.

To do this comprehensively, the team of an occupational therapist and the designer, can assess the person and the environment respectively while considering each others expertise. Although most injuries or disabilities have a common set of symptoms, it is often true that each person's particular set of symptoms varies widely.

Analysis of the Individuals Needs

How a person "*lives*" with and tolerates these symptoms will vary with the individual.

It is also true that some conditions present themselves differently or have an unpredictable course. Lifestyle in terms of roles, responsibilities and desires must be explored.

A comprehensive assessment of a person's capabilities would include looking at the physical, sensory, perceptual, cognitive and emotional components of function.

An **Occupational Therapist** is a trained professional educated to assess these components as they relate to functional abilities in order to make recommendations which would result in optimizing each person's independence.

- By considering medical history, prognosis and skill level the therapist analyzes one's ability to complete grooming and hygiene skills.

- Specific activities such as oral hygiene, shaving, toileting, bathing, cosmetic application and the ability to complete hair care are assessed.

- Strengths and areas of concern are determined. A treatment plan is developed which would include techniques, strategies, environmental modifications and adaptive equipment.

While some of these recommendations are universal, some are specific to the individual.

The teaming of skills of a kitchen or bathroom designer and an occupational therapist will provide the optimal solution.

MOBILITY

Mobility is the ability to move around an identified space safely and efficiently. A person's ability to move may be impaired due to many factors. Relative to the purpose of kitchen and bathroom design, the cause of the impairment and how movement and function are affected are essential to the success of the design choice.

Mobility Impairments

Impairment of mobility may mean the person can freely and easily move around the kitchen or bathroom but needs to sit at certain intervals of time perhaps due to decreased endurance.

At the other end of the spectrum, impaired mobility may mean reliance on a wheelchair. Each of these individuals can successfully function in the kitchen or bathroom if given the "*right*" setup.

If mobility is impaired due to conditions involving joint inflammation and resulting degeneration, techniques known as "*joint protection*" and "*energy conservation*" are employed. This approach is utilized in such conditions as osteo and rheumatoid arthritis (inflammation of joints) and ankylosing spondylitis to reduce the strain on joints. Joints feel painful, swell and get red resulting in lack of movement.

For example, an individual suffering from rheumatoid arthritis should be able to gather necessary items all at one time and in one location, and then prepare the meal while seated to avoid swelling joints. The incorporation of a conveniently located, all purpose work surface at sitting height with easy access to the refrigerator, sink and electrical outlets would greatly enhance that individual's ability to function pain free. The design should also allow for the sliding of heavy objects such as cans and casserole dishes along the countertop to and from the food preparation area and the oven/range top.

For individuals in need of walking aides (canes, walkers, wheelchairs), the ability to carry things is often compromised. Utility carts designed for the transport of foods, dishes, etc. are often times an inexpensive yet safe solution.

Designing a kitchen with consideration of countertop and wheelchair heights is essential for any person who uses a wheelchair.

Work space and setup should be designed to reduce unnecessary walking and lifting so energy is conserved for the tasks related to meal preparation.

Convenience Considerations

Grooming and hygiene activities can be completed with less effort if done after gathering all items in one location.

- Ideally, an all purpose work surface at a comfortable sitting height adjacent to a lavatory should be planned.

- Close access to a mirror and electrical outlets will greatly enhance that individual's ability to function in a pain free workspace.

- Storage should be designed to reduce unnecessary walking and lifting so energy can be conserved for grooming and hygiene.

- A built-in vanity area with access to drawers and a water source will accomplish this need. An open kneespace at the vanity would allow for wheelchair accessibility as well.

- Cabinet and countertop arrangements which allow the sliding of items is oftentimes an inexpensive yet safe solution.

- Caution should be taken in making such a recommendation, with attention to a person's balance and how he/she lifts and moves their feet. Judgment must be assessed by a trained professional.

- Clients with spinal cord injuries, multiple sclerosis, or amputations can be easily accommodated to allow for independent access and use of the bathroom. Wheelchair accessible space for safe and independent transfers from wheelchairs to the toilet and bathtub or shower could mean dignity for the individual as well as relief for the care provider.

- Consideration of wheelchair heights is essential to the success of any person who is operating from a wheelchair.

- A solution as simple as a raised toilet seat or raised toilet seat height may mean the ability to toilet oneself thereby perserving the individual's dignity and prevent the possibility of falls.

- Many types of adaptive seats and lifts are available for bathtubs and showers *(See chapters 8 and 9).*

- Many assistive devices are also available.

- For specific types of transfer, *(refer to Appendix 7).* Safe independent use of these devices requires proper selection and training through the services of a therapist.

BALANCE

Balance and mobility are closely aligned and should be assessed together. Balance or a state of equilibrium can be compromised by many injuries or illnesses.

Neurological conditions such as Multiple Sclerosis and Parkinson's Disease as well as orthopedic conditions which relate to bones, muscles and joints (e.g. hip or other leg fractures, leg length discrepancy, arthritic conditions, leg amputations,) are only some of the conditions which may result in balance problems.

Design Concerns

The functional considerations would include; walking and carrying things, bending over to obtain objects from a low height, reaching up to access items from above shoulder height to bring them safely to the countertop or lavatory, getting in and out of a bathtub or shower and getting on and off a toilet seat safely.

Design Solutions

Solutions includes a lavatory with open kneespace and rearrangement of cabinetry so storage is within easy reach, (e.g. approximately waist height). This reduces the chance of slips or falls and should be strongly considered. Individuals with decreased balance and/or mobility need greater security. Kitchen solutions may range from the easy addition of a utility cart for the transport of items, to the placement of microwaves and wall ovens at accessible heights. An accessible height would allow for easy reach for the item (approximately waist height) and would require little or no lifting or lowering to get it to the countertop.

COORDINATION

Coordination or the ability to control movement can be assessed by observing the ability to move around the environment in a smoothly executed manner and to use various bathroom items and tools safely and efficiently.

Motor control can be affected by many different injuries and disabilities. For example, many neurological conditions such as Cerebral Vascular Accidents (stroke), Multiple Sclerosis, Parkinson's Disease, Traumatic Brain Injury and Cerebral Palsy as well as Peripheral Nerve Injuries (i.e. Carpal Tunnel Syndrome) result in a decrease in motor control. Symptoms such as spasticity, tremors, weakness and impaired sensation can result in incoordination.

When planning a kitchen for someone with incoordination, begin by observing the individual's ability to move around the environment. *Can the individual move in a smoothly executed manner and use various kitchen tools safely?* In fact, safety is the most pressing issue for someone with incoordination in the kitchen.

Safety and Convenience

The most pressing issue for someone with incoordination in the bathroom is safety. Positions which foster better motor control such as sitting may help an individual gain control over their muscles.

When the use of both sides of the body at the same time is compromised, adaptive equipment that stabilizes objects may be extremely helpful. Items such as a suction denture or nail brush allow for independence with the use of one arm and hand.

Tremors or incoordination may result from fatigued muscles so energy conservation and work simplification techniques discussed earlier would again be essential. Individuals with incoordination may find an increase in ability when provided with a different handle (i.e., built-up, weighted, or curved) or a universal cuff to attain items they would otherwise have to do without.

Assistive technology that eliminates and simplifies steps such as faucets with preset water temperatures on the shower will help provide independence for a person with incoordination.

STRENGTH

Strength is the ability of a muscle or a muscle group to produce or resist a physical force. This concept is often mixed up with **endurance, which is the ability to continue an activity despite increasing physical or psychological stress.**

It is true however that weaker muscles tend to have decreased endurance. Conditions in which muscle strength is impacted may include: Multiple Sclerosis, Spinal Cord Injury, Muscular Dystrophy, and Cerebral Vascular Accident (stroke). Other conditions such as those related to cardiac (heart) and pulmonary (lung) conditions (e.g. heart arrhythmias and Congestive Obstructive Pulmonary Disease - C.O.P.D.), depression and pain can result in decreased endurance versus loss of muscle strength.

Strength Solutions

In terms of functional outcome, it does not matter if the issue is strength, endurance or both. The key is for the individual to learn how to pace themself so energy can be devoted to those components of activities determined to be essential. In addition to pacing,

energy conservation and work simplification techniques should be employed.

Adaptive equipment is available to reduce energy drains and allow that person to redirect their effort for the best result - independence.

For kitchens, small work triangles, reducing steps, along with group preparation and work areas which feature easily reached kitchen utensils and storage will assist an individual who may have physical strength impairments.

SENSATION

Sensation is the ability by which stimuli are perceived and conditions outside and within the body are distinguished and evaluated. Sensation requires one to be able to take in stimuli, process it (by itself as well as with other input) and then respond appropriately. The processing of sensory information and a person's response to it will be discussed in more detail in the next section on perception and cognition.

Consider all the Senses

When looking at sensory stimuli and processing in a bathroom, there is not one sensory input which can be excluded.

We need to be able to see, hear, feel, taste, smell and know our position in that environment. If any of these are compromised due to injury or illness, compensatory strategies and environmental modifications can allow for functional independence.

Design Solutions

Sensory losses such as impaired vision can be accommodated for by the use of enlarged visual cues (e.g. colors on faucets) or Braille.

Diminished touch needs to be closely assessed by a trained professional to determine the extent of the impairment. *For example,* the loss of ability to determine hot and cold can be devastating for someone as she may not realize the water is too hot until after the fact. Sensory retraining to help people learn to use other senses to compensate for the loss of a particular sense can make the difference between independence and devastation. The case in point would be to train the person with diminished hot/cold to rely on vision to a far greater extent especially when adjusting water temperature for bathing.

In addition, a person may have diminished (light or depth) sensory pressure which functionally may translate to not feeling a severe cut. In this instance, the cut would go unattended after shaving. We see this type of sensory loss in the feet and possibly the hands of diabetics. The result can be a devastating infection.

Impaired sensation may result in many issues pertinent to kitchen and bathroom skills; however, compensatory techniques to assist the person in using other cues from their body or the environment have proven to be very useful and improve safety consciousness. When there is reduced sensation, mirrors to check difficult to see areas can be of greater help in preventing other problems such as skin breakdown or infections.

PERCEPTION/COGNITION

Perception and cognition are easily defined; however, their boundaries are nebulous.

Perception can be viewed as the conscious recognition and interpretation of sensory stimuli through unconscious associations.

On the other hand, **cognition can be seen as the mental process characterized by knowing, thinking, learning, and judging.**

In simplistic terms, we take information in from the environment and about ourselves through our senses. This information is then processed and associated with other information so we form our own perceptions. These perceptions are part of the formation of our knowledge base which is what we use to think, learn and judge our world and ourselves. How many times have you seen three or four different people call the same color tile by three or four different names: blue, green, aqua or teal. Each person, based on their color perception and knowledge of color labels will argue his or her answer as being correct.

Perceptual and cognitive dysfunction can be seen as the result of some type of injury or change to the brain. Traumatic brain injury, cerebral vascular accident and brain tumor are a few of the possible diagnoses which can cause problems in this area of function.

Perception Types

The area of perception can be divided by type of sensory input. *For example*, perception may include:

• visual,

• auditory,

• tactile, etc.

Each of these can then be subdivided into more specific areas. Visual perception can include:

• figure-ground (the ability to distinguish foreground from background)

• depth perception (ability to determine how far away one object is as compared to another)

• visual memory (the ability to remember what you have seen)

• visual sequential memory (the ability to remember a visual sequence)

• visual closure (the ability to see the whole from parts of the whole)

• spatial relationships (the ability to see an object orientation in space), etc., etc.

A similar type of subdivision can be made for each area of perception as well as the complex addition of a motor or movement response, i.e. visual-motor integration.

Understanding Perception Problems

A person with figure-ground perception problems might have difficulty finding a brush or a comb in a drawer full of brushes or combs. An organizer of some type may help the person scan and find the particular object more easily.

Color choice and use of contrasting materials can play an integral part in relieving this type of perceptual issue throughout the bathroom space without compromising beauty and design.

Cognition

Cognition is a complex component to function as it includes:

- attention
- memory (short and long term)
- planning
- organization
- problem solving
- decision making
- judgment

Most individuals who would be using a bathroom independently may have minimal cognitive dysfunction. Attention, memory loss or confusion related to multi-step tasks are the areas which can be most easily addressed by a kitchen or bathroom designer/Occupational Therapist team.

- Environmental devices such as dual cues (i.e. blinking light and soft bell) will serve to keep a person focused.
- Single function controls on faucets would be another consideration.

Cognitive concerns can have a strong impact on safety. A trained health care professional can assess the level to which a person can function independently and safely.

ADAPTATIONS AND MODIFICATIONS

There are many adaptive kitchen and bathroom devices available commercially. The market has seen tremendous growth in both high and low tech solutions available for institutional and residential applications.

Care needs to be given to choices made recognizing beauty, design and function. The key to success is listening to and observing the client. Selection must be matched not only to the desired function, but to the specific abilities of the individual.

Consideration of other variables such as prognosis (whether a particular injury or disability will get better, stay the same or get worse), current and future roles and responsibilities (i.e. care for others, career) and personal motivation for use of the space in question (a person who wants or is ready to be independent versus one who is not motivated at a given point in time).

Many adaptations are not commercially available. These need to be fabricated by the team of client, family, bathroom designer, Occupational Therapist, and sometimes a rehab engineer.

chapter 18

The

Client

In any designer/client relationship, understanding the client and establishing mutual respect is critical to the success of a kitchen or bathroom design project. This need for trust is even more important when the client has a disability that limits his or her opportunities to collect information about the project.

- You must speak comfortably to the client.

- You must establish what the client needs and wants and whether or not you can meet those requirements.

APPROACHING THE CLIENT

This chapter presents information to better enable you to show respect and collect information to confirm and solidify the relationship when the client has a disability.

A respectful approach to the client with a disability requires observance of certain etiquette and attitudes.

- People with disabilities need to be recognized as people first, in thought and words.
- They don't wish to be thought of as sick or as objects of pity or even admiration.
- Also, politically correct euphemisms like "*the vertically challenged*" or "*differently abled*" are not popular.
- Avoid negative terms like "*confined to a wheelchair*".

In other words, positive references and direct honest conversation works best.

The following conversational guidelines and examples will help. If you aren't sure how to refer to a disability, ask your client. If you feel you have spoken out of turn, acknowledge it and apologize.

Attitude	Negative	Positive
• Avoid negative description	afflicted with polio	person who has had polio
	crippled with arthritis	person with arthritis
	confined to a wheelchair	person who uses a wheelchair, or a wheelchair user
	victim of M.S.	person who has M.S.
	Disabled and Normal people	people with disabilities and people without disabilities
• Put people first and avoid grouping	the disabled	people with disabilities
	the blind	people with blindness or visual impairments
	the deaf	people with deafness or hearing impairments
• Emphasize abilities, not limitations	confined to a wheelchair	uses a wheelchair
	can't climb stairs	stairs are an obstacle or a barrier
• Use appropriate terminology for specific disabilities	the blind	boy who is blind, girl who has low vision, man who is visually impaired
	birth defect	congenital disability
	the deaf	person who is hearing-impaired
	crippled	person with mobility impairment

CONVERSATION GUIDELINES

These guidelines for conversation with a client who has a disability are universally appropriate.

- Position yourself to speak at eye level.
- Respect your client's privacy. You need to know certain things to better serve her, but it is her decision what she chooses to share with you.
- Respect the client's assistive devices and don't interfere with his use of them.
- Ask specific questions about the client's needs and abilities as outlined in **NKBA's Universal Design Survey**.

- Listen and record what is said. Remember that while you may have more awareness of design options, your clients have the awareness of their needs.

There is a tendency to get caught up in terminology. These guidelines are intended to help you avoid that.

If you focus on the person and not the disability, you will most likely have positive results.

THE CLIENT SURVEY

The client survey included on the following pages is expanded from the NKBA Business Management forms to incorporate appropriate questions regarding disabilities. It is a checklist from which you will determine the questions to ask your client. From time to time, you will find the need to customize this survey to fit various projects.

A Helpful Hint

An occupational or physical therapist or a doctor who works with your client will have an understanding of your client's present and expected future abilities that you as a kitchen or bathroom designer probably don't have. If your client agrees, include these profession-als in completing the survey and collecting in-formation.

Set up a home consultation or a confer-ence call to provide the opportunity for input from the therapist, or visit the rehabilitation center with your client.

The ideal teaming of a kitchen or bath-room designer with an occupational therapist and perhaps a rehab engineer can truly make a difference in the success of a project.

Form #4025

UNIVERSAL KITCHEN PLANNING CLIENT SURVEY

NATIONAL KITCHEN NKBA & BATH ASSOCIATION ®

Name: _____ Date: _____

Address: _____

City, State, Zip: _____

Phone:_____ Work: _____

Jobsite Address:_____

City, State, Zip: _____

Directions:_____

_____

Appointment: _____

Date:_____ Address: _____

Time:_____ City/State/Zip:_____

Comment: _____ Phone:_____

_____

Allied Professional: _____

_____

_____

Pertinent Information: _____

_____

_____

_____

SAMPLE

I. THE CLIENT - PHYSICAL PROFILE

Sight: _____

Do you wear glasses for reading? _____ for distance? _____

Any visual impairments that influence the type/amount of lighting needed? _____

Hearing: _____

What issues regarding your ability to hear will affect the design process? _____

Tactile/Touch: _____

Can you feel hot and cold? _____

Taste/Smell: _____

Do you know of any change in your sense of taste? _____ smell? _____

Strength & Function: _____

What can you lift? _____ carry? _____

Do you have more strength on one side than the other? _____

Do you use both hands fully? _____ palms only? _____

How is your grip? _____ Left Side? _____ Right Side? _____

How is your balance? _____ Standing? _____ Bending? _____

Areas of Physical Limitation: _____

Does your mobility or balance vary by time of day? _____

Is there an assistant who helps sometimes? _____ All the time? _____

What adaptive equipment do you use? _____

Weight? _____ Height? _____

Prognosis: (Is condition stable? Is further deterioration anticipated? Is improvement anticipated?)

_____

Consultants: _____

Physician _____ telephone: _____

Occupational Therapist _____ telephone: _____

Comments from doctor and Occupational Therapist:

_____

_____

_____

Transfer Information: (Prefer right, left, or forward?)

_____

_____

Special Safety Concerns:

_____

_____

Reach and Grasp Profile:

Have your client position themselves as shown where applicable, fill in the appropriate reach/grasp measurements.

COUNTER DEPTH

DEGREES OF FLEXION

STANDARD SIGHT LINE

REACH
25"
(64cm)

OPTIMUM CONTROL HEIGHT

LOW REACH

LOWEST REACH

Reach and Grasp Range - Standing

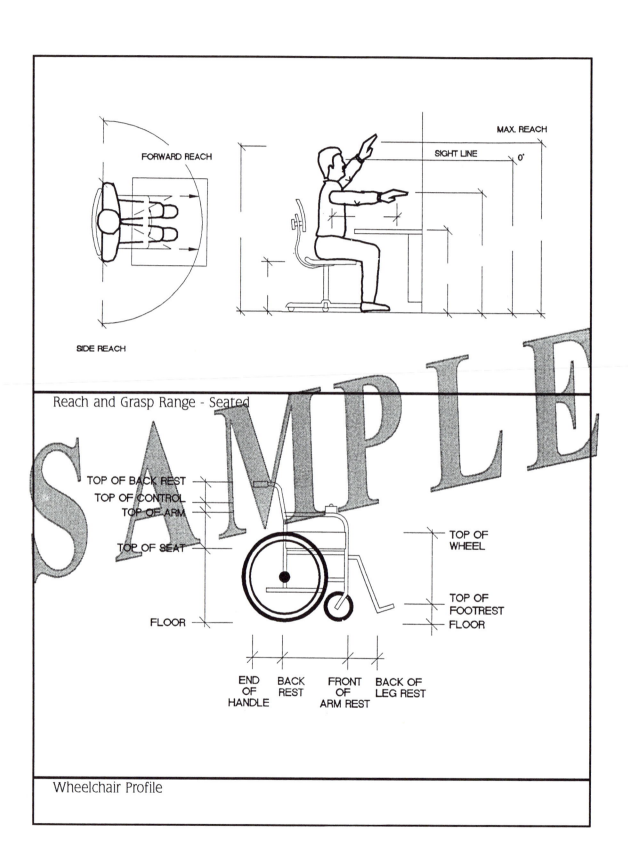

FORWARD REACH

SIDE REACH

MAX. REACH

SIGHT LINE

0°

Reach and Grasp Range - Seated

TOP OF BACK REST
TOP OF CONTROL
TOP OF ARM

TOP OF SEAT

FLOOR

TOP OF
WHEEL

TOP OF
FOOTREST
FLOOR

END
OF
HANDLE

BACK
REST

FRONT
OF
ARM REST

BACK OF
LEG REST

Wheelchair Profile

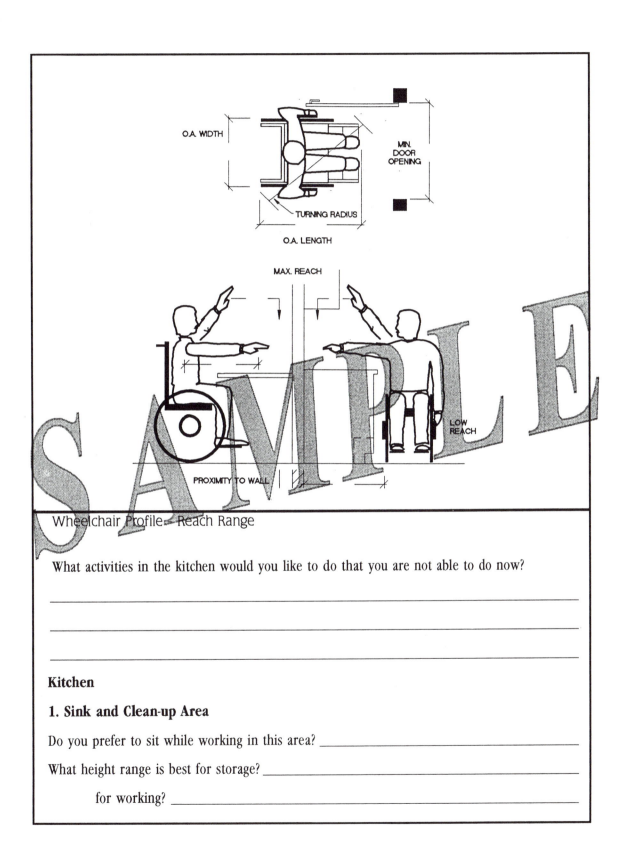

Wheelchair Profile - Reach Range

What activities in the kitchen would you like to do that you are not able to do now?

_____

_____

_____

Kitchen

1. Sink and Clean-up Area

Do you prefer to sit while working in this area? _____

What height range is best for storage? _____

      for working? _____

Is the present height and depth of the sink comfortable for you? _____

   present height _____ preferred height _____

Does the present faucet operate easily for you? _____

   preferred location & style _____

Is the present dishwasher located so that you can use it easily? _____

Do you wish a knee space at the sink area? _____

_____

_____

2. Cooking Area

Cooktop - Can the controls be safely & easily reached? _____

   read? _____ used? _____

Can all burners be safely used & reached? _____

Is the present height comfortable for you? _____

   present height _____ preferred height _____

Oven - Can the controls be safely and easily reached? _____

   read? _____ used? _____

Is the present height comfortable for you? _____

   present height _____ preferred height _____

Is there a safe way to transfer hot items out of the oven? _____

Microwave - Can the controls be safely and easily reached? _____

   read? _____ used? _____

Is the present height comfortable for you? _____

   present height _____ preferred height _____

Knee Space - Is there clear knee space near the appliances? _____

At which appliances do you most need knee space? oven _____ cooktop _____

   microwave _____

3. Refrigerator/Freezer

Is most of the refrigerator space usable? _____

Is the freezer usable? _____

Can you easily open and close the doors? _____

Do you wish ice/water on the door? _____

4. Storage	**presently**	**preferred**
Where do you store?		
Food_____		
Tableware _____		
Pots & Pans _____		
Mix/Measure equipment ____		
Small appliances _____		
coffeemaker _____		
blender _____		
food processor _____		
juicer _____		
toaster _____		
can opener _____		
mixer _____		
other _____		
Waste _____		
Laundry _____		

Is your existing hardware easy to use? _____

     present style _____preferred _____

Current cabinet accessories _____

Desired cabinet accessories_____

5. Counter and Table Heights

current height _____ preferred height _____

Is there enough work space near each of the appliance work centers? _____

At which areas would you most like knee space?_____

_____

6. Lighting, contrast, and ventilation

Is there enough lighting for cooking?_____for cleaning? _____

for food preparation? _____for general illumination? _____

What problems do you have currently with lighting and contrast in the kitchen? _____

_____

Is the ventilation adequate? _____

Can you safely and easily reach vent controls? _____

7. Controls

Is the current height safe and easy to use? _____

current height_____ preferred height_____

Outlets _____

Electric Switches _____

8. Moving Around

Is there room to move safely and easily around the kitchen? _____

Where would you most like to see more access? _____

9. Safety Features

_____

_____

10. Any other concerns

_____

_____

_____

Form #4025

UNIVERSAL BATHROOM PLANNING CLIENT SURVEY

Name: _____ Date: _____

Address: _____

City, State, Zip: _____

Phone: _____ Work: _____

Jobsite Address: _____

City, State, Zip: _____

Directions: _____

_____

Appointment: _____

Date: _____ Address: _____

Time: _____ City/State/Zip: _____

Phone: _____ Comment: _____

_____

Allied Professional: _____

_____

_____

Pertinent Information: _____

I. THE CLIENT - PHYSICAL PROFILE

Sight:

Do you wear glasses for reading? _____ for distance? _____

Any visual impairments that influence the type/amount of lighting needed? _____

Are you taking any medications that affect your sight? _____

Hearing:

What issues regarding your ability to hear will affect the design process?_____

Tactile/Touch:

Can you feel hot and cold?_____ texture?_____

Taste/Smell:

Do you know of any change in your sense of taste? ____ smell? _____

Strength & Function:

What can you lift? _____carry? _____

Do you have more strength on one side than the other? _____

Do you use both hands fully?_____ palms only?_____

How is your grip?_____Left Side? _____ Right Side? _____

How is your balance? _____Standing? _____ Bending? _____

Areas of Physical Limitation:

Does your mobility or balance vary by time of day? _____

Is there an assistant who helps sometimes? _____ All the time? _____

What adaptive equipment do you use?_____

Weight?_____Height?_____

Prognosis: (Is condition stable? Is further deterioration anticipated? Is improvement anticipated?)

Consultants:

Physician _____ telephone:_____

Occupational Therapist _____ telephone:_____

Comments from Physician and Occupational Therapist:

_____

Transfer Information: (Prefer right, left, or forward?)

_____

Special Safety Concerns:

_____

Reach and Grasp Profile:

Have your client position themselves as shown where applicable, fill in the appropriate reach/grasp measurements.

COUNTER DEPTH

DEGREES OF FLEXION

STANDARD SIGHT LINE

REACH

OPTIMUM CONTROL HEIGHT

LOW REACH

LOWEST REACH

Reach and Grasp Range - Standing

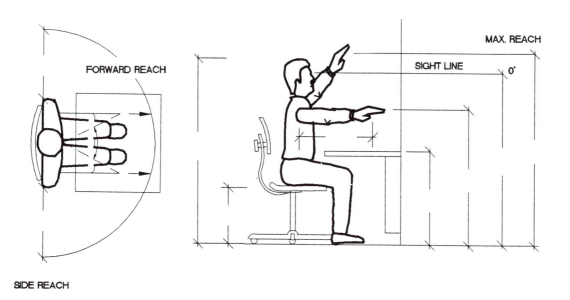

FORWARD REACH

MAX. REACH

SIGHT LINE

0°

SIDE REACH

Reach and Grasp Range - Seated

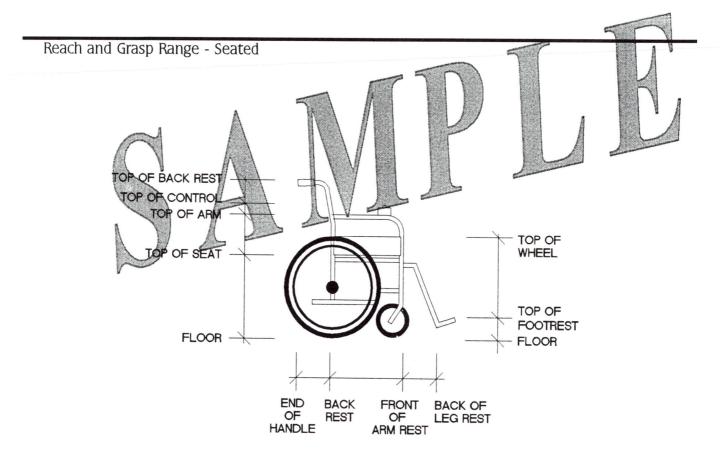

TOP OF BACK REST

TOP OF CONTROL

TOP OF ARM

TOP OF SEAT

TOP OF WHEEL

TOP OF FOOTREST

FLOOR

FLOOR

END OF HANDLE

BACK REST

FRONT OF ARM REST

BACK OF LEG REST

Wheelchair Profile

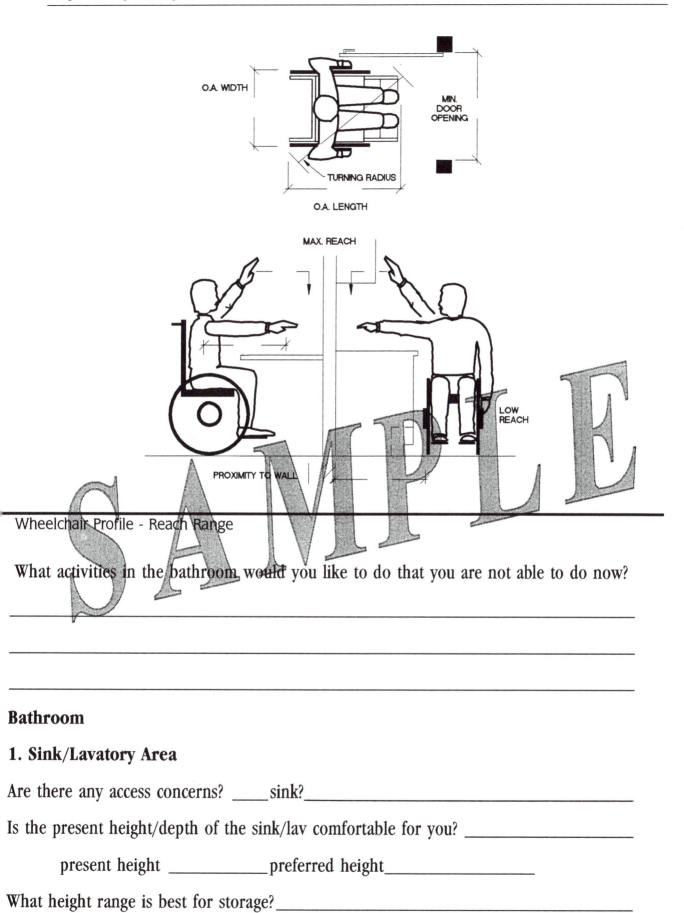

Wheelchair Profile - Reach Range

What activities in the bathroom would you like to do that you are not able to do now?

_____

_____

_____

Bathroom

1. Sink/Lavatory Area

Are there any access concerns? _____ sink?_____

Is the present height/depth of the sink/lav comfortable for you? _____

      present height _____ preferred height_____

What height range is best for storage?_____

Is there a need for open space below the sink and vanity? _____

_____

Does the present faucet operate easily for you?_____

     preferred location & style _____

Do you wish a knee space at the sink/lav area? _____

Comments/Concerns _____

_____

2. Bathtub/Shower Area

Do you prefer a bath? _____ or shower? _____

Is your bathtub easy and safe to get into and use? _____

Is there a bathtub/shower seat? _____ should one be included in the plan_____

Is there a hand-held spray? _____ should one be included in the plan_____

Can the controls be reached from both a sitting and standing position?_____

Are the controls easy to use? _____

     present style and location _____

     preferred style and location_____

Is the bathtub/shower floor non-slip? _____

How will you approach/transfer to the bathtub/shower? _____

_____

_____

Comments/Concerns_____

_____

3. Toilet Area

Is the present toilet at a height that is safe and comfortable for your approach/transfer?

_____

Do you prefer a standard height toilet or a raised height toilet?_____

Will you use an elevated seat? _____

What height must the seat be? _____

Present clearances

     left _____

     right _____

     front _____

Preferred clearances

     left _____

     right _____

     front _____

TOILET			
# A	B	C	D
1			
2			
3			
4			

Is the toilet paper dispenser within your reach? _____

     present location _____

     preferred location_____

Is the flush lever easily and safely used? _____

     present location _____

     preferred location_____

4. Support System

Where do you need grab bars in the toilet area?_____

_____

Where do you need grab bars at the bathtub/shower? _____

_____

Do you need any other grab bars or railings? _____

5. Storage

Is there adequate storage within your reach?_____

_____

Are the medicine cabinet and shelves within your reach? _____

_____

Are the storage areas safely and easily opened? _____

_____

For what items do you need storage? _____

_____

Any unusual sized items? _____

_____

Do you have any supportive or hygiene equipment that requires storage? (list items and

dimensions) _____

_____

6. Counter Heights

current height_____ preferred height _____

Is there enough work space? _____ knee space?_____

7. Accessories and Controls

Are towel racks easily and safely used? _____

_____

Are towel racks likely to be used as grab bars? _____

_____

Are the light/fan switches easy to use? _____

present height and style_____

preferred height and style _____

Are the electrical outlets GFCI?_____

Are outlet locations safe and easy to use? _____

    present height _____

    preferred height _____

8. Moving Around

What problems exist in entering and moving around in the bathroom? _____

_____

What style door do you prefer? pocket _____ hinge_____other _____

What is your door swing preference? (check clear floor space outside door) _____

Where would you like the door handle located? _____

9. Lighting and Ventilation

Is there enough lighting

    for bathing _____

    in the lav/mirror area _____

    in the toilet area _____

    for general illumination _____

Is the bathroom well ventilated? _____

10. Other Concerns/Comments

Is there a safe and easy exit in case of fire? _____

Are the windows operable? _____

Comments _____

_____

c h a p t e r *19*

Marketing Universal Design Services

Given that universal design needs to be part of all good kitchen and bathroom design, designers with these skills should market them as part of the expertise that they bring to the drawing board.

Just as a thorough understanding of fixtures and equipment or spatial considerations is part of your background, universal design should become part of your knowledge base as well.

It is important to understand that this is not design that is different for people who are different, but design that is expanded to better serve a more diverse target clientele.

In a given advertising or promotional campaign, you might choose to emphasize universal design skills. When doing so, traditional marketing concepts apply, with the target possibly changing or broadening. Also, certain marketing strategies may be emphasized more.

APPLYING MARKETING SOLUTIONS

STEP 1 - Identify Target Market

Applying general marketing solutions to universal design - the first step is to identify the target. In addition to your standard business target, you may wish to focus marketing efforts on people with specific disabilities or people who are middle-aged or older or people with young children. Keep in mind that universal design skills benefit everyone, so while you may focus on one group in one marketing effort, you will want to remember the others.

For example, universal design concepts make independent living more possible for people who are older, but these same benefits apply to people in the so-called prime of life, for their parents, for their own future and for their children, allowing the bathroom to work better and safer for more of the people in it.

People who benefit directly from universal design are part of your market already. The key may be to more thoroughly identify with the universal design aspects of your client's needs. In addition to your usual avenues for marketing, you may reach this population through hospitals and rehabilitation centers, home-health care equipment stores, independent living centers and advocacy groups focusing on a particular aspect of aging or disability. Other contacts include lawyers and real estate agents.

STEP 2 - *Understand Your Target*

The next traditional marketing step is to understand your target in terms of motivation, priorities and buying trends. Usually, this can be done through NKBA market research, trade publications or consumer news.

You will want to expand your sources to research and publications that deal with the specific target. These might be special interest groups like the **American Association for Retired Persons (AARP)** or local and national magazines and newsletters or papers that target your same clientele.

NETWORKING

Even more than with traditional kitchen and bathroom design, networking is a key aspect of marketing universal design services and design for people with specific disabilities. The greatest single source of business is referral from past clients or from other professionals.

If a person's occupational therapist or a friend or family member with a similar disability refers the person to you, there is a confidence or trust initiated.

TEAM APPROACH

A team approach may be the key to expanding your penetration to this market and to the total success of each project. Beyond the familiar allied professionals, consider medical people, particularly occupational and physical therapists and rehabilitation engineers who are experts in adaptive devices and assistive technology. They will add to your credibility, expand the information available to you and open new avenues for networking.

To help you understand the nature of the role an occupational and physical therapist plays in the life of your clients, a description is listed for you here. These non-traditional, allied professionals are among new resources you can use.

OCCUPATIONAL THERAPISTS

Occupational therapists help individuals with mentally, physically, developmentally or emotionally disabling conditions to develop, recover or maintain daily living and work skills. They not only help patients improve basic motor functions and reasoning abilities, but also compensate for permanent loss of function.

Their goal is to help patients have independent, productive and satisfying lifestyles.

Occupational therapists use activities of all kinds ranging from using a computer to caring for daily needs, such as dressing, cooking and eating.

For those with permanent functional disabilities, such as spinal cord injuries, cerebral palsy or muscular dystrophy, therapists provide such adaptive equipment as wheelchairs, splints and aids for eating and dressing. They also design or make special equipment needed at home or at work.

Therapists develop and teach patients to operate computer-aided adaptive equipment, such as microprocessing devices that permit individuals with severe limitations to communicate, walk, operate telephones and television sets and control other aspects of their environment.

PHYSICAL THERAPISTS

Physical therapists improve the mobility, relieve the pain and prevent or limit the permanent physical disabilities of patients suffering from injuries or disease. Their patients include accident victims and disabled individuals with conditions such as multiple sclerosis, cerebral palsy, nerve injuries, burns, amputations, head injuries, fractures, low back pain, arthritis and heart disease.

Therapists evaluate a patient's medical history; test and measure their strength, range of motion and ability to function; and develop written treatment plans. These plans, which may be based on physician's orders, describe the treatments to be provided, their purpose and their anticipated outcomes. As treatment continues, they document progress, conduct periodic re-evaluations and modify treatments, if necessary.

THE NETWORKING CONCEPT

Professional networking can take place through professional and community involvement. Attending, participating and speaking at NKBA events, speaking to rehabilitation centers, visiting nursing associations or independent living centers, or participating in local advocacy and support groups are a few examples. These activities will give you contacts and information and allow you to promote yourself and get a clear picture of the group you are serving.

STEP 3 - Focused Advertising

The last step in the marketing process is to reach your target through focused promotions. You can write articles for newsletters or write your own newsletter and send it to past clients and professional contacts. Sometimes the advertising budget favors spending time instead of money, so speak to and write to these groups.

Maintain a mailing list and follow up on your contacts. Keep in mind that repeat business is more common in clients with disabilities or clients who are aging.

Remember that universal design skills will not only enable you to better meet the needs of a client with a particular disability, these skills will also enable you to design a kitchen or bathroom that is safe and accessible to all people. Use and sell these skills with your entire target market as one aspect of what makes your kitchen or bathroom design services superior.

POST OCCUPANCY EVALUATIONS

One way to become better at what you do is through the **Post Occupancy Evaluation.**

Many firms conduct Post Occupancy Evaluations in an effort to broaden not only their own knowledge of design, but to expand their marketing potential. A Post Occupancy Evaluation is simply a way to evaluate whether or not your design solution actually solved your client's problems.

A systematic evaluation of your completed projects can tell you things you never imagined and prepare you for the next job you do.

Conduct the Post Occupancy Evaluation four to nine months after the client begins using the room on a full-time basis. This allows time for the client to use the storage, fixtures and equipment and for the room and the design concepts to be experienced under the demands of various usage.

USING THE DESIGN SURVEY

The Post Occupancy Evaluation is performed in person using the design survey you used to obtain the design criteria when you began the project. However, it is a good idea to plan for the Post Occupancy Evaluation at the time you close the sales portion of the job. Explain what you would like to do, why you are doing it and why the clients' participation will be important.

With the original design survey in front of both you and the client, read through the survey and re-direct the questions to your client. Client comments should be tape recorded (ask permission first) or recorded through note taking. This exercise will allow you and your client to re-examine the success of the project. You should add some additional questions that are unique to the job and that will assist you the next time you design a similar project. These particular questions should address design features and the products used. *Did they like the special-height cabinets? Or the universally accessible features?*

Be sure to pay particular attention to what the clients say with regard to doing something differently if they could do it over again. Whenever possible, include all of the family members who use the space.

LEARNING THE IMPACT OF YOUR DESIGN

During the Post Occupancy Evaluation process, you will receive information on the design, the products used and your clients' reaction to their new space. There is no better way to learn how your work impacts people's lives. You will learn if your design solved the problem and obtain qualitative information on specific products and features you find yourself using on a regular (or not-so-regular) basis. You'll be able to document user acceptance of design guidelines, colors, lighting techniques, new equipment and materials and more. If they had to choose those products or that design feature again, would they? This is what you really want to know. This information will be most valuable the next time a client wishes to use that product or incorporate that design element. Your professionalism will be perceived as a real asset to a client through the decision-making process.

Through Post Occupancy Evaluations, design firms that market themselves as service-oriented companies can expand their professional expertise while gaining important marketing information. By using Post Occupancy Evaluations in the planning process, you can justify your thought process through previous project documentation and experience. When information is documented, it instantly becomes credible. It is logical; it can be verified by others; and it is extremely difficult to dispel. Such experiences can yield rewards that advertising could never accomplish. Post Occupancy Evaluations will expand your expertise, involve your clients in the process and create repeat business for the future.

Over time, complete marketing strategies will become evident based on the types of work that you perform. You will be amazed at the uses for this information as you plan spaces and become known as the firm who specializes in service.

a p p e n d i x 1

Universal Kitchen Design Checklist

GENERAL KITCHEN DESIGNER TIPS

☐ Concentrate the work triangle, limit needless steps.

☐ Consider clear floor space and traffic flow when planning island or peninsula.

☐ Use "*easily accessed*" storage of all supplies and utensils.

☐ Use non-glare finishes, especially for older eyes.

☐ Provide good, adaptable and adjustable lighting throughout the space to make area comfortable for younger and older eyes.

☐ Use lower wall cabinets or pull down storage to bring more storage into the 15" - 48" (38cm - 122cm) universal reach range.

☐ Choose lighter colors on cabinets, counters, floors and wall coverings to benefit eyes that are aging or impaired.

☐ Plan lower windows to allow more people to see outside, including children and people using wheelchairs.

☐ Plan pull-out work counters placed at lower than 36" (91cm) counter height to accommodate people who are shorter or who sit to work.

☐ Choose non-skid floors - check slip resistance rating.

☐ Designing contrasting or raised countertop edges to cue people with visual impairments.

☐ Remove cabinet doors to make access easier.

☐ Use tambour units to other appliances garages to put heavy objects at countertop height.

☐ Use full extension drawer glides for maximum accessibility.

☐ Use glare-free task lights.

☐ Design for long spans of continuous countertop to allow for sliding items on counter as opposed to having to carry them from center to center.

☐ Install timers to insure that any appliance that should not be running will be automatically shut off.

☐ Limit cabinet door sizes to 18" (46cm) and consider bi-fold doors to lessen interference with clear floorspace.

☐ Use tilt down fronts as an area to access switches or plugs that would otherwise be difficult to reach.

☐ Consider automatic doors that open and close based on a pressure pad and voice activated lights to free up hands.

☐ Place switches and outlets in the universal reach range of 15" - 48" (38cm - 122cm) above the finished floor.

☐ Consider touch latch cabinet doors to eliminate the need to grasp knobs or pulls.

☐ Use wire or architectural pull in lieu of knobs.

☐ Use adjustable (hydraulic) office type chair to create flexibility in the working height.

☐ Design a back or garage loading pantry and recycling center to eliminate the need to carry bulky items great distances.

☐ Design a recycling center that has bins that are easy to remove without great lifting.

☐ Use rolling carts to transport many items at one time.

☐ Install repairable counter surfaces.

☐ Use drawers in lieu of doors to make access easier.

☐ Install hot water dispenser within reach of seated or shorter use.

☐ Install standard cabinets at a lower height when feasible.

☐ Provide a variety of countertop heights: 30", 36" and 42" (76cm, 91cm, and 107cm) provide comfortable work surfaces for people of varied heights.

☐ Provide an easily-accessed step stool to reach upper cabinets. Models available with or without railings, for installation in the toe-kick, on the inside of cabinet doors, or collapsible for easy storage.

☐ Use shallow pantry cabinets or roll-out shelves to increase accessibility.

☐ Store heavy objects at the safest and most convenient height.

☐ Consider a built-in ironing board in base cabinet drawer for easy accessed use.

☐ Store dishes in wall cabinets placed on the floor with an added toekick to make access easy and convenient for everyone.

☐ Design projects so that they do not appear to be clinical.

☐ Keep appliance controls, outlets and switches at the front of base cabinetry or low enough to be reachable.

☐ Use levers or touch controls and avoid smooth round control knobs.

☐ Test a control to see if it can be operated with a closed fist.

☐ For greatest accuracy plan controls close to the body at elbow height.

☐ Suggest a vinyl jar opener or a vinyl knob cover to improve grip on knobs.

☐ Choose controls that do not require sustained holding.

☐ Be aware of simple assistive devices:

☐ A wall mounted holder to help open jar lids.

☐ A potato peeler with a clamp requires just one hand for use.

☐ Pan holders keep the pan from turning while stirring.

☐ A pan drainer allows one to drain off hot liquids with one hand.

☐ A gripper to add to silverware, small objects and handles.

☐ Select small appliances on a basis on weight, balance and control.

☐ Ask manufacturer for braille (overlays) on appliance controls.

☐ Keep guard rails around burners of gas and electric appliances.

☐ Try to choose switches and controls that are audible, large print and easy to read.

Sink/Clean Up Center Tips

☐ Consult with the manufacturer and when possible, raise the dishwasher up 6" to 16" (15cm to 41cm) for better access.

☐ Choose faucet handles that require minimum grip use. Crosshandles work, blade handles are better, and single lever, scald-control fittings are the most universal.

☐ Consider faucets with retractable heads, particularly in limited reach applications.

☐ Plan soap dispensers for easier access, requiring less movement and less hand strength and coordination.

☐ Mount soap dispensers, instant hot water dispensers and faucets on the side for easier reach.

☐ If area under sink is left open for wheelchair and seated access: insulate water pipes and sink bottom to eliminate burns or cuts.

☐ Use rear drain location to provide maximum space in front.

☐ Position dishwasher to be used from either side, paying attention to clear floor space.

☐ Provide casters for trash unit to take to table, workspace or garage.

☐ Install integral or undermounted sink to aid in easy cleanup.

☐ Plan adaptable or flexible knee space at the sink to allow for occasional or future desire to sit while working.

☐ Use GFCI outlets.

☐ Consider automatic faucets that are activated by sensors with pre-set temperatures.

☐ Install pull-out accessories under sink for easy access.

☐ Choose sinks that allow the user to reach the bottom (maximum 6 1/2" depth (17cm) for seated or users of shorter stature).

☐ Use pop-up drains and sinks that feature work covers to aid in access.

Refrigeration/Preparation Center Tips

☐ Give preference to side-by-side refrigerators since they place both refrigerated and frozen sections at an easily accessible height.

☐ Consider quick access doors to eliminate having to open the unit entirely making it easier to access most used items.

☐ Choose ice'n'water dispensers in the door as they require less hand strength and coordination.

☐ Consider smaller refrigerators in raised positions, placing more storage in the universal reach range.

☐ Install a built-in jar opener for people with arthritis or less strength in their hands.

☐ Install plug strips at a convenient location to eliminate a potential long reach for those with limited mobility.

☐ Block out base cabinets and keep most used items during preparation in tambours at the back to create easy access.

☐ Vary work counter heights.

☐ Plan an open knee space or a lower pull-out work surface next to the refrigerator for seated users (does not work well with side by side).

☐ Use a model with 180° door swing for best access.

COOKING/RANGE/OVEN CENTER TIPS

☐ Consider electric ranges over gas for safety where a user has cognitive or physical disabilities.

☐ Consider side hinged oven doors for easier approach and access in some applications. However, a drop down oven provides its own shelf, it is is built to do so.

☐ Lower cooktop for children and people in wheelchairs.

☐ Install angled mirror above cooktop to aid in seeing contents of cooking vessels.

☐ Use cooktops that have staggered burners to eliminate the need to reach over a hot element.

☐ Consider turning two burner units sideways, placing all four burners parallel to the front edge.

☐ Eliminate the need to reach across hot elements by avoiding rear controls and choosing side or preferably front controls.

☐ Consider lock out covers or program lock out systems to prevent operating of cooking units unless a responsible cook is present.

☐ Use back lit range controls to make them easier to read.

☐ Consider installing a second switch in the front of the cabinet adjacent to the range to put the hood switch within the universal reach range.

☐ Install knobs that are at least 1 1/2" (4cm) in diameter for easy grasping, preferably with a lever design, or use touch pads.

☐ Use Braille control overlays or raised letter indicators that can be seen and felt.

☐ Use bright running lights so that people with visual impairments will notice that the ranger top is on.

☐ Mount ovens so that the bottom rack is close in height to adjacent transfer surface.

☐ Install a kill switch: a switch that would shut unit off if pot boils dry or is not properly set on burner.

☐ Consider magnetic induction, safe because no heat is used, and it shuts off if pan boils dry or is not properly set on element.

☐ Recommend lightweight cookware.

☐ Plan a heat resistant shelf under the oven to allow for easy transfer of hot pans from the oven.

☐ Plan heat resistant surfaces adjacent to cooking surfaces to cut down on the need to lift hot pots. a smooth cooking surface allows the cook to slide those pots onto adjacent heatproof surfaces.

CHECKLIST EXAMPLES

Through the courtesy of the Maytag company, the following sketches further demonstrate helpful universal design applications.

A swing-out stool under a sink can accommodate a person who needs to sit for short periods of time as well as be pushed away to make room for a wheelchair.

A multi-tiered counter offers comfortable countertop heights for all users. A side-mounted faucet at the sink allows for easier reach.

Raising the clothes dryer places the dryer door level with the washer lid, reducing back strain when loading and unloading.

An angled non-fog mirror installed above a cooking surface permits a seated user to see what's cooking. Retractable doors allow easy wheelchair access and close for a finished look when not in use.

A stacked washer and dryer right at home in the kitchen, is favored by mature consumers and anyone who desires to avoid lifting and bending. These units also save valuable floor space.

Electrical switches and outlets normally difficult to reach are mounted in the front of a tilt-down drawer concealed from curious children. A plug strip at a convenient location can serve the same purpose, shortening the long reach to the backsplash for those with limited mobility.

The proximity of the dishwasher and dish storage to the dining table provides step saving cleanup.

Windows can be lowered so that the entire family can enjoy the view.

appendix 2

Access Kitchens

As part of a research and training development project, the Access Kitchens were created by two teams of Certified Kitchen Designers.

THE DESIGN TEAM MEMBERS

The designers were given a space, a client profile and the assignment to create an accessible kitchen within those parameters. The teams were made up of the following Certified Kitchen Designers.

- Mary Jo Peterson, CKD, CBD Mary Jo Peterson Design Consultants, Brookfield, CT;

- Ken Smith, CKD, CBD, Denver, Colorado;

- Jim Krengel, CKD, CBD, Kitchens by Krengel, St. Paul, MN;

- Joy Piske, CKD, Winnipeg, MB, Canada

These two project descriptions and the resulting design solutions are featured here for your review. You will notice that not all of the NKBA® "40 Design Guidelines of Kitchen Planning" were met in every instance. It is important to remember that the guidelines are there for you as a designer to use as a "measurement" to assimilate a competency. It is not always possible to meet every guideline.

ACCESS PROJECT #1 - TOWNE KITCHEN

Client Profile

Gene and Audrey Towne are building an addition to include a new kitchen. They are in their late 60's and would like to plan this space so that they can stay in their home as they grow older.

Their home is on Long Island, in a small community where they can walk or use available elder-taxi service to maintain independence outside the home.

Their goal in this remodeling/addition project is to create a space that is adaptable to any physical changes they may experience so that they can choose to stay in their familiar surroundings and truly "*age in place*".

Physically right now, they both have sight and hearing changes typical of their age, Audrey has some arthritis, and they both have less stamina than they once had. It might be useful to incorporate a lower counter with a chair for seated work or to plan a space where a stool might be used when cooking food.

They stress that they are doing this project to extend their independence at home as much as they can.

Design Solution

This kitchen was designed to meet the needs of the Townes, allowing them to be independent for several more years to come and to meet the aesthetic requirements for all people. It is a space that allows the Townes to spend as much or as little time in the room as they desire, due to the fact that social issues as well as physical issues were addressed.

The pantry storage was incorporated into the kitchen because there was concern about future accessibility of such a space and the open plan requires fewer steps.

The door openings were both nicely sized and did not require any changes to them. The windows in the proposed eating area were just 18" (46cm) off the floor which we felt would provide not only a nice view but more light making it a pleasant space to be in all day long.

The kitchen designed is an "L-shaped" plan with an island, the most functional arrangements, requiring the least steps. The sink is located in the island since it allows Mrs. Towne to be able to be in both visual and verbal communication with her husband, whether he is at the island snack bar or the corner table. The raised bar further disguises any mess at the sink area for people seated at the kitchen table or in the dining room.

A reasonably good work triangle was created. The oven is a low work center, easily accessible from the dining room, as well as from the snack bar. A rolling cart under the lowered baking center allows for storage and a knee space if needed. The decision to provide two (2) microwaves was made easily. One was for the main cooking tasks and the other placed near the table would allow the Townes to re-heat something that had cooled at the table without having to get back up, and to cook some menu items in that kitchen area.

There is generous countertop work space throughout the kitchen. A large expanse of low work counter with a stool stored below it can aid Mrs. Towne. She is intrigued by the raised dishwasher and knows that it will be just the perfect solution for her arthritis and painful bending that sometimes occurs.

Walkways were not increased beyond the NKBA® standards since a wheelchair was not an issue. Further, because of the nice flow of this plan, it would still be easy for either partner in a wheelchair to access this space.

The corner hutch with upper glass doors is something that Mrs. Towne feels she will enjoy daily as she intends to display memorabilia of her children and grandchildren. The angled front was selected to allow traffic to flow smoothly as the years go by. The pantry/tall cabinets on the dining wall will provide all of the storage they will need. The shallow depth was selected since it will make access to tall items easier. The angles were selected to repeat the look in the kitchen as well as to aid traffic flow.

The desk/message center/entertainment center was really exciting to both of the Townes. Having a TV in the kitchen along with a compact stereo system will allow them to truly enjoy this space.

The kitchen was designed to accommodate the reduced strength that an older couple will experience. Handles have been selected instead of knobs. They have chosen a light finish cabinet at the suggestion of the designer to reflect more light back into the room without glare. A magnetic induction cooktop was chosen due to its many built in safety features such as automatic shutoff and the cool cooking surface. It is also easy to clean. The low work center near the oven features granite to allow transfer of hot items directly on the surface and there is a matching "*hotspot*" of granite near the cooktop inlaid into the solid surface countertop. Solid surface was chosen for its ease in maintenance and repair. The entire kitchen is outfitted with general, task and ambient lighting with great flexibility.

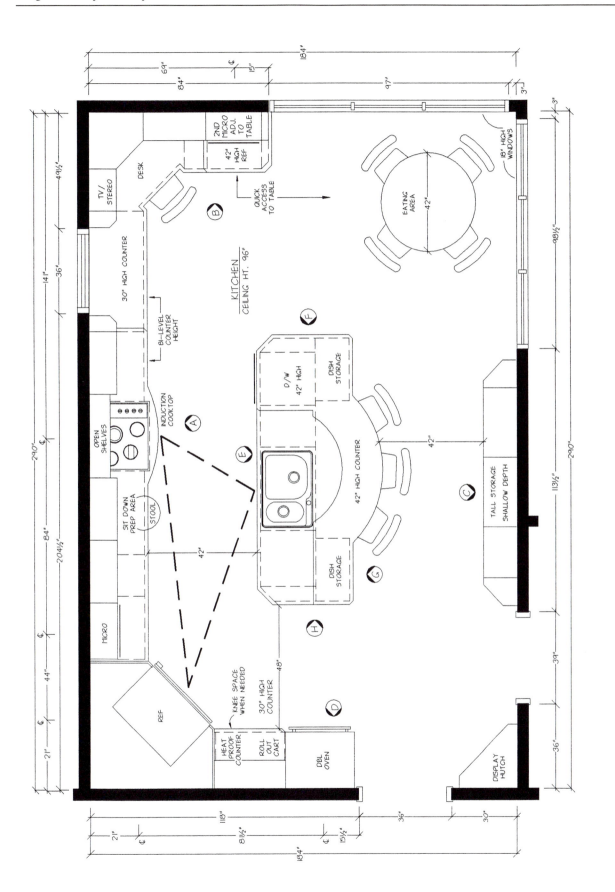

ACCESS PROJECT #1 - Towne Kitchen - Krengel/Piske, Designers.

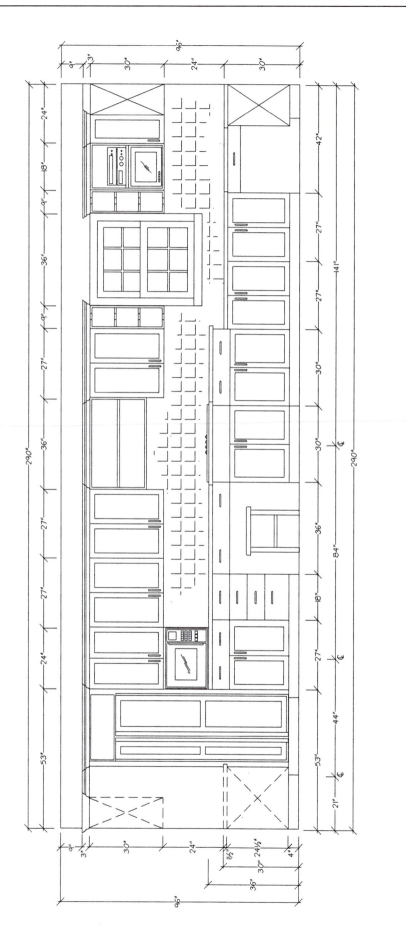

ACCESS PROJECT #1 - Towne Kitchen - Krengel/Piske, Designers.

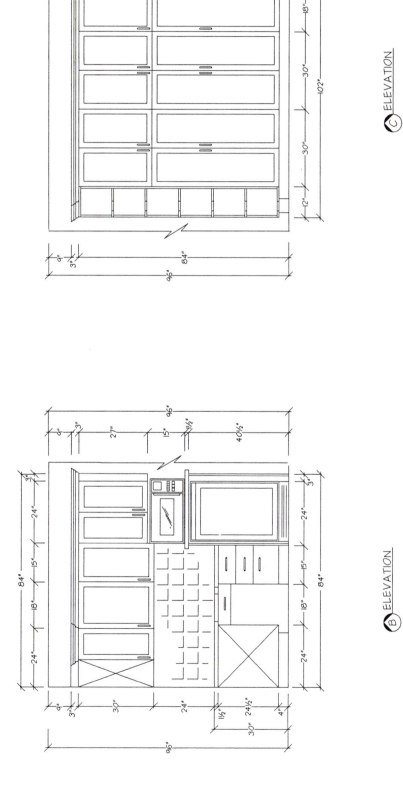

ACCESS PROJECT #1 - Towne Kitchen - Krengel/Piske, Designers.

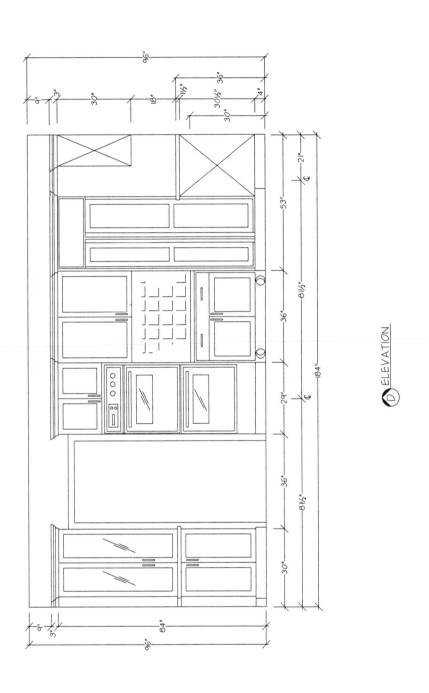

ELEVATION

D

ACCESS PROJECT #1 - Towne Kitchen - Krengel/Piske, Designers.

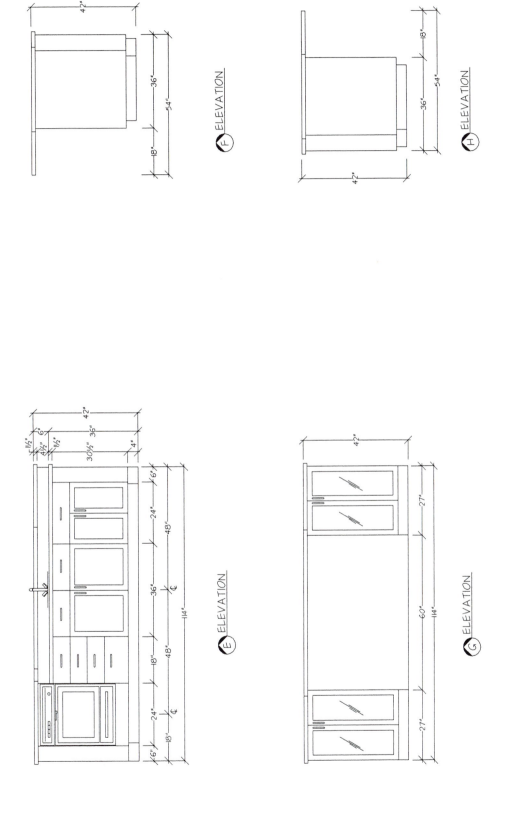

ACCESS PROJECT #1 - Towne Kitchen - Krengel/Piske, Designers.

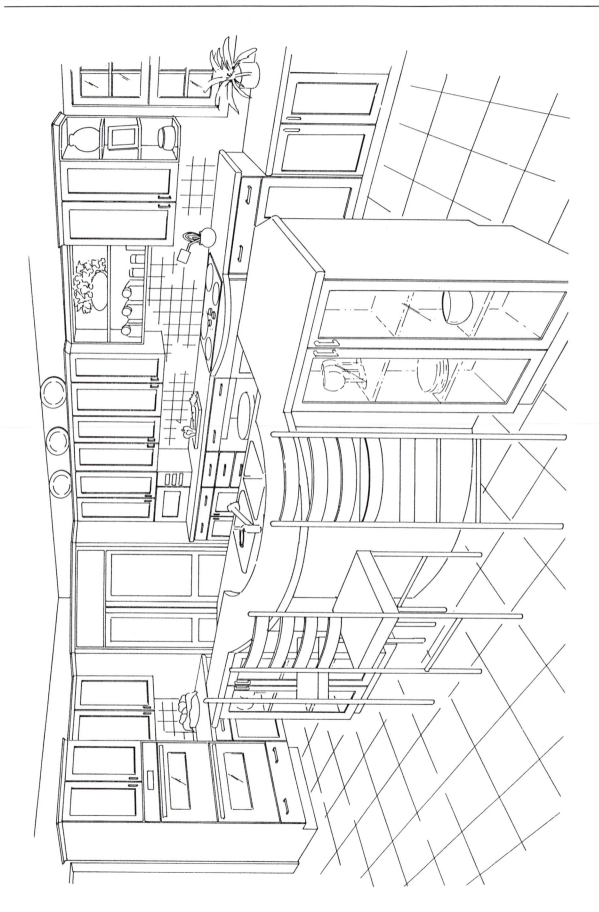

ACCESS PROJECT #1 - Towne Kitchen - Krengel/Piske, Designers.

ACCESS PROJECT #1 - Towne Kitchen - Krengel/Piske, Designers.

ACCESS PROJECT #2 - SAMPSON KITCHEN

Client Profile

Pat and Tom Sampson are ready to re-model their kitchen. They are in their late 50's and Pat's mother is coming to live with them. Given that they would like to stay in their home as they get older, and given that Pat's mother has some mobility-impairments, they wish to pay special attention to creating a space that will work for them for many years.

Aside from wearing glasses to read and having some arthritis, Pat and Tom are fully mobile and non-disabled. Pat's mother, Irene, uses a wheelchair to get around and is able to stand only long enough to transfer. She has limited sight, hearing and sense of smell, and is sometimes forgetful. She functions independently now and Pat and Tom would like their new kitchen to allow her to get around and do some of the family food preparation.

Pat enjoys cooking and it is important to her that in her kitchen, both work stations and storage will function for her present high use. In addition, she wishes to provide for her mother to assist her and to be able to do some food preparation on her own. As much as possible, Pat would like to make the space work well now and have key features that are either wheelchair accessible or easily adaptable should she find herself in a wheelchair. Pat and Tom would also like to consider their grandchildren as they plan, particularly the microwave oven for candy making that they do with their grandmother.

The walls and windows in the space will not change, but when asked, Pat and Tom agreed that the dining room door could be eliminated. The sink can be moved minimally. They wish to maintain their hall pantry, and their eating area.

Design Solution

With needs varying from grandchildren to a mother in a wheelchair, the Sampsons present a true challenge in universal planning and design. Pat is concerned that needed storage not be lost while at the same time wishes to provide for her mother to do at least some of the preparation and cooking. Considering these things and the fact that Pat and Tom also have some arthritis, the proposed plan is intended to be functional and adaptable to possible changing needs.

The work flow begins at the refrigerator, a side-by-side unit with ice and water in the door. This configuration allows for access within the universal range of 15" - 48" (38cm - 122cm) off the floor.

A model was chosen with pass thru handles as opposed to a continuous concealed pull as this allows for adding a gripping device if needed. Easy access to ice and water is a plus for everyone. Above the refrigerator, full depth cabinetry is accessorized with tray dividers for accessible storage. The counter and cabinetry have been increased in depth to allow for enclosing the refrigerator which is aesthetically pleasing. At the same time this provides extra depth for appliance storage at counter height which does not interfere with the work surface. Unnecessary gripping or lifting is eliminated as appliances may be used in place or slid forward for use. The base cabinet includes a pull out work surface at a lowered height for seated use. The corner base storage is generous and includes shelves that pull out and down to counter height. Completing the area are task lights mounted in the front under the wall cabinet.

Around the corner to the sink area, this cabinet is built with a removable face frame and doors and a decorative/protective panel houses the plumbing. If at some point seated use is desired at the sink the cabinet front can be removed to create a knee space. In the meantime this area houses recycling bins. The sink was chosen carefully to be 6 1/2" (17cm) deep and with rear drains to make the knee space optimum. To the right of the sink another work area is provided with a dishwasher and full extension drawer storage below and wall storage above, again with task lighting. The use of drawers in place of a door in the base cabinet eliminates one motion and the need to maneuver around a door.

Around the corner, the cooking area has been installed at a dropped height to allow for seated use. This section of the counter is granite to be heat proof allowing for sliding of pots off the cooktop and onto the counter - again minimal lifting. The cooktop is induction, safe and easy to use (cooktop automatically shuts off when pan is empty or not in use, controls are dual cued and high contrast). The downdraft system provides ventilation that can be controlled from a seated position.

Across from the main work triangle is a secondary work storage area. A pantry consists of deep drawers on full extension slides in the lower section and roll-outs in the upper section. A tall cabinet houses the microwave, installed so that the door drops down at 32" (81cm). The drop down door provides its own shelf. Adjacent is a lowered-height work area with a sink, rolling cart and knee space. Finally the oven is installed at 30" (76cm) off the floor, providing ease of transfer of hot items.

Overall the spread U-shape provides an open feeling that belies the space constraints. Clear floor spaces have been increased while maintaining storage.

Control and lighting in the room include task lighting (1 switch), over the sink lighting (1 switch), dining light (decorative fixture - dimmer switch) and general illumination (recessed lighting - dimmer switch). A master memory panel allows for pre-set adjustment of lighting. One master switch shuts off all power to the kitchen, except the refrigerator, as a safety check. Additional safety features include a fire extinguisher, mounted on the wall near the entry from the front foyer, a lock out feature on the dishwasher and oven, and a light that blinks when any appliance is in use beyond a certain set time.

Flooring is solid vinyl tile, providing easy care and some slip-resistance, with a contrasting border. Counters are light in color with a contrast front edge that blends with the granite areas and helps clarify the edge. The overall effect is a kitchen that is warm and friendly and flexible to work for a variety of cooks.

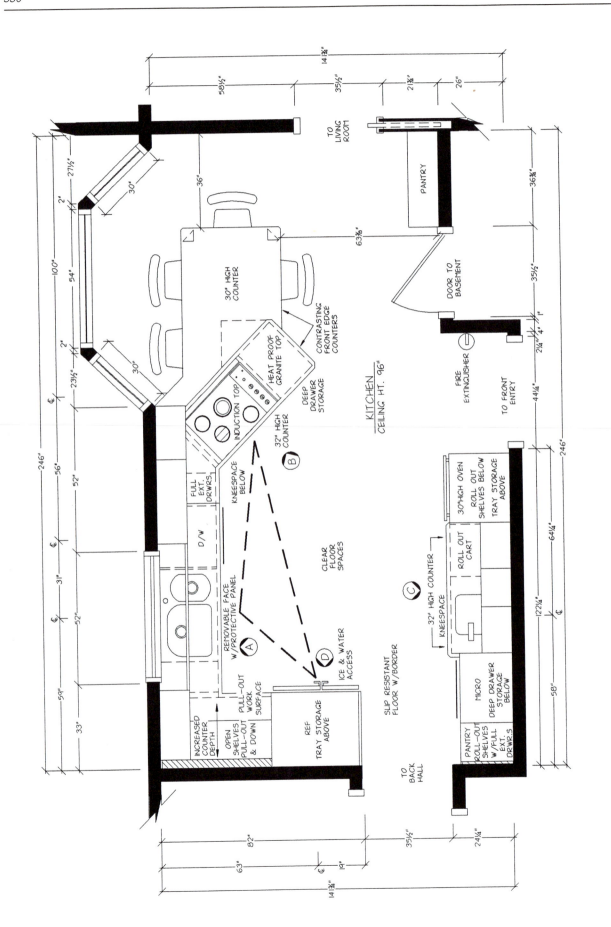

ACCESS PROJECT #2 - Sampson Kitchen - Peterson/Smith, Designers.

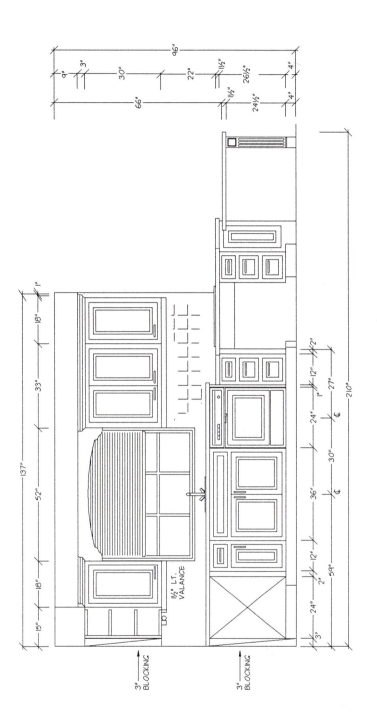

ACCESS PROJECT # 2 - Sampson Kitchen - Peterson/Smith, Designers.

A ELEVATION

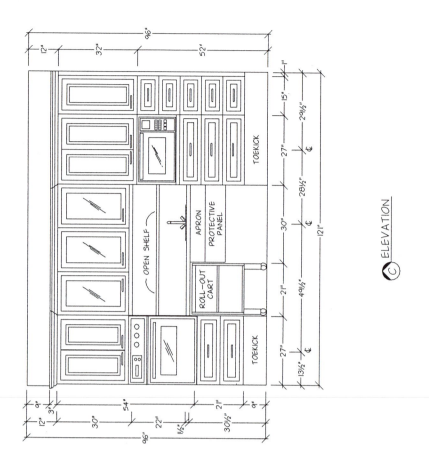

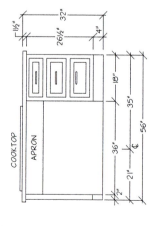

ACCESS PROJECT #2 - Sampson Kitchen - Peterson/Smith, Designers.

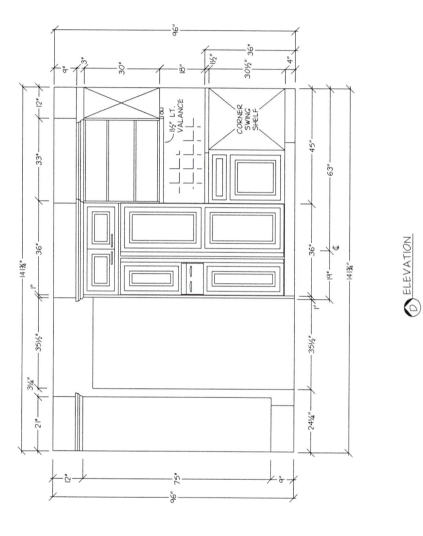

ELEVATION

ACCESS PROJECT #2 – Sampson Kitchen – Peterson/Smith, Designers.

ACCESS PROJECT # 2 - Sampson Kitchen - Peterson/Smith, Designers.

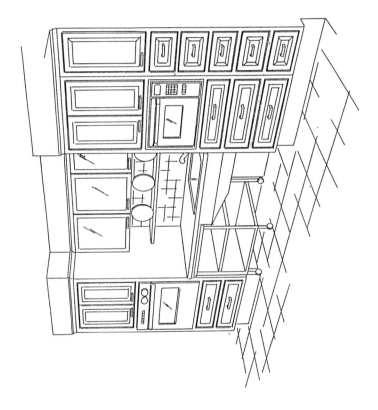

ACCESS PROJECT #2 - Sampson Kitchen - Peterson/Smith, Designers.

a p p e n d i x 3

Universal Bathroom Design Checklist

GENERAL BATHROOM DESIGNER TIPS:

☐ Use *"Easily accessed"* storage - visible storage is good except where privacy is desired.

☐ Use non-glare finishes, especially for older eyes.

☐ Provide non-glare, adaptable lighting throughout the space to make area comfortable for younger and older eyes.

☐ Lower mirror and wall storage for people with limited reach range.

☐ Lighter colors are especially beneficial for older eyes, with contrast at fixtures or edges. There are iridescent inlay materials available.

☐ Lower windows allow a seated user to see outside.

☐ Non-skid floors are safer for people using walkers and crutches.

☐ A flush or nearly flush threshold is safer for visually/mobility impaired users.

☐ Use drawers and tambour units instead of doors to make access easier.

☐ Adjustable-height sinks are available for use by all.

☐ Use full-extension locking drawer glides for maximum accessibility, strength and safety.

☐ Have timers installed to insure that any fixtures or grooming equipment that should not be running will be automatically shut off.

☐ Automatic doors that open and close based on a pressure pad, or pocket doors improve mobility.

☐ Voice activated lights: *"ON"*, *"OFF"*, *"DIM"*.

☐ Lowered light switches controls, and outlets make it easier for children and people in wheelchairs to reach.

☐ Touch- latch cabinet doors eliminate the need to grasp knobs or pulls, especially a problem for arthritic fingers.

☐ Use wire or architectural pulls in lieu of knobs.

☐ Use lighted interiors on cabinets to aid in visibility.

☐ Install repairable surfaces in areas where surfaces may be scarred or scorched accidentally.

☐ Store heavy objects at the safest and most convenient height.

☐ Design your projects so that they do not appear to be clinical. Like anyone, people with disabilities deserve beautiful design and function.

☐ Provide a built-in step stool in the toe space to create a step for users of shorter stature.

☐ Lower accessories, towel bars, toilet paper holder, etc, to be within a more universal reach range.

☐ Always plan reinforcment in the walls around bathtub/shower and toilet for the possible later installation of addional grab bars.

☐ A cabinet on wheels can meet additional bathroom storage needs.

☐ Add a seat to help in transfer and dressing.

TOILETS

☐ A board or bench seat may help in transferring to the toilet.

☐ Choose a toilet with a seat at wheelchair height for easy transfer.

☐ Add a base under the toilet to raise the seat to wheelchair height.

☐ Elongated toilets are easier for aligning with a wheelchair.

☐ The flushing lever should be on the approach side of the toilet.

☐ A toilet in the shower is easily cleaned and doubles as a shower seat.

☐ Use a padded or non-slip toilet seat with a shower toilet.

☐ Plan the sink and mirror outside of the shower area.

☐ Add a flush lever extension to the toilet.

☐ Use a toilet paper holder with a controlled flow.

☐ Mount the toilet paper holder at 26" (66cm) high in front of the toilet.

☐ A recessed holder won't interfere with approach.

BATHTUBS AND SHOWERS

☐ Consider showers with curtains, not doors.

☐ Shower curtains should be longer than floor length to help retain water in the shower area.

☐ Padded vinyl shower seats can be slatted for drainage.

☐ Wood or textured vinyl backs on shower seat prevent sticking.

☐ Consider a fold-away shower seat for transfer from wheelchair.

☐ Choose an adjustable-height hand-held shower with a single-lever mix valve.

☐ Specify a pressure-balancing mix valve to prevent hot water surges.

☐ Insure that the diverter is a lever and within the universal reach range.

☐ The hand-held shower should detach from a wall mount with vertical adjustment.

☐ The flexible shower hose should be at least 72" (183cm) long.

☐ Some hand-held showers have a water volume control button.

☐ Make sure that the showerhead bar does not interfere with grab bars.

☐ For free hands, install a safety belt in the shower.

☐ Bathtubs with a flat bathtub bottom may offer more stability.

☐ Insure that the floor of the bathtub is slip resistant.

☐ Choose a lever type bathtub drain control.

☐ Choose a lever-type faucet.

☐ To wash your back, choose a pistol grip bath brush.

☐ Consider difficulty of transfer over deck mounted shower doors on a bathtub.

☐ Glass doors, even when tempered, can break easily.

LAVATORIES

☐ Recognize the impact on clear floor space of sinks with legs and pedestals.

☐ Insulate pipes under approachable sinks to prevent burns.

☐ Pressure-balancing levers prevent a sudden change in water temperature.

☐ Consider adding a spray at the lavatory for washing hair.

☐ Start your mix valve at a temperature of 115°F (46°C).

☐ Identify the edge of the lavatory with a colored strip.

☐ Use red on the hot water control and blue on the cold.

GRAB BARS

☐ Grab bars are generally located 33" - 36" (84cm - 91cm) high on back and side walls of bathtub/shower.

☐ Grab bars are generally located behind the toilet and on each side.

☐ Angled grab bars are very dangerous.

☐ Grab bars should not break or chip or have sharp or abrasive edges.

☐ They must not rotate within their fittings.

☐ The bar should contrast from the wall to ensure accurate vision.

☐ Use flat finishes, as glare may visually distort shiny grab bars.

☐ Special finishes are available for a sure grip.

appendix 4

Access Bathrooms

Also part of a research and training development project, our team of designers were asked to create two bathroom spaces.

These two project descriptions and the resulting design solutions are featured here for your review. You will notice that not all of the " *41 Design Guidelines of Bathroom Planning*" were met in every instance. It is important to remember that the guidelines are there for you as a designer to use as a "*measurement*" to assimilate a competency. **It is not always possible to meet every guideline.**

ACCESS PROJECT #1- JASON'S BATHROOM

Client Profile

Sally and Tom Edwards have three children, the oldest being Jason, age 18, who was involved in a car accident and has no use of his legs. As a family, they have decided to remodel the main floor bedroom and bathroom to be Jason's room. Jason intends to go on to college in a year and may move away from home, but this plan will provide him with a room whenever he is home.

Jason uses a wheelchair and has full use and strength in his upper body. He is able to

transfer using his tremendous upper body strength and coordination, and enjoys most moving in generous spaces.

The family would like the new bathroom to be spacious and contemporary, and to include bathtub and shower options, either as one unit or as separate units. There is a need for closed storage of some equipment that Jason uses for personal hygiene, and open storage for the usual bathroom gear.

The intended space is the existing bathroom and closet. The walls separating the closet from the existing bathroom and surrounding the shower may be removed. The wall between these spaces and the bedroom may be moved as far as the bedroom window, and somewhere in that space, a new closet must be provided. Any plumbing can be moved, but it would be best not to move the toilet.

The Shower Area

The 36" x 36" (91cm x 91cm) transfer shower provides easiest use for Jason. He will roll next to the shower, adjust the controls (set off center towards the room) and then backup to make a parallel transfer onto the shower seat. This will be done using his wheelchair and the shower grab bars for support. The decorative shower curtain then is pulled for his shower.

The shower may also be used by standing persons by flipping up the seat, or if desired they may flip it down and shower in a seated position. The pressure balanced temp control will prevent any risk of burning.

Bathtub Area

Offset controls (set closer to room) allow for ease in filling the bathtub with water. If assistance is desired, the dignity bathtub allows Jason or others to transfer to the built in transfer seat. Once on the seat, Jason would rotate into the bathtub and lower himself hydraulically.

Once in the bathtub, Jason can activate the whirlpool by the air switch located in the front side of the bathtub. A second control and hand-held spray allows for refilling or warming of the bathtub during use.

The beauty of this particular bathtub is that in a lowered position the seat is totally flush with the bottom of the bathtub, unusual in lifts and providing ease of use and comfort for anyone wishing to bathe.

In the bathtub area grab bars and hand rails are provided for safe and easy maneuvering. An additional grab bar is to be used as a towel bar. The windows in the bathtub area open by remote control, convenient for anyone given the bathtub location. The deck area provides convenient towel storage/display.

From the bathtub, moving towards the toilet and personal hygiene area, grab bars in brass, non-slip finish line the walls, creating a chair rail effect and allowing for assistance at any point. The rolling storage provides for Jason's personal hygeine needs and can be moved easily to be adjacent to the toilet with built-in bidet. This toilet was chosen for its height which suits Jason. A second grab bar mounted below the standard grab bar serves as a tower bar. This application eliminates the risk of Jason using an accessory installed

to hold towels as a grab bar. In other words, every horizontal bar in the room, whether intended for towels or support has been installed to support Jason's weight.

In the vanity area, storage includes drawers on full extension slides and open shelves within Jason's reach range. The higher section of the tall vanity cabinet provides additional storage behind a door.

The vanity counter has been placed at 32" (81cm), a universal height with an apron and a decorative protective panel to house the plumbing.

The sink is 6 1/2" (17cm) deep with a rear drain and lever faucets to facilitate universal access. The counter extends and angles back to provide generous work space, contributing to the rich and open feeling of the room while providing 51" (130cm) of clear kneespace for grooming.

Controls and switches are installed 44" (112cm) off the floor to the left of the entry allowing for separate controls of lighting in the shower (1) bathtub area (dimmer), vanity area (dimmer), toilet area (1), and general illumination (dimmer) as well as auxiliary heat/fan and a remote control for the windows in the bathtub area.

The floor, shower, bathtub area and counters are made of solid surface material for ease of care and slip resistance, as well as a rich look. The contrast borders add a decorative detail while also enhancing *way-finding* in the space.

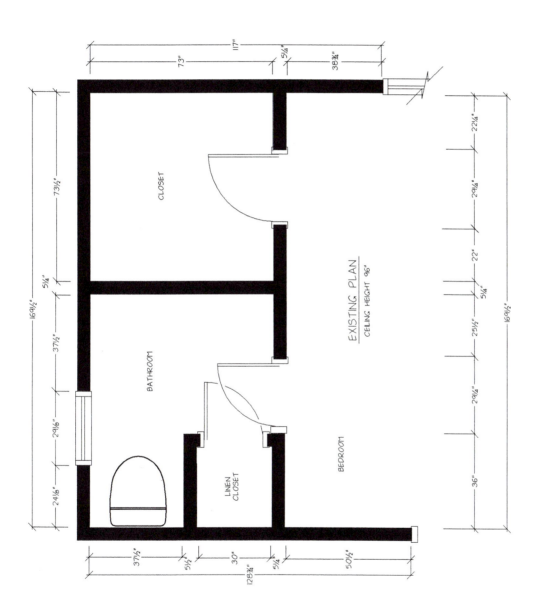

EXISTING PLAN
CEILING HEIGHT 96"

CLOSET

BATHROOM

LINEN
CLOSET

BEDROOM

ACCESS PROJECT #1 - Jason's Bathroom - Peterson/Smith, Designers.

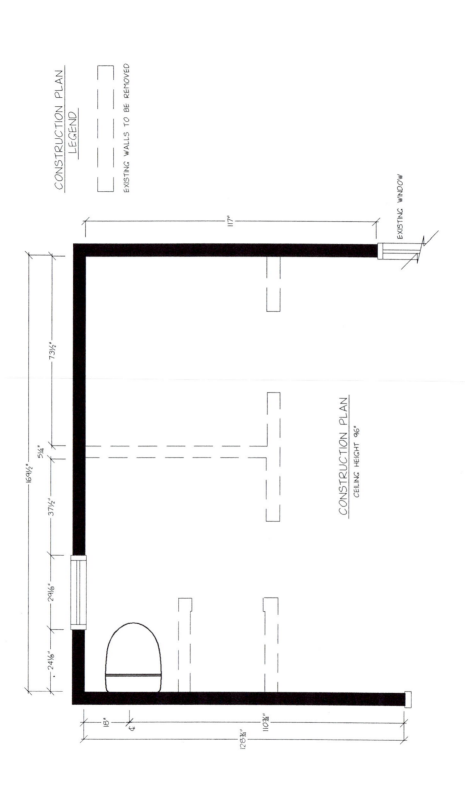

CONSTRUCTION PLAN
LEGEND

EXISTING WALLS TO BE REMOVED

EXISTING WINDOW

117"

73½"

5¼"

169½"

37½"

29⅝"

24⅛"

CONSTRUCTION PLAN
CEILING HEIGHT 96"

18"

℄

128¾"

110¾"

ACCESS PROJECT #1 - *Jason's Bathroom* - Peterson/Smith, Designers.

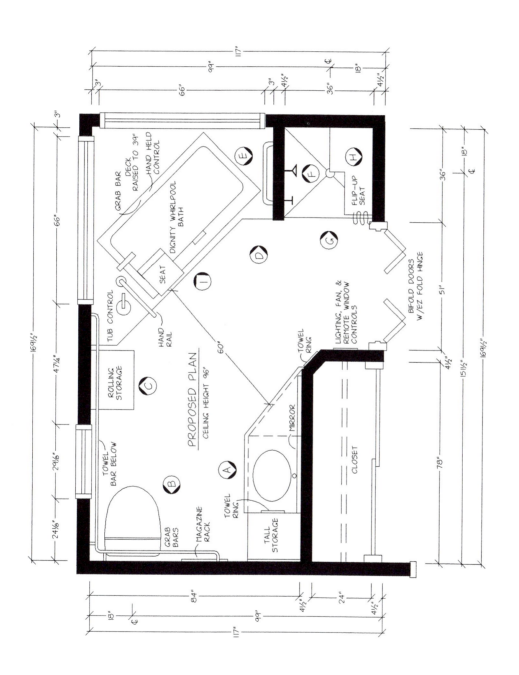

PROPOSED PLAN
CEILING HEIGHT 96"

GRAB BAR

DECK RAISED TO 39"

HAND HELD CONTROL

DIGNITY WHIRLPOOL BATH

SEAT

TUB CONTROL

HAND RAIL

ROLLING STORAGE

TOWEL BAR BELOW

GRAB BARS

MAGAZINE RACK

TOWEL RING

TALL STORAGE

MIRROR

CLOSET

TOWEL RING

LIGHTING, FAN, & REMOTE WINDOW CONTROLS

BI-FOLD DOORS W/EZ FOLD HINGE

FLIP-UP SEAT

ACCESS PROJECT #1 - Jason's Bathroom - Peterson/Smith, Designers.

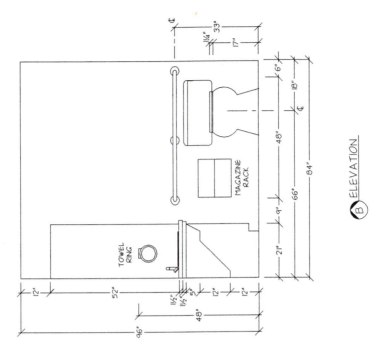

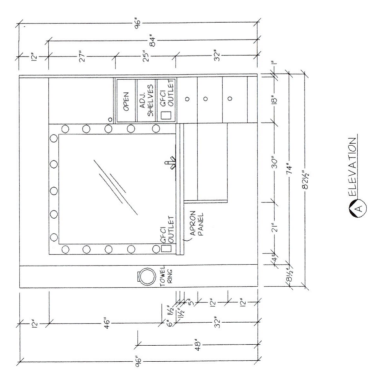

ACCESS PROJECT #1 - Jason's Bathroom - Peterson/Smith, Designers.

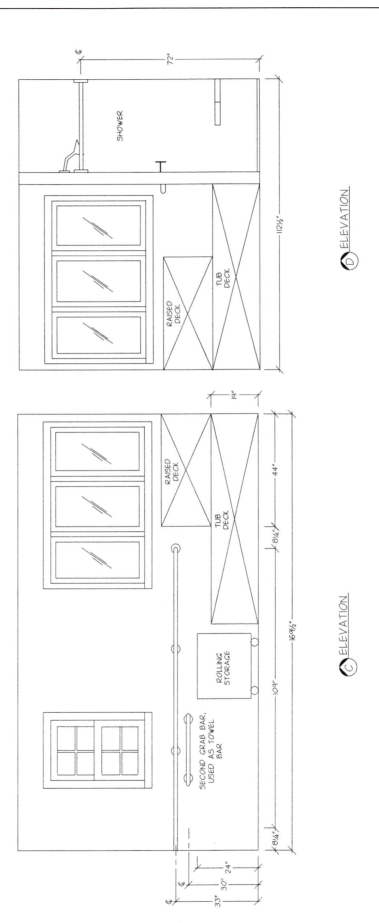

ACCESS PROJECT #1 - Jason's Bathroom - Peterson/Smith, Designers.

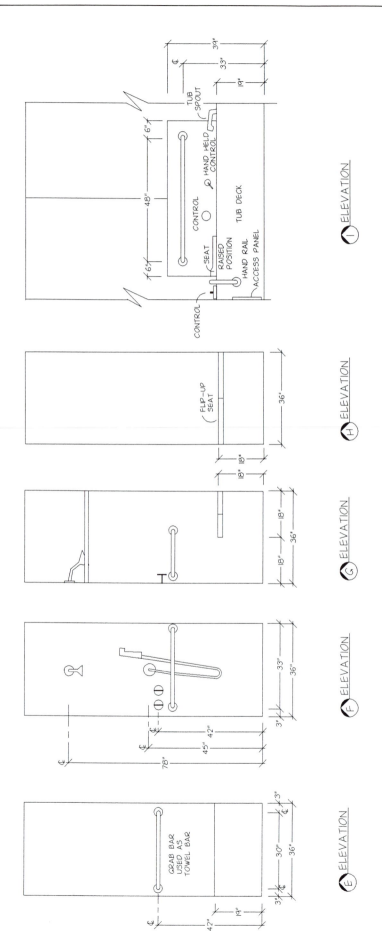

ACCESS PROJECT #1 - Jason's Bathroom - Peterson/Smith, Designers.

ACCESS PROJECT #2 - THE SCHULZE BATHROOM

Client Profile

Howard and Nancy Schulze, age 60 and 54 years, respectively, are remodeling the hall bathroom and the master bathroom in their home. After living in their home since it was built 30 years ago, they are ready for a change, and as they have decided to remain in this home indefinitely after retirement, they want bathrooms that will meet their current and future needs.

They are happy to see the space gutted - in fact, the more change the better. They would like to borrow space from the hall bathroom to enlarge the master bathroom. They want the hall bathroom to provide a combination bathtub/shower, one sink and the water closet. They would like a fresh look and a smaller, safer space.

The focus of this project is the master bathroom. Howard would like a huge and wonderful shower and a whole new look. Nancy feels the same and does not look for more storage in the bathroom but stresses wanting a bigger and more open feel to the room. The basic needs are a water closet, one sink with minimum storage and no bathtub, but a fun shower.

Because the Schulze's plan to live here indefinitely and because Howard has recovered from a hip replacement and Nancy has the beginnings of arthritis, universal and accessible features are important, particularly in the master bathroom.

Increased lighting, decreased background noises, universal controls, safe surfaces, space for maneuvering and easy access to the shower must be incorporated.

While Howard and Nancy are truly fit and without limitations today, they wish to plan a space that is without barriers, not only for their present needs, but for varying needs of others and themselves in the future.

Design Statement

Howard and Nancy Schulze were easy to work with. We were able to achieve nearly all of their requirements due to their flexibility and positive attitudes toward life.

Since the master bathroom was the most important to both of them, we focused on this area, making certain to give them each of the items requested and provide them with a fun, functionally and aesthetically pleasing space.

The doorway was enlarged to accommodate a future wheelchair when and if it should become necessary and a large floor-space (which isn't usually possible in a bathroom) to allow for a comfortable turn around of a wheelchair. The shower has been designed to allow a wheelchair to roll right into the space, and the vanity features an attractive open space below it so that a future wheelchair can be used if necessary.

Due to Howard's hip replacement and also for the sake of good universal design, a sit down area has been planned in the shower. The large space will accommodate both Howard and Nancy as they still enjoy intimate time together. The shelf in the shower will hold items frequently used without bending, and the glass block will allow additional light into the shower space.

Both the shower and toilet areas feature grab bars in new, fun colors. Both Howard and Nancy like the idea of something other than chrome because chrome looks too institutional to them.

The floor is non-slip tile that will be maintenance free. The cabinets have pulls and also are in a light finish. There is both general lighting in the bathroom, a light above the toilets for reading, a light in the shower and lighting on both sides and above the mirror.

The biggest controversy was removing part of the closet. Howard finally agreed that the smaller closet would become his in order to have a larger bathroom.

The shower features several showerheads as well as pressure-balancing valves to eliminate the possibility of scalding.

The hall bathroom has been reduced dramatically in size, but since the children are gone there is little need for the additional space. Howard hardly ever uses a bathtub, but Nancy likes to luxuriate in a bathtub from time to time, and they both agree that a bathtub is important when they are not feeling

well. The bathtub and toilet feature grab bars and the bathtub fittings have anti-scald controls.

Both vanities have been specified as 34" (86cm) finished height for ease of use. Pocket doors will be used in both areas to conserve space and provide for additional safety because many bathroom accidents involve a person falling against a door.

These bathroom modifications will enable them to live both comfortably and safely in the home that they have grown to love.

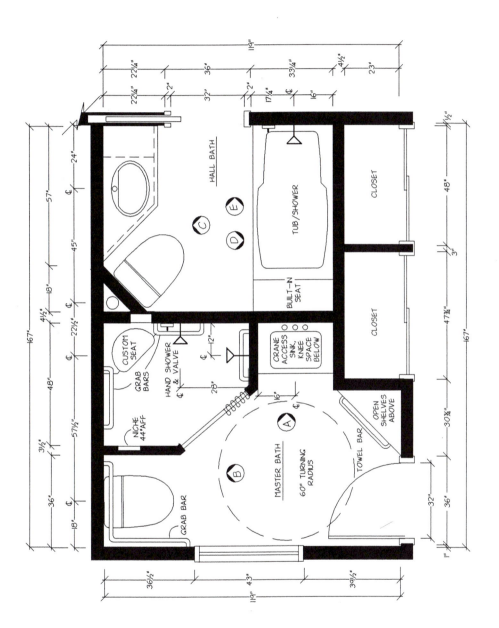

ACCESS PROJECT #2 - *Schulze Bathroom - Krengel/Piske, Designers.*

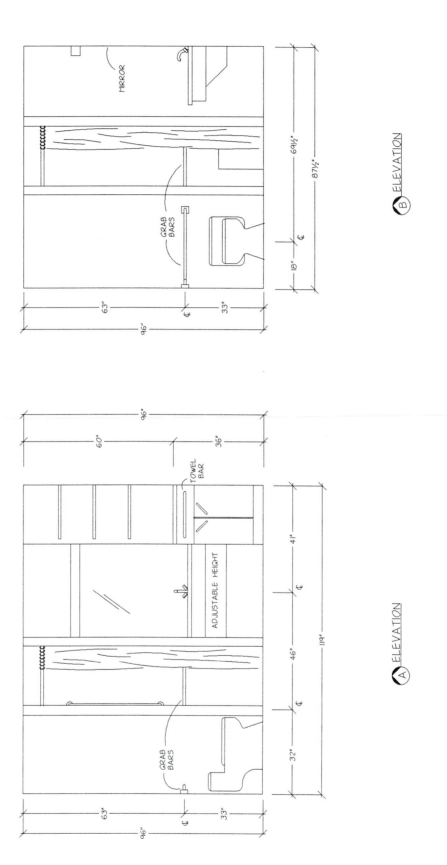

ACCESS PROJECT #2 - Schulze Bathroom - Krengel/Piske, Designers.

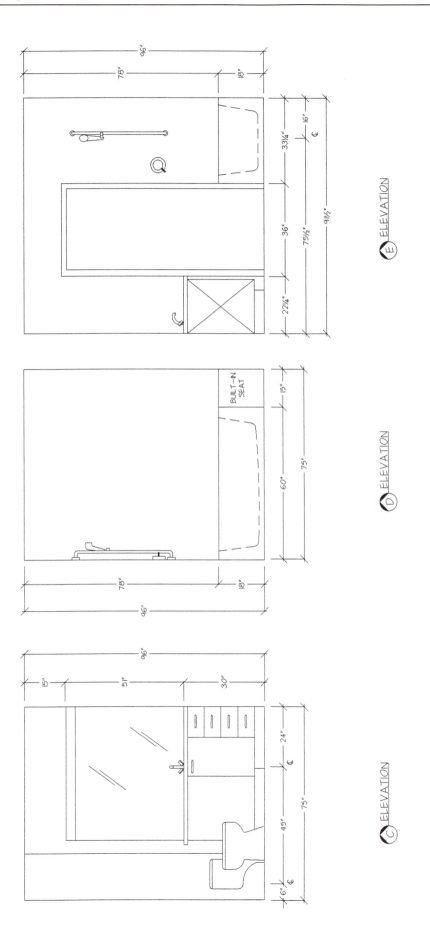

ACCESS PROJECT #2 - Schulze Bathroom - Krengel/Piske, Designers.

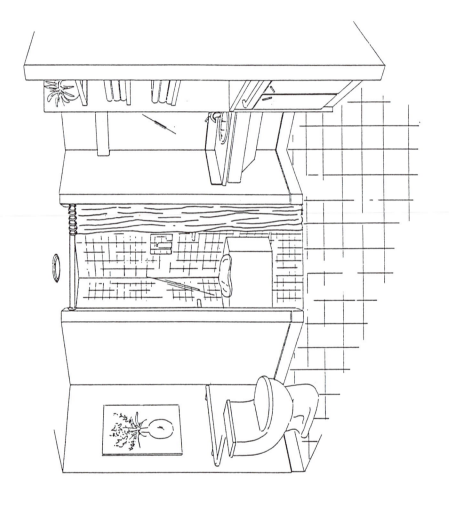

ACCESS PROJECT #2 - *Schulze Bathroom* - Krengel/Piske, Designers.

appendix 5

Laws and Standards

At this time there are no laws regulating universal design in private, single-family homes. There are, however, laws and standards that serve as a starting point in designing universal spaces, plus local and state codes that impact residential construction. The main laws and standards are outlined here.

ARCHITECTURAL BARRIERS ACT

In 1968, the **Architectural Barriers Act** was passed to regulate buildings used or funded by the federal government. The **Uniform Federal Accessibility Standards (UFAS)** were published in 1984. The purpose of UFAS was to set "*uniform standards for the design, construction and alteration of buildings so that physically handicapped persons will have ready access to and use of them in accordance with the Architectural Barriers Act.*" **UFAS** represented the most comprehensive standard to that date and was a good effort to minimize the differences among the federal standards and the access standards recommended for facilities that did not fall under the **Architectural Barriers Act**. The technical provisions of UFAS were for the most part the same as the 1980 edition of the **American National Standards Institute A117.1**, "*Specifications for Making Buildings and Facilities Accessible to and Usable by Physically Handicapped People.*"

FAIR HOUSING AMENDMENTS ACT

In 1988, the **Fair Housing Amendments Act** was passed into law as an amendment to the **Civil Rights Act of 1968**. The **Civil Rights Act** prohibited discrimination in sale, rental, or financing of dwellings based on color, religion, sex or national origin. The **Fair Housing Amendments Act (FHA)** added people with disabilities and people with children to the list. In 1991, the **Final Fair Housing Accessibility Guidelines** were published to "*provide builders and developers with technical guidance on how to comply with the specific accessibility requirements of the Fair Housing Amendments Act of 1988.*" This standard and law applies to multi-family construction where there are four or more units under one roof. While the requirements of the law are mandatory, these precise guidelines are not: "*Builders and developers may choose to depart from the Guidelines and seek alternate ways to demonstrate that they have met the requirements of the Fair Housing Act.*" The Act provides that "*compliance with ANSI 117.1 or with local laws that required accessibility, would be adequate.*"

AMERICANS WITH DISABILITIES ACT

In 1990, the **Americans with Disabilities Act (ADA)** was passed into law, requiring non-discrimination in many areas of life against people with disabilities. Title II of the

Act relates to places of state and local governments (federal continues to be regulated by UFAS) and Title III relates to places of public accommodation and services operated by private enterprises. In 1991, the **ADA Accessibility Guidelines (ADAAG)** were produced to set *"guidelines for accessibility to places of public accommodation and commercial facilities by individuals with disabilities."* At this time **ADAAG** does not cover private residences.

AMERICAN NATIONAL STANDARD FOR ACCESSIBLE AND USABLE BUILDINGS AND FACILITIES

First issued in 1961, the current **ANSI Standard for Accessible and Usable Buildings and Facilities (A117.1)** was revised in 1992. This standard was created as a model code *"for adoption by government agencies and for organizations setting model codes to achieve uniformity in the technical design criteria in building codes and other regulations."* It is also intended to provide technical design guidelines to make buildings and facilities accessible to and usable by persons with physical disabilities. It is in compliance with or is the basis for much of the information given in the other standards. And it includes information relating to the kitchen and the bathroom, among other things.

This brief overview on most of the major laws and guidelines regarding accessibility should help clarify how they relate to bathroom design. Tremendous research and involvement on local, state and national levels have led to these guidelines, and it is not the intent of this chapter to create *"experts"* on these laws and codes. If a situation arises that may not be covered, contact the appropriate agency and work from their guidance. In most cases, information and some amount of technical assistance are free.

In addition, these laws and codes and the organizations that developed them provide minimum guidelines and space requirements. It is important to note that these standards are minimums and not hard-and-fast rules. They will serve as a basis from which to expand and create truly universal bathrooms.

ARCHITECTURAL AND TRANSPORTATION BARRIERS COMPLIANCE BOARD

The **Architectural and Transportation Barriers Compliance Board**, known as the **Access Board** was established to ensure compliance with the **Architectural Barriers Act**. In addition, the **Access Board** was given authority to develop minimum standards of accessibility and to provide technical assistance. It is a great source of information and clarification on standards relating to accessibility.

Today there is a trend toward greater and greater uniformity among the various codes and guidelines, and the **ANSI** code is referred to most often. It is again in the review process for possible revision. The **Access Board** states as a goal that the **ADAAG** will be constantly revised and improved to insure its effectiveness. Proposed changes to **ADAAG** include a section on residential housing, including bathrooms for public housing covered under Title II.

a p p e n d i x 6

Products Sources and Resources

In designing universal kitchens and bathrooms, some new and some existing products will be used. The single-lever faucet is an example of an existing product that has always worked well in terms of universal use. Sometimes an existing product can be worked into a design in a non-traditional way. To be universal in use, the same faucet located to one side of a sink instead of at the back will put it within reach of more users. Finally, there are a number of products new to the market that have been designed for universal use.

THE IMPORTANCE OF RELIABLE SOURCES

To maintain a complete and current file of the new products on the market would be nearly impossible. Technology and a growing awareness of universal design are bringing new products and new twists on existing products on an almost daily basis. Because of this, it is important to have good sources for information and a method for evaluating new products. To become aware of new products relating to universal design, there are several existing sources of information listed later in this appendix. Among them, two are particularly useful.

- **Abledata** is a database on products for people with disabilities. Information is available by purchasing the program or for a small charge by calling Abledata directly. When you provide them with a description of needs or the desired product, they will give you information on the manufacturers in their databank who produce such a product along with general pricing.

- The **1995 Accessible Building Product Guide** is a current listing compiled by Universal Designers and Consultants.

Listed at the back of this chapter are business and educational research service centers focusing on universal design. They can help to first identify new products and equally important, to help evaluate them. Once a possible product has been identified, it must be evaluated. This becomes particularly important with products that are new to the market and somewhat untested or unfamiliar. Along with the obvious, consider the level of technology involved.

Although technology can provide amazing options, the less complex a product, the easier it will be to use and maintain. If a client lacks a comfort level with a product, it will not be used. To that end, provide opportunities for the client to test-use the product when possible. If this is not possible, network to find others who have used the product. They may be other designers, referrals from the manufacturer or distributors, or other related professionals. Manufacturers may have independent market research on the product.

The following product evaluation guide lists points to consider in the evaluation process.

PRODUCT EVALUATION GUIDE

I   **The Process**

    A.   Determine the task to be done

    B.   Assess client abilities (use survey)

    C.   Evaluate Product/Technology

        1.   What does it do and what can't it do?

        2.   How complicated is it?

        3.   How does it compare to its competitors?

        4.   Ask opinion of others on your team (doctor, therapist, supplier)

        5.   Ask other designers

        6.   Ask for formal evaluation results

        7.   Ask where the product is sold

II.   **Points to Consider**

    A.   Installation (can it be installed to meet client needs)

    B.   Safety (general and added checks - auto shutoff)

    C.   Design (least amount of energy used)

    D.   Cuing (size of graphics, dual cuing)

    E.   Color and Contrast for Visibility

    F.   Maintenance (who, what, how often, how expensive)

    G.   Reach Range and Line of Sight

    H.   Comfort Zone (appearance, location, ease of use)

    I.   Time on Market, warranty, reliability of manufacturer

    J.   Specifications (match with client

RESOURCES

There are numerous resources, in print and through people and agencies specializing in universal design and design for people with various disabilities.

This resource list is divided into printed materials, other sources of information, and suggestions for obtaining information in your area.

SECTION 1 Books and Printed Materials

☐ Accent on Living, Directory of Products, Sources, Organizations and Dealers. Available from Cheever Publishing, Inc., RR2 Gillum Road and High Drive, P.O. Box 700, Bloomington, Il, 61704.

☐ The Accessible Bathroom. Host. Jablonski, Lori, and Nickels, Karen, 1991. Available from Design Coalition, Inc., 2088 Atwood Ave., Madison, WI, 53704.

☐ Access Information Bulletins. Available from National Advocacy Program, Paralyzed Veterans of America, 801 18th Street, NW, Washington, DC 20006.

☐ Accessible Environments: Toward Universal Design. Mace, Ron, Graeme Hardie and Jaine Place. Available from Center for Universal Design, NCSU, Box 8613, Raleigh, NC 27695.

☐ Accessibility in Georgia: A Technical and Policy Guide to Access in Georgia, 1986. Barrier Free Environments, Inc. Available from client Assistance Program, Division of Rehabilitation Services, Seventh Floor, 878 Peachtree Street, NE. Atlanta, GA 30309

☐ Accessibility Reference Guide, An Illustrated Commentary on U.B.C. Chapter 31 and CABO/ANSI A117.1-1992. International Conference of Building Officials (IBCO). Available from the ICBO Order Department at, 5360 Workmenmill Road, Whittier, CA 90601.

☐ The Accessible Housing Design File. Barrier Free Environments, Inc., New York: Van Nostrand Reinhold, 1991. Available from International Thomson Publishing, 7625 Empire Drive, Florence, KY 41042.

☐ The Accommodating Kitchen: Accessibility with Substance ... and Style, Maytag Consumer Information Center, Newton, IA 50208.

☐ Adaptable Housing. U.S. Department of Housing and Urban Development, 1987. Available from HUD User, P.O. Box 6091, Rockville, MD 20850.

☐ Aging in the Designed Environment. Christenson, M., New York: Haworth Press, 1990. Available from Haworth Press, 10 Alice Street, Binghamton, NY 13904.

☐ American National Standard - Accessible and Usable Buildings and Facilities (ANSI A117.1-1992). Available from Council of American Building Officials, 5203 Leesburg Pike, #708, Falls Church, VA 22041.

☐ Americans with Disabilities Act Guidelines for Buildings and Facilities, 1992. Available from Architectural and Transportation Barriers Compliance Board, 1331 F Street, NW, Suite 1000, Washington, DC 20004.

☐ The Arts and 504: A 504 Handbook for Accessible Arts Programming. Available from Office for Special Constituencies, National Endowment for the Arts, 1100 Pennsylvania Ave., NW, Washington, DC 20506.

☐ Assistive Technology Sourcebook. Enders, A. & M. Hall, 1991, Available from RESNA Press, Washington, DC.

☐ Bathroom Industry Technical Manuals. Cheever, Ellen M., McDonald, Marylee, DePaepe, Annette, and Geragi, Nick, 1996. Available from the National Kitchen & Bath Association, 687 Willow Grove St., Hackettstown, NJ, 07840.

☐ Bathroom Lifts. Mullick, Abir. Available from Center for Inclusive Design and Environmental Access, School of Architecture and Planning, University of Buffalo, 390 Hayes Hall, Buffalo, NY, 14214.

☐ Beautiful Barrier-Free: A Visual Guide to Accessibility. Leibrock, C., & Behar, S., 1993. Available from International Thomson Publishing, 7625 Empire Drive, Florence, KY 41042.

☐ Benches and Seats. Mullick, Abir, Available from Center for Inclusive Design and Environmental Access, School of Architecture and Planning, University of Buffalo, 390 Hayes Hall, Buffalo, NY, 14214.

☐ Building for a Lifetime. Wylde, M., Adrian Barron-Robbins and Sam Clark, 1994. Available from Tauton Press, Inc., 63 S. Main St., Newtown, CT 06470.

☐ The Complete Guide to Barrier-Free Housing: Convenient Living for the Elderly and the Physically Handicapped. Branson, G.D., Available from Betterway Books, 1507 Dana Avenue, Cincinnati, OH 45207.

☐ CAH Selected Readings List. Available from Center for Universal Design, North Carolina State University, Box 8613 Raleigh, NC 27695.

☐ A Comprehensive Approach to Retrofitting Homes for a Lifetime. NAHB Research Center for HUD. Available from NAHB Research Center, 400 Prince George Blvd., Upper Marlboro, MD 20774.

☐ A Consumer's Guide to Home Adaptation, 1989. Available from Adaptive Environments Center, 374 Congress St., Suite 301, Boston, MA 02210.

☐ Design for Aging - An Annotated Bibliography, 1980-1992. Available from Aging Design Research Program, AIA/ACSA Council on Architectural Research, 1735 New York Ave., NW, Washington, DC 20006.

☐ Design for Independent Living: Housing Accessibility Institute Resource Book, 1991. Available from Center for Accessible Housing, North Carolina State University, Box 8613 Raleigh, NC 27695.

☐ The Do-Able Renewable Home. Salmen, John P.S., 1991. Available from AARP, 601 E Street, NW, Washington, DC 20049.

☐ E.C.H.O. Housing: Recommended Construction and Installation Standards. Available from American Association of Retired Persons, 1909 K Street, NW, Washington, DC 20049.

☐ Fair Housing Accessibility Guidelines, US Department of Housing and Urban Development, 1991. Available from Fair Housing Information Clearing House, P.O. Box 9146, McLean, VA, 22102.

☐ Fair Housing Design Guide for Accessibility. Davies, T.D., & Beasley, K.A., 1992. Available from Paradigm Design Group, 801 8th St. N. W., Washington, DC 20006.

☐ The First Whole Rehab Catalog: A Comprehensive Guide to Products and Services for the Physically Disadvantaged. Abrahms, A.J. & M.A., Abrahms, 1991. Available from Betterway Books, 1507 Dana Avenue, Cincinnati, OH 45207.

☐ Handbook for Design: Specially Adapted Housing, VA pamphlett 26-13, April 1978. Available from: Assistant Director for Construction and Valuation (262), Veterans Administration, 810 Vermont Avenue, NW, Washington, DC, 20420.

☐ Harris Communications, Inc., 1995. Catalog products for people with hearing impairments. Available from: Harris

Communications, Inc., 6541 City West Parkway, Eden Prairie, MN 55344-3248.

☐ Home Safety Guide for Older People: Check it out, fix it up. Pynoos, J. and E., Cohen, 1990. Available from Serif Press, Inc., Attn: Melissa Junior, 1331 H Street, NW, Suite 110 Lower Level, Washington, DC 20005.

☐ Housing Accessibility Information System. Available from NAHB Research Center, 400 Prince George Blvd., Upper Marlboro, MD 20774.

☐ Housing as We Grow Older. Barner, P. (Ed.), 1992. Available from NRAES Cooperative Extension, 152 Riley-Robb Hall, Ithaca, NY 14853-5701.

☐ Housing Disabled Persons, 1990. Available from Canada Mortgage and Housing Corporation (CMHC), 700 Montreal Road, Ottawa, Ontario K1A OP7.

☐ Housing Interiors for the Disabled and Elderly. Raschko, B., 1982. Available from International Thomson Publishing, 7625 Empire Drive, Florence, KY 41042.

☐ Independence in the Bathroom, May, 1992. Available from The Rehab Engineering Center at the National Rehab Hospital and ECRI. 102 Irving Street N.W., Room 1068, Washington, DC 20010-2949.

☐ Kitchen Industry Technical Manuals, Cheever, Ellen M.; DePaepe, Annette; Geragi, Nick; McDonald, Marylee, 1996. Available from National Kitchen & Bath Association, 687 Willow Grove Street, Hackettstown, NJ 07840.

☐ Lighting Kitchens and Baths. Grosslight, Jane, 1993. Available from Durwood Publishers, Box 37474, Tallahassee, FL, 32315.

☐ Low Vision Information, 1993. Available from The Lighthouse, Inc., 111 East 59th Street, New York, NY 10022.

☐ Mobile Homes: Alternative Housing for the Handicapped, 1976. Available from

Barrier Free Environments, Inc., Highway 70 West, Water Garden, PO Box 30634, Raleigh, NC 27622.

☐ Open House Guidebook. Available from Canada Mortgage and Housing Corporation (CMHC), 700 Montreal Road, Ottawa, Ontario K1A OP7.

☐ Paraplegia News. Available from PVA Inc., 2111 East Highland, Suite 180, Phoenix, AZ 85016.

☐ The Perfect Fit: Creative Ideas for a Safe and Livable Home. Available from American Association of Retired Persons, 1909 K Street, NW, Washington, DC 20049.

☐ The Planner's Guide to Barrier Free Meetings, 1980. Available from Barrier Free Environments, Inc., Highway 70 West, Water Garden, PO Box 30634, Raleigh, NC 27622.

☐ Resources for People with Disabilities and Chronic Conditions. Available from Resources for Rehabilitation, 33 Bedford Street, Suite 19A, Lexington, MA 02173.

☐ The 1995 Accessible Building Product Guide. Salmen, John P.S. and Julee Quarve-Peterson, 1995. Available from John Wiley and Sons or from Universal Designers and Consultants, Inc., 1700 Rockville Pike, Ste. 110, Rockville, MD 20852.

☐ The Safe Home Checkout: Easy Assessment, Simple Solutions. Lisak, J., Culler, K., & Morgan, M., 1991. Available from Geriatric Environments for Living and Learning, 230 West North Ave., Suite 122, Chicago, IL 60610.

☐ Transgenerational Design: Products for an Aging Population. Pirkl, James, 1994. Available from IOnternational Thomson Publishing, 7625 Empire Drive, Florence, KY 41042.

☐ Senior Housing News. Available from National Council on Senior Housing, NAHB,

1201 15th Street NW, Washington, DC 20005.

☐ <u>Staying at Home</u>, Available from American Association of Retired Persons, 1909 K Street, NW, Washington, DC 20049.

☐ <u>UFAS Retrofit Guide: Accessibility Modifications for Existing Building</u>, 1993. Available from International Thomson Publishing, 7625 Empire Drive, Florence, KY 41042.

☐ <u>Universal Design Newsletter</u>. Available from Universal Designers and Consultants, 1700 Rockville Pike, Rockville, MD 20852.

☐ <u>Wheelchair Bathrooms</u>. Schweiker, Harry A. (Jr.), 1971. Available from Paralyzed Veterans of America, 801 18th Street NW, Washington, DC, 20006.

☐ <u>Wheelchair House Designs</u>, 1989, Available from Easter Paralyzed Veterans Association, 75-20 Astoria Boulevard, Jackson Heights, New York 11370-1178.

SECTION II Other Sources

☐ Abledata, 8455 Colesville Rd., Suite 935, Silver Spring, MD 20910.

☐ Accessible Designs - Adjustable Systems, Inc., 94 North Columbus Road, Athens, OH 45701.

☐ Adaptive Environments, 374 Congress Street, Suite 301, Boston, MA 02210.

☐ Adaptive Environments Lab, School of Architecture and Planning, University of Buffalo, 390 Hayes Hall, Buffalo, NY 14214.

☐ American Association of Retired Persons, 601 E Street, NW, Washington, DC 20049.

☐ American Deafness and Rehabilitation Association, P.O. Box 251554, Little Rock, AR 72225.

☐ American Foundation for the Blind, 11 Penn Plaza, Suite 300, New York, NY 10001.

☐ American OT Association, Inc., 1383 Piccard Drive, Rockville, MD 20850

☐ American National Standards Institute (ANSI), 1430 Broadway, New York, NY 10018.

☐ Architectural and Transportation Barriers Compliance Board, 1331 F Street Northwest, Suite 1000, Washington, DC 20004

☐ Association for Safe and Accessible Products, 1511 K Street, NW, Suite 600, Washington, DC 20005.

☐ Barrier Free Environments, Inc., P.O. Box 30634, Raleigh, NC 27622.

☐ Center for Accessible Housing, North Carolina State University, School of Design, Box 8613, Raleigh, NC 27695-8613.

☐ Center for Inclusive Design and Environmental Access, School of Architecture and Planning, University of Buffalo, Buffalo, NY 14214-3087.

☐ Center for Universal Design, North Carolina State University, School of Design, Box 8613, Raleigh, NC 27695-8613

☐ Disabled American Veterans National Service Headquarters, 807 Maine Ave., SW, Washington, DC 20024.

☐ Disability Rights Education Defense Fund, 1633 Q Street, NW, Suite 220, Washington, DC 20009.

☐ Eastern Paralyzed Veterans Association, 7520 Astoria Blvd., Jackson Heights, NY 11370-1178.

☐ EZ Fold Hinges - Kiwi COnnections, 82 Shelburne Center Road, Shelburne, MA 01370.

- [ ] E-Z Shelf - E-Z Shelf Ltd., Unit 103, 17369 Rowan Place, Surrey, BC, V3S-5K1, Canada.

- [ ] Hear You Are, Inc., 4 Musconetcong Ave., Stanhope, NJ 07874.

- [ ] Independent Living Research Utilization Project, 2323 S. Shepard Street, Suite 1000, Houston, TX 77019.

- [ ] Lifease, 2451 15th St. N.W., Suite D, New Brighton, MN 55112.

- [ ] The Lighthouse, Inc., 111 East 59th Street, New York, NY 10022.

- [ ] Maddock, Inc., Catalog for Orthopedic and ADL products.

- [ ] National Center for Disability Services, 201 I.U. Willets Rd., Albertson, NY 11507.

- [ ] National Council on Independent Living, 2111 Wilson Blvd, Suite 405, Arlington, VA 22201.

- [ ] National Eldercare Institute on Housing and Supportive Services, Andros Gerentology Center, USC, University Park, MC-0191, Los Angeles, CA 90089.

- [ ] National Institute on Disability and Rehabilitation Research, US Department of Education, 400 Maryland Ave., SW, Washington, DC 20202.

- [ ] National Rehabilitation Engineering Center on Aging, 515 Kimball Tower, University at Buffalo, Buffalo, NY 14214-3079.

- [ ] National Rehabilitation Information Center, 8455 Colesville Rd., Suite 935, Silver Spring, MD 20910.

- [ ] North Carolina Assistive Technology Project, 1110 Navaho Drive, Suite 101, Raleigh, NC 27609-7322.

- [ ] ProMatura, 428 N. Lamar Blvd., Oxford, MS 38655.

- [ ] Sammons 1994 Catalog for Orthopedic and ADL products, Sammons, PO Box 5071, Bolingbrook, IL 60440.

- [ ] Trace Research and Development Center, 1500 Highland Ave., Madison, WI 53705.

- [ ] Universal Designers and Consultants, Inc., 1700 Rockville Pike, Suite 110, Rockville, MD 20852.

- [ ] Volunteers for Medical Engineering, 2201 Argonne Drive, Baltimore, MD 21218.

SECTION III Suggestions for Local Sources of Information

- [ ] Independent Living Centers

- [ ] Local chapter of advocacy groups. Easter Seals, Paralyzed Veterans, American Association of Retired Persons, etc.

- [ ] State Office of Disabilities - sometimes called Governors Commission or Council on the Rights of People with Disabilities, or Protection and Advocacy Program

a p p e n d i x 7

Bathroom Fixture Transfer Techniques

Understanding how a person will approach and transfer to a bathtub, a shower, or a toilet/bidet will help the bathroom designer to make the best use of clear floor space in the bathroom.

The following information on transfer is taken from the **Accessible Housing Design File**.

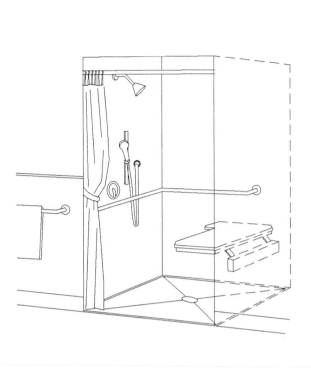

Molded plastic 36" x 36" (91cm x 91cm) Transfer Shower.

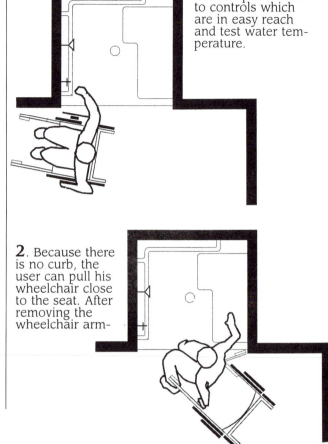

1. User pulls close to controls which are in easy reach and test water temperature.

2. Because there is no curb, the user can pull his wheelchair close to the seat. After removing the wheelchair arm-

Use of the 36" x 36" (91cm x 91cm) Transfer Shower by wheelchair users.

3. the user transfers from his wheelchair to the shower seat. Transferring is made easier and safer because the shower seat is generally mounted at the same height as the wheelchair seat.

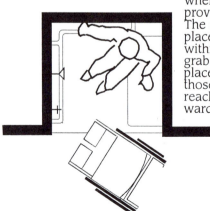

4. Using the grab bar for support, the user slides over to the corner where the shower walls provide lateral support. The size of the shower places the controls within easy reach. The grab bar provides a place to rest the arm for those who cannot easily reach forward and backward.

Use of the 36" x 36" (91cm x 91cm) Transfer Shower by wheelchair users.

Parallel Transfer onto a Built-In Transfer Seat From a Wheelchair

1. User pulls parallel to transfer surface at head of bathtub, removes arm rest

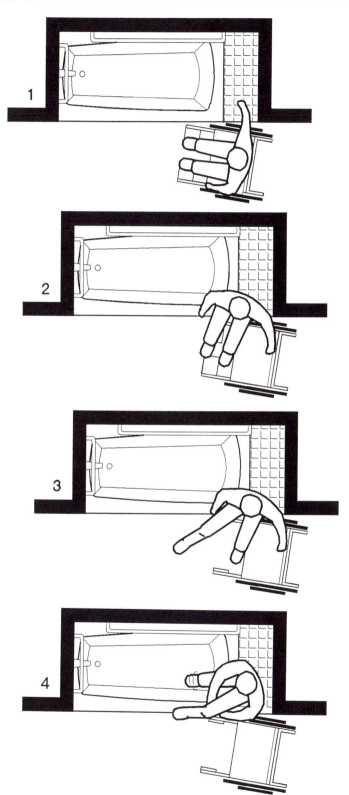

2. and holding onto wheelchair, begins to slide over onto the transfer surface.

3. Once securely in position,

4. the user lifts their legs, one at a time, over the bathtub rim and places them into the bathtub.

5. Gripping the grab bar and the wheelchair for support, the user slides forward on the transfer surface.

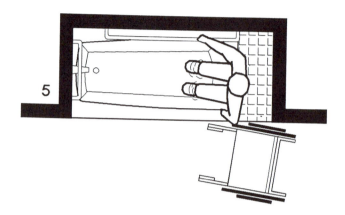

6. Using the grab bar and the bathtub rim, she lowers herself into the water.

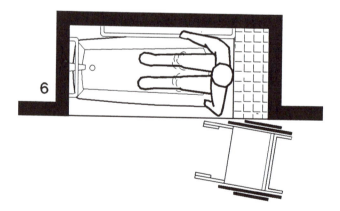

Transfer from a wheelchair into a bathtub (continued)

Forward Transfer from a Wheelchair into a Bathtub

1. User pulls close to bathtub, swings footrests to side, lifts legs over bathtub rim, and pulls chair tight to wall of bathtub.

2. After sliding forward in his chair and onto the bathtub rim, the user reaches for the grab bar in preparation for transferring.

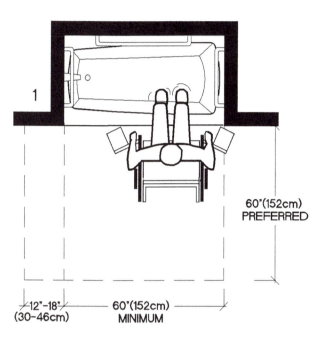

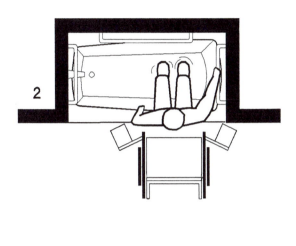

60"(152cm)
PREFERRED

12"-18"
(30-46cm)

60"(152cm)
MINIMUM

3. Grasping both the bathtub rim and the grab bar on the back wall, the user slides off the bathtub rim and lowers himself into the water

4. for a relaxing bath!

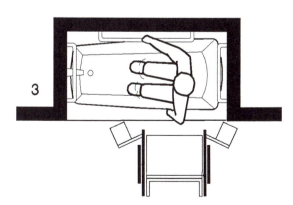

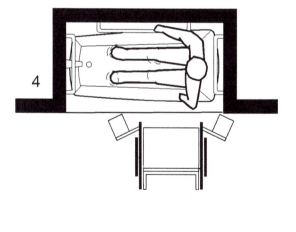

Wheelchair to Toilet Transfer Diagonal Approach

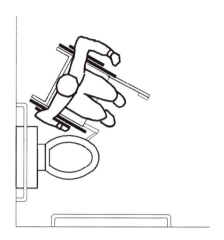

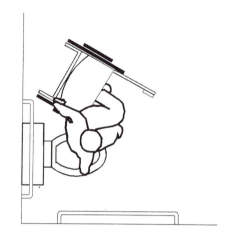

1. The user parks at a comfortable angle with the chair seat against the toilet.

2. After swinging the footrests out of the way and possibly removing the armrest, the user makes a sliding transfer using the grab bars and chair for support.

Common wheelchair to toilet transfer techniques.

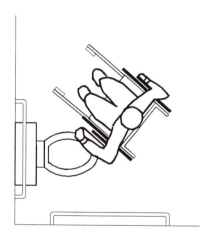

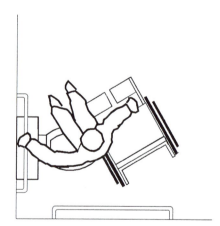

3. This method may be used to achieve a left-handed transfer in a right-handed room or vice versa.

Wheelchair to Toilet Transfer with Attendant Assistance

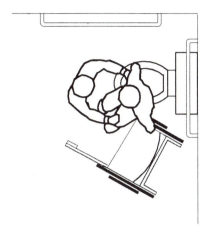

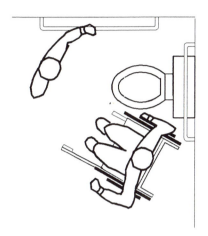

1. The user is positioned diagonally with the wheelchair seat close to the toilet. The attendant stands in front.

2. After swinging the footrest to the side, the attendant lifts the person to a standing position, rotates them, and places them on the toilet seat.

Common wheelchair to toilet transfer techniques. Diagonal approach with attendant assistance.

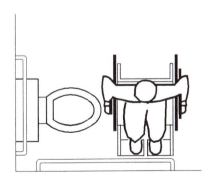

3. The user positions their chair at a 90 degree angle to the toilet, locating the wheelchair seat as close as possible to the toilet

4. After removing one armrest and using the grab bar and toilet for support, the user makes a sliding and pivoting transfer onto the toilet seat.

Common wheelchair to toilet transfer techniques. Perpendicular approach.

b i b l i o g r a p h y

- American Association of Retired Persons. Understanding Senior Housing for the 1990's. AARP, 1992.

- American Association of Retired Persons and ITT Hartford, The Hartford House - A Home for a Lifetime, 1994.

- American Foundation for the Blind. Building Bridges, 1993.

- American Foundation for the Blind. Aging and Vision, 1987.

- American National Standards Institute, American National Standard - Accessible and Usable Buildings and Facilities (ANSI A117.1-1992), Council of American Building Officials, 1992.

- Americans with Disabilities Act - Questions and Answers. U.S. Equal Employment Opportunity Commission and U.S. Department of Justice Civil Rights Division, 1992.

- Americans with Disabilities Act Title III Technical Assistance Manual. US Department of Justice.

- Americans with Disabilities Act Accessibility Requirements. U.S. Architectural and Transportation Barriers Compliance Board (Access Board), 1991.

- Barrier Free Environments, Inc. Adaptable Housing. U.S. Department of Housing and Urban Development, 1987.

- Barrier Free Environments, Inc. The Accessible Housing Design File. Van Nostrand Reinhold, 1991.

- Barrier Free Environments, Inc. UFAS Retrofit Guide. VanNostrand Reinhold, 1993.

- Beasley, Kim, AIA. "Home Sweet Home." Paraplegia News, September, 1994.

- Boyce, Peter, lighting designer, Lighting Research Center, Renesslaer Polytechnic Institute, Troy, New York. Interview.

- Branson, G.D. The Complete Guide to Barrier-Free Housing: Convenient Living for the Elderly and the Physically Handicapped. Betterway Publications, Inc., 1991.

- Bulletin #5: Using ADAAG. The Access Board, February, 1993.

- Bureau of the Census, Housing and Household Economic Statistics Division. (statistics), November, 1994.

- Bureau of the Census, Population Division, Age and Statistics Branch. (statistics), November, 1994.

- Center for Accessible Housing. Fact Sheets.

- Cheever, Ellen M.; McDonald, Marylee; Geragi, Nick; and DePaepe, Annette. Kitchen Industry Technical Manual, Volume 3, Kitchen Equipment and Materials. National Kitchen and Bath Association and University of Illinois Small Homes Council, 1993.

- Cheever, Ellen M.; McDonald, Marylee; Geragi, Nick; . Bathroom Industry Technical Manual, Volume 3, Bathroom Equipment and Materials. National Kitchen and Bath Association and University of Illinois Small Homes Council, 1992.

- Cheever, Ellen M.; McDonald, Marylee; Geragi, Nick, and DePaepe, Annette. Bathroom Industry Technical Manual, Volume 4, Bathroom Planning Standards and Safety Criteria. National Kitchen and Bath Association and University of Illinois Small Homes Council, 1992.

- Christiansen, M. Aging in the Designed Environment. Haworth Press, 1990.

- Cochran, W., Restrooms. Paralyzed Veterans of America, 1981.

- Cullinan, Gould, Silver, Irvine. "Visual Disability and Home Lighting." Lancet March, 1979.

- Cullinan, T.R. "Visual Disability and Home Lighting." Journal of Rehabilitation Research 3, 1980.

- DeLuca, Michael, Kitchen and Bathroom Lighting ... Made Easy, National Kitchen & Bath Association, 1997.

- Dietsch, Deborah K. "Improve Gray Architecture." Architecture, October, 1994.

■ Eastern Paralyzed Veterans Association. Barrier-Free Design: The Law - Connecticut, March, 1992.

■ Federal Register - Volume 56, no. 144 ADA Accessibility Guidelines for Buildings and Facilities, 1991.

■ Federal Register - Volume 56, no. 44 Final Fair Housing Accessibility Guidelines, 1991.

■ General Services Administration, Department of Defense, U.S. Department of Housing and Urban Development, and U.S. Postal Service. Uniform Federal Accessibility Guidelines, 1988.

■ Grosslight, Jane. Lighting Kitchens and Baths. Durwood Publishers, 1993.

■ Hart, Leslie. "Design for Special Needs." Kitchen and Bath Business, December 1992.

■ Hiatt, Lorraine. "Effective Trends in Interior Designing". Provider, April, 1986.

■ Hiatt, Lorraine. "The Color and Use of Color in Environments for Older People." Nursing Homes, 1980.

■ Hiatt, Lorraine. "Touchy about Touching". Nursing Homes, 1980.

■ Hiatt-Snyder, Lorraine. "Environmental Changes for Socialization." Journal of Nursing Administration, January, 1978.

■ Horton, Jules, lighting designer, Horton-Lees, 200 Park Avenue South, Suite 1401, New York, New York. Interview.

■ Jerome, Jeffrey, Director, and David Ward, Curator. Future Home. Tour and interviews, Phoenix, MD, June 1994.

■ Kiewel, Harold Dean, AIA, 4770 White Bear Parkway, White Bear Lake, MN, 55110. Interview - January, 1995.

■ Kira, Alexander, The Bathroom. Penguin Books, 1976.

■ Lehman, Betsy. "Making a House Livable for Elderly." Boston Globe, July 22, 1985.

■ Leibrock, C., & Behar, S. Beautiful Barrier-Free: A Visual Guide to Accessibility Van Nostrand Reinhold, 1993.

■ Leibrock, Cynthia. Easy Home Access, 1985.

■ Mace, Ronald L., Graeme J. Hardie and Jaine P. Place. Accessible Environments: Toward Universal Design. Center for Accessible Housing.

■ McKay, Hayden, lighting architect, Hayden McKay Lighting Design, 31 West 21st St., New York, NY. Interview - November, 1994.

■ Miller, Katie and Elizabeth Hite. Accessibilities for Everybody. University of Kansas.

■ Moore, Lois J. and Edward R. Ostrander, In Support of Mobility: Kitchen Design for Older Adults, Cornell University, 1992.

■ Mullick, Abir, Benches and Seats. Suny, Buffalo,

■ Mullick, Abir, Bath Lifts. Suny, Buffalo,

■ National Center for Health Statistics. (statistics), 1994.

■ National Council on Aging. (statistics), 1993.

■ National Council on Disability, ADA Watch - Year One, 1993.

■ New York State Rural Housing Coalition, Inc. "Designing Housing to Meet Special Needs." Rural Delivery, June 17, 1993.

■ Nissen, LuAnn, Ray Faulkner and Sarah Faulkner. Inside Today's Home. Harcourt Brace College Publishers, 1992.

■ Nolan, William and Joseph Boehm. "Forever Young." Better Homes and Gardens, October, 1994.

■ Null, Roberta. "Environmental Design for the Low Vision Elderly." Journal of Home Economics, Fall, 1988.

■ Paskin, Nancy and Lisa-Anne Soucy-Maloney, Whatever Works - Confident Living for People with Impaired Vision. Lighthouse, Inc., 1992.

■ Raisch, Marsha. "A Kitchen for All Seasons." Better Homes and Gardens Kitchen and Bath Ideas, Fall, 1994.

■ Rascho, B. Housing Interiors for the Disabled and Elderly. Van Nostrand Reinhold, 1982.

■ Research and Training Center on Independent Living, University of Kansas. Guidelines for Reporting and Writing About People with Disabilities. National

Institute of Disability and Rehabilitation Research, 1987.

■ Rosenberg, Robert, O.D., <u>Lighting and the Aging Eye</u>, Lighthouse Low Vision Services, 1994.

■ Shapiro, Joseph. <u>No Pity</u>, Times Books, 1994.

■ Sit, Mary. "Home Sweet Home." <u>Exceptional Parent's Guide for Active Adults with Disabilities</u>, Spring, 1992.

■ Tetlow, Karin. "Contrasting Colors". <u>Interiors</u>, September, 1993.

■ <u>Understanding Developmental Disabilities</u>. Indiana Governor's Council on Development Disabilities.

■ United States Department of Labor, Bureau of Labor Statistics, <u>Occupational Outlook Handbook</u>, Beran Press, 1994.

■ White, Betty Jo; Mary H. Yearns; Glenda Pifer; Robert Null. "Future Environments: Forecasts and Issues." <u>Journal of Home Economics</u>, Spring, 1989.

■ Wrightson, William and Campbell Pope. <u>From Barrier Free to Safe Environments: The New Zealand Experience</u> World Rehabilitation Fund, Inc., 1989.

■ Wylde, M., Adrian Barron-Robbins and Sam Clark, <u>Building for a Lifetime</u>, Tanton Press, Inc., 1994.

■ Yepsen, Roger. "A Home for Life." <u>Practical Homeowner</u>, 1987.

■ Zola, Irving Kenneth, Ph.D. <u>Living at Home - The Policy Convergence of Aging and Disability</u>.

index

A

B

W